The Essence of COM
A PROGRAMMER'S WORKBOOK

ISBN 0-13-016581-6

90000

9 780130 165817

PRENTICE HALL PTR MICROSOFT® TECHNOLOGIES SERIES

NETWORKING

- Microsoft Technology: Networking, Concepts, Tools
  Woodard, Gattuccio, Brain

- NT Network Programming Toolkit
  Murphy

- Building COM Applications with Internet Explorer
  Loveman

- Understanding DCOM
  Rubin, Brain

- Web Database Development for Windows Platforms
  Gutierrez

PROGRAMMING

- Windows Shell Programming for C++
  and MFC Developers
  Seely

- Windows Installer Complete
  Easter

- Windows 2000 Web Applications Developer's Guide
  Yager

- Developing Windows Solutions with Office 2000
  Components and VBA
  Aitken

- Win 32 System Services:
  The Heart of Windows 98 and Windows NT,
  Third Edition
  Brain

- Multithreaded Programming with Win32
  Pham, Garg

- Developing Professional Applications
  for Windows 98 and NT Using MFC,
  Third Edition
  Brain, Lovette

- Introduction to Windows 98 Programming
  Murray, Pappas

- Windows CE: Application Programming
  Gratten, Brain

- The COM and COM+ Programming Primer
  Gordon

- Understanding and Programming COM+:
  A Practical Guide to Windows 2000 DNA
  Oberg

- Distributed COM Application Development Using Visual
  C++ 6.0
  Maloney

- Distributed COM Application Development Using Visual
  Basic 6.0
  Maloney

- The Essence of COM, Third Edition
  Platt

- COM-CORBA Interoperability
  Geraghty, Joyce, Moriarty, Noone

- MFC Programming in C++ with the Standard Template
  Libraries
  Murray, Pappas

- Introduction to MFC Programming
  with Visual C++
  Jones

- Visual C++ Templates
  Murray, Pappas

- Visual Basic Object and Component Handbook
  Vogel

- Visual Basic 6: Error Coding and Layering
  Gill

- ADO Programming in Visual Basic 6
  Holzner

- Visual Basic 6: Design, Specification,
  and Objects
  Hollis

- ASP/MTS/ADSI Web Security
  Harrison

- Visual Basic Style Guide
  Patrick

BACKOFFICE

- Designing Enterprise Solutions with Microsoft
  Technologies
  Kemp, Kemp, Goncalves

- Microsoft Site Server 3.0 Commerce Edition
  Libertone, Scoppa

- Building Microsoft SQL Server 7 Web Sites
  Byrne

- Optimizing SQL Server 7
  Schneider, Goncalves

ADMINISTRATION

- Windows 2000 Hardware and Disk Management
  Simmons

- Windows 2000 Server: Management and Control,
  Third Edition
  Spencer, Goncalves

- Creating Active Directory Infrastructures
  Simmons

- Windows 2000 Registry
  Sanna

- Configuring Windows 2000 Server
  Simmons

- Supporting Windows NT and 2000 Workstation
  and Server
  Mohr

- Zero Administration Kit for Windows
  McInerney

- Tuning and Sizing NT Server
  Aubley

- Windows NT Cluster Server Guidebook
  Libertone

- Windows NT 4.0 Server Security Guide
  Goncalves

- Windows NT Security
  McInerney

- Windows NT Device Driver Book
  Baker

CERTIFICATION

- Core MCSE: Windows 2000 Edition
  Dell

- Core MCSE
  Dell

- Core MCSE: Networking Essentials
  Keogh

- MCSE: Administering Microsoft SQL Server 7
  Byrne

- MCSE: Implementing and Supporting Microsoft
  Exchange Server 5.5
  Goncalves

- MCSE: Internetworking with Microsoft TCP/IP
  Ryvkin, Houde, Hoffman

- MCSE: Implementing and Supporting Microsoft Proxy
  Server 2.0
  Ryvkin, Hoffman

- MCSE: Implementing and Supporting Microsoft SNA
  Server 4.0
  Mariscal

- MCSE: Implementing and Supporting Microsoft Internet
  Information Server 4
  Dell

- MCSE: Implementing and Supporting Web Sites Using
  Microsoft Site Server 3
  Goncalves

- MCSE: Microsoft System Management Server 2
  Jewett

- MCSE: Implementing and Supporting
  Internet Explorer 5
  Dell

- Core MCSD: Designing and Implementing Desktop
  Applications with Microsoft Visual Basic 6
  Holzner

- Core MCSD: Designing and Implementing Distributed
  Applications with Microsoft Visual Basic 6
  Houlette, Klander

- MCSD: Planning and Implementing SQL Server 7
  Vacca

- MCSD: Designing and Implementing Web Sites with
  Microsoft FrontPage 98
  Karlins

PRENTICE HALL PTR MICROSOFT® TECHNOLOGIES SERIES

The Essence of COM

A PROGRAMMER'S WORKBOOK

Third Edition

David S. Platt

PH
PTR

Prentice Hall PTR, Upper Saddle River, NJ 07458
www.phptr.com

Library of Congress Cataloging-in-Publication Data

Platt, David S.
    The essence of COM: a programmer's workbook / David S. Platt.–3rd ed.
        p. cm. – (Prentice Hall PTR Microsoft technologies series)
    Includes index.
    ISBN 0-13-016581-6
        1. Object-oriented programming (Computer science) 2. COM (Computer architecture)
    I. Title. II. Series.

    QA76.64. P617 2000
    005.7–dc21   00-027306

Acquisitions Editor: *Michael Meehan*
Editorial Assistant: *Linda Ramagnano*
Marketing Manager: *Bryan Gambrel*
Manufacturing Buyer: *Maura Goldstaub*
Cover Design: *Design Source*
Cover Design Director: *Jerry Votta*

Published by Prentice Hall PTR
Prentice-Hall, Inc.
Upper Saddle River, NJ 07458

Prentice Hall books are widely used by corporations and government agencies for training,
marketing, and resale.

The publisher offers discounts on this book when ordered in bulk quantities.
For more information, contact Corporate Sales Department,
phone: 800-382-3419; fax: 201-236-7141;
email: corpsales@prenhall.com
Or write Corporate Sales Department, Prentice Hall PTR, One Lake Street, Upper Saddle River, NJ 07458.

Printed in the United States of America

10 9 8 7 6 5 4 3 2 1

ISBN 0-13-016581-6

Prentice-Hall International (UK) Limited, *London*
Prentice-Hall of Australia Pty. Limited, *Sydney*
Prentice-Hall Canada Inc., *Toronto*
Prentice-Hall Hispanoamericana, S.A., *Mexico*
Prentice-Hall of India Private Limited, *New Delhi*
Prentice-Hall of Japan, Inc., *Tokyo*
Pearson Education Asia Pte. Ltd.
Editora Prentice-Hall do Brasil, Ltda., *Rio de Janeiro*

To my parents, Ellen and Ben Platt

CONTENTS

Preface

On the Teaching and Learning of COM

WHY I WROTE THIS BOOK

COM has a reputation for being hard to learn. A client once told me that he knew of only two programmers in the entire world who understood it, both of whom worked for Microsoft and spent their days writing puzzles for each other. But really, nothing could be further from the truth. COM has an elegant simplicity to its architecture and an internal self-consistency that the Windows API lacks. It's just a different way of looking at the world. This book is an attempt to clear things up, to present in a simple and easily digested fashion the stuff I had to learn the hard way.

As I hope to demonstrate in this book, learning COM isn't that hard. It may take you a little while to get the basic concepts, though I've done my best to build easily accessible ramps into it. But once the light bulb goes off, probably after about two weeks of head banging, you will have the keys to all of COM. Learning the Windows API was largely a matter of memorizing arbitrary function calls without any central organizing principle, sort of like memorizing all those boring equations in college organic chemistry. Learning COM as presented in this book is more like learning the basic principles that cause the entire universe to operate. Remember college physics? The simplest equations, such as $F = MA$, describe all macroscopic motion, from the falling of a feather to the collision of galaxies.

MARCH OF THE YEARS

I sent the first edition of this book to press at the end of August 1996, going on four years ago. That's an awfully long time in the software business. I did a second edition about a year later, Christmas of 1997. This edition is headed to press in the spring of 2000. The changes reflect not so much the changes in COM, although God knows there are plenty of those (DCOM, threading, and asynchronous operation, to name just a few), but the changes in my understanding. I remember reading a certain part of the first edition and thinking, "I can't believe I actually looked at the world that way then." As I changed my mind about my 1972 George McGovern ideals when I started having to write my own checks to the IRS, so I changed my mind about many things in COM once I actually started using them on projects.

I occasionally envy my Harvard colleagues in the Department of Classics, whose material hasn't changed in 2000 years. This area of software is really snowballing. COM is everywhere, at the foundation of everything. This book is my attempt to keep up with it, and keep you up with it as well.

IT GOT SMALLER

Anyone who has seen the second edition of this book, the one with the airplane on the cover, will notice that this book is about 60% the size of that one. It's not just that I got shoulder pain hauling around a backpack with that book in it, and it's not just that I almost killed my cat when I accidentally dropped it on her. You know the old cliché that inside every large program, there's a small program struggling to get out. The prime goal of writing this book from the first day was succinctness: to get the basic ideas out so people could understand them easily. I wanted to hack a narrow path through the jungle from end to end. The second edition just had too much stuff in it; the signal-to-noise ratio was too low. So in this book, I thought about what I really used in COM and tried to slim it down. I took out everything having to do with the MFC. Jeff Prosise would probably disagree, but I think the MFC has reached its evolutionary dead-end point. I took out a lot of the user interface stuff that I don't use any more, except for the Clipboard and drag-and-drop samples that I've found so useful as a visual demonstration of the first principles of COM. The result was about a 40% reduction. Too bad the government can't do a similar job.

SAMPLE CODE AND FREE QUARTERLY COM/COM+ DEVELOPMENT NEWSLETTER ONLINE

Instead of putting this book's sample code on CD-ROM, I've decided to put it on my Web site, www.rollthunder.com. It's easier for me to update and add to. You don't have to remember where you put that disk. And it's free to anyone, even if you didn't buy the book. Tell your friends.

While you're on my Web site, why don't you check out my free quarterly e-mail newsletter, entitled *ThunderClap*. Each issue contains a technical article on timely COM or COM+ development topics. Recent issues have covered automatic synchronization of objects in COM+, COM+ compensating resource managers, and a COM+ event system spy program. It is also free to anyone, so please come help yourselves.

HOW TO USE THIS BOOK

If you are new to COM, **READ CHAPTERS 1 AND 2 FIRST!!** Do not attempt to jump to other chapters until you feel comfortable with these. In these chapters I introduce the new programming model and vocabulary of COM without which subsequent chapters will make no sense. I hate the term "paradigm shift"; it's been so badly overused as to have lost all meaning, but COM does turn your head around.

You don't really own your knowledge of software until you've written some yourself. The end of each chapter contains self-study programming exercises with detailed instructions. The prepackaged labs pretty much follow the text, so they aren't hard. The extra credit sections at the end of some labs are designed to stretch your mind a bit more.

When you are actually writing your programs, keep this book handy on your desk. My students tell me that it is the first source they refer to, because it's easy to find what they want and easy to absorb when they do find it. They only go off to a thicker book when they can't find what they want in this book. One student even has two copies, one at home and one at work.

WHY ALL THE EMPTY PAGES?

The reason I have them is to align the two-page sound bites over a spread of two facing pages. When a topic doesn't fit on a single page, my experience has shown that students find the material much easier to absorb if it is spread across two facing pages. I can't stand pages that say "This page intentionally left blank." Does it never occur to anybody that this statement is self-negating? THE %$#^$@ PAGE ISN'T BLANK, IT CONTAINS THAT ONE LYING SENTENCE!! If the author can't even get that dinky little piece right, how can I believe anything else he says? Instead, my empty pages truthfully say, "This page intentionally contains no text other than this sentence." Call me a curmudgeon.

SEND ME FEEDBACK

I love to hear from my readers, to find out which parts of the book were most useful. Also, I guarantee that, despite my best efforts and those of my reviewers, some errors remain in this book, and I'd sure appreciate it if you'd tell me about them so they can be fixed in the next edition. My e-mail address is dplatt@rollthunder.com. My web site, www.rollthunder.com, will contain updates and corrections to the book.

PROGRAMMING CLASSES AVAILABLE

A self-study guide like this one is great (I hope), but the fastest way to get going in programming is to have an in-house hands-on class. I'll come to your company and teach exactly the parts of COM and COM+ that you care about. Contact me by e-mail at the address in the preceding paragraph.

ACKNOWLEDGMENTS

I need to thank the following people, without whom this book would never have been completed. Mehrdad Givehchi, who did a great job reading the book and finding errors. If he ever gets sick of programming, he's got a great future as a technical editor. Pat Duggan, who found so many typos in my previous book that he earned a free copy of this one. Kraig Brockschmidt, for discussions on the philosophy of OLE and of life in general. I need to thank all those people who helped me figure out things about COM. The staff at *Microsoft Systems Journal* and Microsoft's Developer Relations Group were especially helpful when I was researching COM threading for a couple of MSJ articles on the topic (February and August 1997). Thanks to Dave Edson, Sara Williams, Charlie Kindel, Nat Brown, Dave D'Sousa, and Eric Maffei. When I teach at Boston University's WinDev conferences, I learn much from attending talks presented by the other instructors. Thanks go to Don Box, Jeffery Richter, Jeff Prosise, Ken Ramirez, Joe Najjar, and Richard Hale Shaw. Thanks also to Mike Meehan, Jane Bonnell, and my wife Linda. Last but not least, thanks to everyone who bought or recommended the first two editions, on behalf of my creditors. I hope you like this one as much.

— David S. Platt
Ipswich, MA, January 2000

Chapter 1

Introduction:
Using Objects

A. CONCEPTS AND DEFINITIONS

1. COM, the *Component Object Model*, is Microsoft's top-level, all-encompassing binary and wire specification for the interoperation of one software component with another, across multiple processes, machines, and (one day, Microsoft hopes) hardware and operating systems. OLE is a collection of higher-level functionality, primarily related to the user interface, that uses COM for communicating between components. It is not always clear exactly where COM stops and OLE begins. Philosophical debate on the topic is about as productive as debating how many pinheads can dance on an angel.

2. The nomenclature of the OLE/COM/ActiveX world is confusing to say the least. If you search through the Microsoft Developer Network CD-ROM, you will see an incredible array of different meanings attached to the various terms, changing drastically over time and occasionally returning to their starting points. There is no single set of meanings for them and there never really was. Here are the derivations of the terms as you will see them used in the literature today:

OLE first shipped in 1991 with Windows 3.1 and used Dynamic Data Exchange (remember good ol' DDE?) as its underlying communication protocol. OLE originally stood for "Object Linking and Embedding", because that's what it did and that's all it did. Then OLE 2.0 came out in 1993, significantly enhancing the original object linking and embedding functionality, containing such cool enhancements as in-place activation and linking that actually worked. OLE 2.0 replaced DDE with COM as its underlying communication protocol, and as such was the first major use of COM. It also added the programmability of OLE Automation, which nobody was quite sure how to use yet. At this point, Microsoft declared that OLE was no longer an acronym for object linking and embedding. Instead, it was just a combination of random syllables that Microsoft liked enough to trademark, that referred to the entire set of technologies built on top of COM. Here matters stood for a couple of years. Kraig Brockschmidt's book *Inside OLE*, published in 1995, dealt with the entire set of COM-based technologies and refers to them all as OLE. The first edition of the book you are now holding, written beginning in 1995, was entitled *The Essence of OLE with ActiveX*.

Around 1996, when most developers started writing 32-bit apps for Windows 95, they noticed that the way OLE used COM was a cool way of architecting software. Developers started writing their own objects and their own interfaces in a similar manner. Also, the operating system started requiring the use of COM technology, for example, for programming the Windows 95 user interface. It wasn't object linking and embedding and it wasn't automation; what the heck was it? The term COM started to be used more and more frequently on its own, which is probably what should have happened in the first place. The term OLE is no longer used as the catch-all it once was. Some writers are trying to make it revert to its original meaning, object linking and embedding, but that would leave COM-related user interface technologies, such as drag-and-drop and Clipboard handling, without a term. I've coined a new word for this type of confusion: MINFU, for Microsoft Nomenclature Foul-Up.

The term ActiveX is another winner. In my column on Byte.Com I expound at length on the origin and subsequent diluting into oblivion of this term. To quickly summarize here, the term "ActiveX" has no technical meaning whatsoever, although it did have several different meanings at various times. It is today a branding prefix, the same as the letters "Mc" in front of all the food at the restaurant with the golden arches. It means "Microsoft-warm-fuzzy-good", no more and no less.

3. When you start an app that uses OLE or COM, you must first initialize it in your app by calling the API function **OleInitialize( )** or **CoInitialize( )**. The former calls the latter internally, as well as setting up support for the user interface portions of OLE. If you don't need this user interface support, then the latter function is all you need. The include files for all OLE and COM functions are supplied via the header file "windows.h", and the import library is "ole32.lib".

If and only if this call succeeds, as shown below, should your app uninitialize the libraries via the function **OleUninitialize( )** or **CoUninitialize( )** when it shuts down. The return type of OleInitialize( ), and of almost every other COM-related function, is of type HRESULT, which is typedefed as a LONG. The high bit of the long is cleared if the call succeeded, set if the call failed. The macro SUCCEEDED( ) tests this bit and returns TRUE if the call was successful. Thus:

```
#include <windows.h>            // includes all OLE and COM files

int WINAPI WinMain(HINSTANCE hInstance, HINSTANCE hPrevInstance,
    LPSTR lpCmdLine, int nCmdShow)
{
    MSG msg;

/*
Initialize OLE Libraries.
*/

    HRESULT hr = OleInitialize (NULL) ;

/*
Run the app.
*/

    <all the other WinMain stuff>


/*
If they were initialized successfully, shut down the OLE Libraries.
S_OK is a constant defined in the system header files.
*/
    if (SUCCEEDED(hr))
    {
      OleUninitialize ( ) ;
    }

    return (msg.wParam);

}
```

B. COMPONENT-OBJECT MODEL

1. In COM, an app does not manipulate the world via API functions, such as ShowWindow( ). Rather, the universe consists of *objects*, which expose one or more *interfaces* to the world. An interface is a group of related functions which operate on the object that exposes them. You cannot access an object's data directly, but only through the functions of the object's interface(s). This model is conceptually somewhat similar to C++ classes with all member variables private. Some interfaces are standard, others are defined by the programmer.

2. You will frequently hear the term "pointer to an object." Although the term gets used a lot as a convenient shorthand, it is really a misnomer. In COM, there ain't no such thing as a pointer to an object. What you have is *a pointer to an interface on the object*. In physical binary terms, you have a pointer to another pointer. This second pointer points to a table of pointers to the interface's member functions. This table of functions is known as a VTBL ("Vee-table"). One of the main advantages to implementing your objects in the C++ language is that the compiler will automatically set up the VTBL for you. However, when you have a pointer to an interface on someone else's object, you cannot assume anything at all about the internal organization of the object. It may well have been written in COBOL. In the following diagram, the location of the VTBL pointer and the object's private data are both shown amorphously, to re-emphasize the fact **that you cannot assume anything at all about the internal organization of an object. When you have a pointer to an interface on an object, you can call that interface's methods. That's all.** You cannot manipulate the internal reference count m_RefCount directly, but only by calling the IUnknown interface methods AddRef( ) and Release( ).

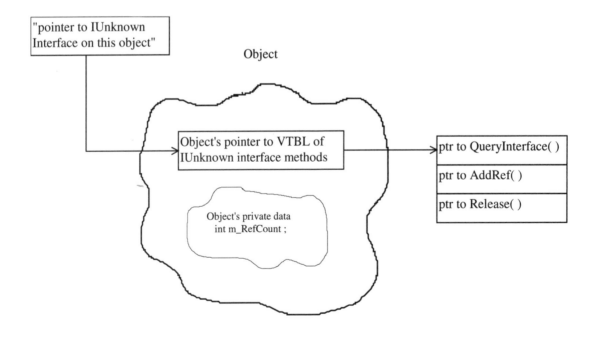

3. Once you have a pointer to an object (remember, this is shorthand for having a pointer to some interface on the object), you communicate with the object by calling the interface's member functions. But how do you get the first pointer to an object? There are several ways. You might call an COM/OLE API function that returns a pointer to an object, such as the following:

CoCreateInstance( )   *// look in registry, launch COM server and get object from it*
OleGetClipboard( )   *// return an IDataObject interface pointer to the clipboard's contents*

Some interfaces have methods that create new objects and return pointers to them. If you have an object of one of these types, you can call the object's method, for example:

IDataObject::EnumFormatEtc( )   *// return an object that enumerates formats the data object has*
IClassFactory::CreateInstance( ) *// create a new object of the class manufactured by the factory*

You might register a callback object whose methods the OS will call and pass you a pointer to an object that it has created, for example:

RegisterDragDrop( )   *// register callback functions for drag-and-drop operations*

Or you might instantiate a C++ object whose VTBL conforms to the requirements of a COM interface, for example:

new CSomeClass( )   *// instantiate an object that implements a COM interface*

C. IUNKNOWN INTERFACE

1. Every COM object, without exception, exposes an interface called *IUnknown* which contains the methods **AddRef( )**, **Release( )**, and **QueryInterface( )**. Each and every interface, without exception, is derived from IUnknown and has pointers to these functions as the first three entries in its VTBL. No matter which interface pointer you have, no matter how you got it, you can always call these three methods, and you frequently will.

The first two methods manipulate an internal reference count that controls an object's lifetime. When an object is first created, its creator must call the object's AddRef( ) method to increment the count. Whenever another user is given a pointer to the object, the object's AddRef( ) method must be called again. When the user is finished with the object, he calls that object's Release( ) method, thereby decrementing the reference count. When the last user calls the object's Release( ) method, the count will reach 0, causing the object to destroy itself. A simple implementation of the methods IUnknown::AddRef( ) and IUnknown::Release( ) might look like this:

```
/*
Increment member variable containing reference count.
*/

ULONG CUnknown::AddRef(void)
{
    return ++m_RefCount ;
}


/*
Decrement member variable containing reference count.  If 0, destroy
object.
*/

ULONG CUnknown::Release(void)
{
    --m_RefCount ;
    if (m_RefCount == 0)
    {
      delete this ;
      return 0 ;
    }
    return m_RefCount ;
}
```

2. Who is responsible for calling AddRef( ) and Release( )? There are two simple rules:

A. Whenever YOU CALL any function or method that returns a pointer to an object, such as OleGetClipboard() or any object's QueryInterface( ) method, the object's AddRef( ) method has already been called for you by the code that supplies the pointer. You must call that object's Release( ) method when you are finished with the object even if you don't do anything with it. It is the object's responsibility to make sure that it continues to exist until you do so.

B. When SOMEONE CALLS YOU and passes an object pointer as a parameter to one of your own callback functions, for example, in drag-and-drop operations, the object's AddRef( ) method has not been called for you. You must call the object's AddRef( ) if you want to store a pointer to the object, and Release( ) it only if you have AddRef'd it.

3. When you get a pointer to an object, what you really have is a pointer to one of its interfaces. Which interface you have depends on how you got the pointer. The object might or might not support other interfaces that interest you; there's no way of telling *a priori*. But since every object is guaranteed to support the IUnknown interface, you can ask the object if it supports some other interface that you care about via the method **IUnknown::QueryInterface( )**.

Interfaces are identified by means of *Interface IDs* (IIDs), 16-byte constants described on the next page. Standard interfaces have their own IID's defined in the system header files, such as IID_IUnknown for the IUnknown interface. When you call QueryInterface( ), you pass it the IID of the interface that you want, and a pointer to an output parameter. If the object supports the requested interface, it will return the success code S_OK (defined as 0) and fill the supplied output parameter with a pointer to the requested interface. If the object does not support the requested interface, it will return a nonzero error code and set the output parameter to NULL. A simple implementation of IUnknown::QueryInterface( ) might look like this:

```
HRESULT CUnknown::QueryInterface(REFIID riid, LPVOID *ppv)
{

/*
Check the IID to see if we support the requested interface.  If we do,
increment the reference count, fill the supplied output variable with a
pointer to the interface, and return the success code.
*/

    if (riid == IID_IUnknown)
    {
        *ppv = (LPVOID)this;
        AddRef();
        return S_OK ;         // success code is 0, repeat zero
    }

/*
We don't support the interface.  Set the supplied output variable to
NULL and return an informative error code.
*/

    else
    {
      *ppv = NULL;
      return  E_NOINTERFACE ; // failure codes are nonzero
    }
}
```

D. GUIDs AND UUIDs

1. The identifier used for uniquely distinguishing any entity in COM that needs it is a 16-byte constant known by the synonymous terms *GUID* (<u>G</u>lobally <u>U</u>nique <u>ID</u>, rhymes with 'squid') or *UUID* (<u>U</u>niversally <u>U</u>nique <u>ID</u>). In the QueryInterface example on the previous page, the interface for which the caller was querying was represented by an *interface ID* or *IID*, which is a GUID used to identify an interface. In Chapter 2, we will see a *class ID* or *CLSID*, which is a GUID used to identify a class of object. The concept comes from OSF RPC. The definition of the GUID structure is:

```
typedef struct _GUID
{
    unsigned long Data1;
    unsigned short Data2;
    unsigned short Data3;
    unsigned char Data4[8];
} GUID;
```

It is the responsibility of the creator of an object class or interface to generate a new GUID to identify it. A program can do this at runtime via the API function **CoCreateGuid( )**. This uses an OSF-approved algorithm that returns a new GUID. When you need a new GUID at development time, you can easily obtain one from the utility app GUIDGEN.EXE, which calls CoCreateGuid( ) internally and places the resulting GUID on the Clipboard for you. Thus:

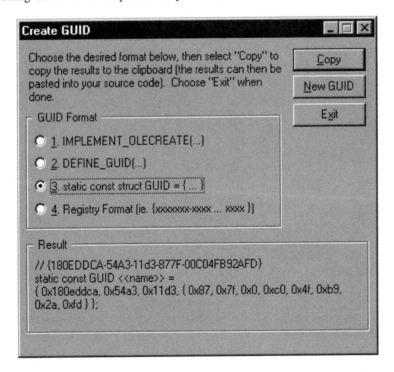

A GUID spans a very large statistical universe. The number of different possible combinations in 16 bytes is 3.4×10^{38}. That's about the square root of the total number of atoms in the universe. Statistically, you don't need to worry about another developer generating the same GUID for his class as you do for yours.

WARNING: The place where you DO see GUID conflicts in real life is when you cut and paste someone else's code without thinking about it. Make sure you change the GUIDs when you reuse someone else's code.

E. HRESULTs

1. As you saw in the QueryInterface example on the previous leaf, all methods of all COM interfaces except AddRef( ) and Release( ) (and a couple of oddballs in the Win95 UI, which shouldn't have been written that way), return a success or failure code called an HRESULT. This is a DWORD, with success or failure information encoded in it. The meanings of the bits are:

Bit	Usage
31	Severity 1 = failure, 0 = success
27-30	Reserved
16-26	Facility (sub-area within COM) in which error occurred
0-15	Specific error code

For example, the error code E_NOINTERFACE, seen in the QueryInterface example, has the hex value of 0x80004002. The severity bit is set, so it indicates a failure. The facility code is 0, which indicates a general error in COM (it actually predates the separation of error codes by facility). The specific error code is 4002. The meanings of the error codes and facility codes are listed in the system header file WINERROR.H.

There are two important things to remember about HRESULTs. First, the success or failure of the method is signaled by the most significant bit, known as the "severity" bit. This bit being set means that the call failed; this bit being clear means that the call succeeded. The macro SUCCEEDED tests only the state of this bit.

The second is that if you are writing your own custom HRESULTS for your own custom interfaces, to avoid conflict with Microsoft standard codes, make sure that you set your facility to FACILITY_ITF (which has the value 0x00040000), and that your code value is greater than 0x1FF.

If you are trying to pass back more information than a single DWORD can handle, you will probably need to use the ISupportErrorInfo interface discussed in Chapter 3.

F. Using Our First COM Object

1. Transfer of formatted data in COM is handled by means of *data objects*, which are objects that support the *IDataObject* interface. A data source application creates a data object and makes it available to the consumer via drag-and-drop, the Clipboard, or other channels. In addition to the IUnknown methods supported by every object, the IDataObject interface contains the following methods:

IDataObject::GetData	*// Get object's data in callee-supplied medium*
IDataObject::GetDataHere	*// Get object's data in caller-supplied medium*
IDataObject::QueryGetData	*// Can data be rendered in specified format?*
IDataObject::GetCanonicalFormatEtc	*// Get formats that produce identical data*
IDataObject::SetData	*// Set object's data*
IDataObject::EnumFormatEtc	*// Get enumerator of object's supported data formats*
IDataObject::DAdvise	*// Establish advise loop on this data object*
IDataObject::DUnadvise	*// Unestablish advise loop on this data object*
IDataObject::EnumDAdvise	*// Get enumerator of advise loops on this data object*

2. Data objects are conceptually similar to individual moveable Clipboards that use delayed rendering and have taken steroids. The single integer that identified a data format in the Clipboard API has been expanded into a FORMATETC structure, allowing the requester of data to be much more specific in indicating its desires. In addition to the original Clipboard format, the caller may specify the type of medium through which the data is to be transferred (global memory, file, metafile, structured storage, etc.), the aspect (level of detail) of the data representation transferred (iconic, thumbnail sketch, or full content), and the output device for which the transferred data is to be formatted.

For the purposes of this book, we will always be using the aspect level DVASPECT_CONTENT, which means "all the data." We will also set the target device to be NULL, which specifies the object's default rendition. For more detailed discussion of the options available in a FORMATETC structure, see Brockschmidt, pp. 497-501. The example on the facing page uses a FORMATETC structure to transfer simple text through an HGLOBAL.

```
typedef struct FARSTRUCT tagFORMATETC
{
    CLIPFORMAT           cfFormat;    // Clipboard format, same as CB API
    DVTARGETDEVICE FAR*  ptd;         // target device to format data for
    DWORD                dwAspect;    // level of detail for data
    LONG                 lindex;      // reserved, must be -1
    DWORD                tymed;       // type of medium for transfer
} FORMATETC ;
```

3. One potential source of a data object is the existing Windows Clipboard. If your app already handles data objects, it is probably easiest to use the same code for handling data from the Clipboard, rather than write a separate handler using the Clipboard API. The API function **OleGetClipboard( )** synthesizes a data object containing the current contents of the Clipboard, whether or not they were put there by an OLE-aware app. The method **IDataObject::QueryGetData( )** interrogates the data object to see if it can supply data in a specified format and medium, conceptually similar to the API function IsClipboardFormatAvailable( ). Finally we release the object by calling its **Release( )** method.

In the following example, we use this mechanism to check the Clipboard's contents before displaying the app's menu. If the Clipboard contains text, we enable the "Paste Text" menu item; otherwise we gray it out. The working app may be found in the sample app \CHAPTER1\DONE\DATA1.EXE. Thus:

```
case WM_INITMENU:
{

/*
Get a data object pointer to the current Clipboard contents.
*/
    IDataObject *lpd ;
    HRESULT hr ;


    hr = OleGetClipboard (&lpd) ;

/*
Fill out a FORMATETC structure, see if the Clipboard data object
contains text.  Gray out EDIT-PASTE menu item if it doesn't, or if
Clipboard is empty (returned data object pointer is NULL).  Otherwise
enable menu item.
*/
    FORMATETC fe ;

    fe.cfFormat = CF_TEXT ;
    fe.ptd = NULL ;
    fe.tymed = TYMED_HGLOBAL ;
    fe.dwAspect = DVASPECT_CONTENT ;
    fe.lindex = -1 ;

    if (!lpd ||  lpd->QueryGetData (&fe) != S_OK)
    {
      EnableMenuItem ((HMENU)wParam, ID_DEMO_PASTETEXT, MF_GRAYED) ;
    }
    else
    {
      EnableMenuItem ((HMENU)wParam, ID_DEMO_PASTETEXT, MF_ENABLED) ;
    }

/*
Release Clipboard data object.
*/
    if (lpd) lpd->Release( ) ;

    return 0 ;
}
```

4. Actually fetching the object's data is done via the methods **IDataObject::GetData( )** and **IDataObject::GetDataHere( )**. They are conceptually identical, except that in the former, the callee both provides and fills the transfer medium, whereas in the latter, the caller provides the transfer medium and the callee fills it. The former is more common; the latter is used primarily in embedding and linking situations. The example on the facing page shows the use of the former in the DATA1.EXE example when the user picks "Paste Text" from the menu.

Transferred data is held in a structure of type STGMEDIUM. This contains space for the supplier of data to specify and supply the storage medium through which the data is being transferred. Since there are several types of storage media with different rules for their release, the function **ReleaseStgMedium( )** is provided, which is guaranteed to properly dispose of a used STGMEDIUM, no matter what its contents. Thus:

```
typedef struct tagSTGMEDIUM {
    DWORD           tymed;              // flags for self-description

// actual data storage

    union {
    HBITMAP         hBitmap;            // Bitmap
    HMETAFILEPICT   hMetaFilePict;      // METAFILEPICT structure
    HENHMETAFILE    hEnhMetaFile;       // 32-bit enhanced Metafile
    HGLOBAL         hGlobal;            // Global memory
    LPOLESTR        lpszFileName;       // File name
    ISTREAM         *pstm;              // OLE stream  (see Chapter 8)
    ISTORAGE        *pstg;              // OLE storage (see Chapter 8)
    };

    IUNKNOWN        *pUnkForRelease;    // IUnknown for release of data
} STGMEDIUM;
```

NOTE: In the example on the facing page, it is still necessary to call GlobalLock( ) and GlobalUnlock( ) as shown on the HGLOBAL returned by the method IDataObject::GetData( ). This is because the Clipboard data object's implementation of this method returns a handle to moveable memory rather than fixed memory. This means that the returned handle is actually an index in a table rather than a pointer, and the function GlobalLock( ) is necessary to fetch the actual memory pointer to which the handle refers. I think this is a hangover from Win16, but it exists and must be dealt with nonetheless.

```
/*
User has picked the EDIT-PASTE command off the menu.  Get data object
from Clipboard and paste its text into our app.
*/

char DisplayText [128] ;

case ID_EDIT_PASTE:
{

/*
Get Clipboard's current contents wrapped in a data object.
*/
    IDataObject *lpd ;

    OleGetClipboard (&lpd) ;

/*
Get data in text format, transferred in an HGLOBAL.
*/

    STGMEDIUM stg ; FORMATETC fe ;

    fe.cfFormat = CF_TEXT ;
    fe.ptd = NULL ;
    fe.tymed = TYMED_HGLOBAL ;
    fe.dwAspect = DVASPECT_CONTENT ;
    fe.lindex = -1 ;

    lpd->GetData (&fe, &stg) ;

/*
Paste data into our app.  GlobalLock( ) and GlobalUnlock( ) are
required because the handle supplied by the data object is to moveable
memory.
*/

    LPSTR cp = (LPSTR) GlobalLock (stg.hGlobal) ;
    lstrcpyn (DisplayText, cp, sizeof(DisplayText)) ;
    GlobalUnlock (stg.hGlobal) ;
    InvalidateRect (hWnd, NULL, TRUE) ;

/*
Release storage medium and data object.
*/

    ReleaseStgMedium (&stg) ;
    lpd->Release ( ) ;

    return 0 ;
}
```

G. WRITING OUR FIRST COM OBJECT

1. To accept data via the user interface drag-and-drop mechanism, an app must provide the operating system with a *Drop Target Object*. This is a C++ object that supports the *IDropTarget* interface, providing methods that the OS shell will call for different situations during a drag-and-drop operation. You must write the code for this object's methods yourself. The object must be created, AddRef( )'d, locked in memory via the function **CoLockObjectExternal( )**, and registered via the function **RegisterDragDrop( )**. Thus:

```
#include "cdroptgt.h"

CDropTarget *lpDropTarget ;

case WM_CREATE:
{

/*
Set up a drop target.  Instantiate a CDropTarget object and CoLock it
to keep it in memory.  Register it with the user interface.
*/

    lpDropTarget = new CDropTarget ( ) ;

    CoLockObjectExternal (lpDropTarget, TRUE, FALSE) ;
    RegisterDragDrop (hWnd, lpDropTarget) ;

    return 0 ;

}
```

When the app no longer wishes to be a drop target, it revokes its drop registration via the function **RevokeDragDrop( )**, unlocks it from memory via the function **CoLockObjectExternal( )**, and releases it with its own Release( ) method, thus:

```
case WM_CLOSE:
{
    RevokeDragDrop (hWnd) ;
    CoLockObjectExternal (lpDropTarget, FALSE, TRUE) ;
    lpDropTarget->Release( ) ;

    DestroyWindow (hWnd) ;
    return 0 ;
}
```

NOTE: The function CoLockObjectExternal is nonintuitive but necessary. If you leave it out, your drop target will work correctly the first time, but not on subsequent drag operations. You can just put it in as shown and stop worrying about it. Or you can consult the MSDN CD-ROM to find the kludge that causes it.

2. The drop target object belongs to a class that you have to write yourself. If you write in C++, inheriting from the public Microsoft-supplied class IDropTarget defined in the system header files, the compiler will properly set up all your VTBLs and your life will be relatively simple. All of IDropTarget's methods (and those of all the other standard interfaces) are defined as pure virtual, which means that you have to implement all of them yourself and you can't change any parameters or leave anything out. Your header file CDROPTGT.H will look something like this:

```
class CDropTarget : public IDropTarget
{

    protected:
        ULONG               m_RefCount ;
        LPDATAOBJECT        m_pIDataSource ;

    public:

        CDropTarget(void) ;
        ~CDropTarget(void) ;

//IUnknown interface members

        STDMETHODIMP       QueryInterface(REFIID, LPVOID FAR *) ;
        STDMETHODIMP_(ULONG)  AddRef(void) ;
        STDMETHODIMP_(ULONG)  Release(void) ;

//IDropTarget interface members

        STDMETHODIMP DragEnter(LPDATAOBJECT, DWORD, POINTL, LPDWORD) ;
        STDMETHODIMP DragOver(DWORD, POINTL, LPDWORD) ;
        STDMETHODIMP DragLeave(void) ;
        STDMETHODIMP Drop(LPDATAOBJECT, DWORD, POINTL, LPDWORD) ;

};
```

The class constructor and destructor will look like this:

```
CDropTarget::CDropTarget(void)
{
    m_RefCount = 1 ;              // calling constructor implies AddRef( )
    return;
}

CDropTarget::~CDropTarget(void)
{
    return;
}
```

NOTE: I like to set my objects' reference counts to 1 in my class constructors. My reasoning is that the constructor is a function that returns a pointer to an object, and any time you call a function that returns a pointer to an object, the pointer has already been AddRef( )'d for your convenience. This is an implementation detail that you can choose to follow or not.   If I didn't do it this way, I would have to AddRef( ) my object on the preceding page immediately after constructing it.

3. The IDropTarget interface contains four methods in addition to the standard IUnknown. The first is **IDropTarget::DragEnter( )**, which is called only once when the mouse first enters the target window with a drag operation in progress. You can use this to examine the offered data object and decide if it contains a data format that your app knows how to handle. Note the similarity of this code to that used in the Clipboard data object example. The main difference is that in the DragEnter( ) method, since the object provider called us, we have to AddRef( ) the data object pointer if we want to keep it. This drop target accepts only plain text and doesn't do anything clever with it.

Your drop target signals the result that would happen if the object was dropped by setting the value pointed to by the last parameter, *pdwEffect*. Since this operation is performed in the DragOver( ) method on the facing page, the DragEnter( ) method simply calls DragOver( ) instead of duplicating its code. Thus:

```
STDMETHODIMP CDropTarget::DragEnter(LPDATAOBJECT pIDataSource,
    DWORD grfKeyState, POINTL pt, LPDWORD pdwEffect)
{

/*
Check to see if the data is in a format we can handle (in this case,
only text).  If so, keep a copy of the data object pointer, which means
that we must AddRef( ) it. Note similarity to Clipboard example.
*/

    FORMATETC fe ;

    fe.cfFormat = CF_TEXT ;
    fe.ptd = NULL ;
    fe.tymed = TYMED_HGLOBAL ;
    fe.dwAspect = DVASPECT_CONTENT ;
    fe.lindex = -1 ;

    if (pIDataSource->QueryGetData (&fe) == S_OK)
    {
      m_pIDataSource = pIDataSource ;
      m_pIDataSource->AddRef ( ) ;
    }
    else
    {
      m_pIDataSource = NULL ;
    }

/*
Call our own DragOver( ) method to set the effect code.
*/

    DragOver(grfKeyState, pt, pdwEffect) ;

    return S_OK ;
}
```

4. The method **IDropTarget::DragOver( )** is called every time the mouse is moved in the target window during a drag operation, similar to a WM_MOUSEMOVE message. The target's job is to signal back to the source the operation (move, copy, link, nothing, etc.) that would take place if the user dropped the data object at the current mouse location. The target does this by setting the output variable pointed to by the parameter pdwEffect to a specified flag as shown below. On input, this parameter contains flags describing the actions that the source will allow. For example, Winhlp32.exe, being a read-only app, allows a copy operation but not a move. Winword.exe allows copy and move operations, but not link. The state of the mouse, CTRL, and SHIFT keys are provided to the drop target in the parameter grfKeyState.

This method is called frequently, so you want to make it as fast and efficient as possible. You don't have to check if the data is acceptable; you did that when it first entered. DragOver( ) is always called, regardless of the effect code returned from your DragEnter( ) method. Thus:

```
STDMETHODIMP CDropTarget::DragOver(DWORD grfKeyState, POINTL pt,
    LPDWORD pdwEffect)
{

/*
If data is in a format we couldn't handle, then set effect code to
indicate nothing would happen if data was dropped here.
*/
    if (m_pIDataSource == NULL)
    {
      *pdwEffect = DROPEFFECT_NONE ;
    }
/*
Otherwise, if CTRL key is up and permitted effects (supplied by drop
source) allow a move, set the effect code to indicate a move.
*/
    else if (!(grfKeyState&MK_CONTROL) && (*pdwEffect&DROPEFFECT_MOVE))
    {
      *pdwEffect = DROPEFFECT_MOVE ;
    }


/*
Otherwise, if effect permits a copy, set effect code to indicate that.
*/
    else if (*pdwEffect & DROPEFFECT_COPY)
    {
      *pdwEffect = DROPEFFECT_COPY ;
    }
/*
Otherwise, even though the data is in a format that we could accept,
the effect code isn't. Set the effect code to indicate that nothing
would happen if data was dropped here.  Unlikely to actually get here
in real life.
*/
    else
    {
      *pdwEffect = DROPEFFECT_NONE ;
    }
    return S_OK;
}
```

5.   The user may drop the data object on the target, which will cause the method **IDropTarget::Drop( )** to be called. Your app takes the data object and does whatever it wants with its data. This signals the end of a drag operation, so you also have to undo any initialization here. Note the similarity of the pasting code to that used in the Clipboard data object operation. Thus:

```
extern int xText, yText ;
extern char DisplayText[ ] ;
extern HWND hMainWnd ;

STDMETHODIMP CDropTarget::Drop(LPDATAOBJECT pIDataSource,
    DWORD grfKeyState,  POINTL pt, LPDWORD pdwEffect)
{
    if (m_pIDataSource)
    {

/*
Get point on screen where data was dropped.   Convert  to client
coordinates,  store  in  global  variables  xText  and  yText,  which will
cause main window to display the text where it was dropped.
*/

        ScreenToClient (hMainWnd, (POINT *)(&pt)) ;
        xText = pt.x ;
        yText = pt.y ;

/*
Fetch text from data object.
*/

        STGMEDIUM stg ; FORMATETC fe ;


        fe.cfFormat = CF_TEXT ;
        fe.ptd = NULL ;
        fe.tymed = TYMED_HGLOBAL ;
        fe.dwAspect = DVASPECT_CONTENT ;
        fe.lindex = -1 ;

        m_pIDataSource->GetData (&fe, &stg) ;


/*
Copy data into string for display in main window and Invalidate to
cause a repaint.
*/
        LPSTR cp = (LPSTR) GlobalLock (stg.hGlobal) ;
        lstrcpyn (DisplayText, cp, 127) ;
        GlobalUnlock (stg.hGlobal) ;
        InvalidateRect (hMainWnd, NULL,  FALSE) ;
```

```
/*
Release data object and storage medium.
*/

     ReleaseStgMedium (&stg) ;
     m_pIDataSource->Release( );


     }

/*
Call our own DragOver( ) method to set the effect code.
*/

    DragOver(grfKeyState, pt, pdwEffect) ;
    return NOERROR;
}
```

6. When the mouse leaves the target window without dropping, your app's **IDropTarget::DragLeave( )** method is called. You use this to undo any initialization that you had done during the DragEnter( ) method. Thus:

```
STDMETHODIMP CDropTarget::DragLeave(void)
{
    if (m_pIDataSource)
    {
      m_pIDataSource->Release();
    }

    return NOERROR;
}
```

Lab Exercises
Chapter 1
Data Transfer Object Consumer

Directory: \EssenceOfCOM\chap01\data1\templ

This lab creates an app that accepts simple text data from the Clipboard by means of a data object. It also implements a drop target object that accepts simple text via drag-and-drop. A skeleton app is supplied for you in the directory listed above; you may want to build it and run it first (it won't do much) to make sure that your development environment is properly configured.

1. Your app must first initialize the OLE/COM libraries. In the file WINMAIN.CPP, add a call to OleInitialize( ) at the start of the function WinMain( ). Add a call to OleUninitialize( ) at the end of WinMain( ).

2. The Demo-Paste Text menu item starts out grayed. We would like to make it respond to the contents of the Clipboard, enabling the menu item if the Clipboard contains text and disabling it otherwise. In the file MAINWIND.CPP, in the WM_INITMENU message handler, add the following code: Call the function OleGetClipboard( ) to get a data object that encapsulates the current contents of the Clipboard. Allocate a FORMATETC structure and fill its fields with the correct parameters for requesting data in the CF_TEXT format via an HGLOBAL transfer medium. Use the data object's QueryGetData( ) method to ask the object if it can supply data in this manner. If it can, enable the menu item, otherwise gray it out. The menu modification code has been supplied for you. Release the Clipboard data object when you are finished.

3. When the user chooses the Demo-Paste Text menu item, we need to get the text from the Clipboard and paste it into the app. In the file MAINWIND.CPP, in the ID_DEMO_PASTETEXT case of the WM_COMMAND message handler, use the function OleGetClipboard( ) to get the Clipboard's contents wrapped in a data object. Allocate a FORMATETC structure and also an STGMEDIUM structure; fill out the fields of the former. This time, use the object's GetData( ) method to actually retrieve the data in text format. Copy the new data from the STGMEDIUM structure into the global string array named DisplayText[ ], which is provided for you. Finally, release the storage medium via the function ReleaseStgMedium( ) and release the Clipboard data object via its own Release( ) method. Your app should now properly paste text from the Clipboard into the upper left corner of its window.

4. Our app now supports the Clipboard; we would like to make it do the same thing via drag-and-drop. A skeleton of a drop target class, called CDropTarget, has been provided for you in the file CDROPTGT.CPP. Examine this file and its header file CDROPTGT.H. You will find the IUnknown methods have been written for you, but the other four methods are empty shells. In the file MAINWIND.CPP, in the WM_CREATE message handler, instantiate a CDropTarget object and use the function CoLockObjectExternal( ) to lock it into memory. Use the function RegisterDragDrop( ) to notify the operating system that your app will accept drop operations. In the WM_CLOSE message handler, use the function RevokeDragDrop( ) to notify the operating system that your window will no longer accept drop operations, unlock it from memory via the function CoLockObjectExternal( ), then free it with its own Release( ) method.

5. Our drop target is connected. Its methods will be called when a drag operation takes place over our window, but so far they don't do anything. Now we have to start implementing the code to make it do what we want. The first method, CDropTarget::DragEnter( ), is called when the mouse first enters the target window. What we need to do here is to check if the data object that the operation contains (passed as the first parameter) can supply the data in the format that we need. Use the object's QueryGetData( ) method to ask the object if it can render its data in CF_TEXT via an HGLOBAL medium. This code will bear an uncanny resemblance to what you did in step 2 above. If the data can be so rendered, save the data pointer in the member variable m_pIDataSource and AddRef( ) it to make sure it will stay valid until we

need it. Otherwise, set the member variable to NULL. You can set the effect code yourself, or, to save duplication, call your own DragOver( ) method described in the next paragraph.

6.   The next method is CDropTarget::DragOver( ), which is conceptually similar to the WM_MOUSEMOVE message. In this case, simply check the value of the data pointer m_pIDataSource. If it is NULL, then our DragEnter( ) method initially decided that the object couldn't supply the data in a format that we wanted, so set the effect to DROPEFFECT_NONE. If it is non-NULL, then we can accept the data. Check the state of the control key, passed in the first parameter. If it's up, and the source permits a move (check the last parameter), then set the effect code to DROPEFFECT_MOVE. Otherwise, if the source permits a copy, then set it to DROPEFFECT_COPY.

7. The DragLeave( ) method is trivial. If the m_pIDataSource pointer is valid, release the object via its Release( ) method. That's all.

8. Now we are left with the Drop( ) method. First, convert the point from the screen coordinates it comes in to the client coordinates that your window wants via the API function ScreenToClient( ). The main window's handle is supplied for you in the global variable hMainWnd. Set the drop point's X value into the global variable xText and its Y value into the global yText. This will cause the WM_PAINT message handler to draw it at the place on the screen where it was dropped. Next, use the data object pointer to get the data from the object in the CF_TEXT format. This will be very similar to step 3 above, including the release of both data object and storage medium. Finally, call your own DragOver( ) method to set the effect code.

EXTRA CREDIT: When dragging text inside your window, use a focus rectangle to show the size of the string being dragged. In your DragEnter( ) method, get the data from the dragged object via its GetData( ) method, then use the function DrawText( ) with the flag DT_CALCRECT to calculate the rectangle that the text would occupy if drawn. Store the rectangle in a member variable. Then in your DragOver( ) method, use the function DrawFocusRect( ) to put a focus rectangle on the screen at the point where the mouse is, showing the rectangle that the text would occupy. You will also have to add another member variable to your drop target for storing the point at which you drew the last focus rectangle, so you can remove it before you draw the new one.

This page intentionally contains no text other than this sentence.

Chapter 2

Object Servers

A. WHY PROVIDE COM OBJECTS?

1. Why would you want to expose your app's capabilities to the world through COM? What's wrong with plain vanilla non-COM DLLs, which were touted as the magic bullet of component software for the first seven or eight years of Windows' existence? COM has at least four advantages as a mechanism for component software.

2. When a client app links to a DLL, the DLL's name is hard coded in an import table inside the client app. When the client app runs, the operating system attempts to find and load all the DLLs named in that table. The DLL must be located in the client app's directory or in the system path. If any are missing, the entire application fails to load, even if the user wasn't planning on using any of the functionality within it, and your computer becomes an expensive paperweight. It is impossible to change the names of the DLLs without breaking the application. Thus:

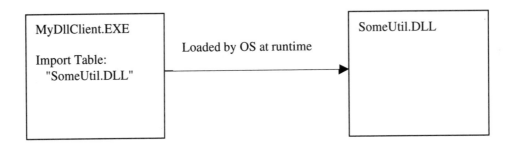

With COM, a client application requests a component by means of a *Class ID* (CLSID), rather than a file name. The CLSID refers to a location in the system registry, which stores the path name to the actual server. In this manner, the names and locations of servers can change without needing to change the client application — you just patch the registry to point to the new server and the client keeps working. Thus:

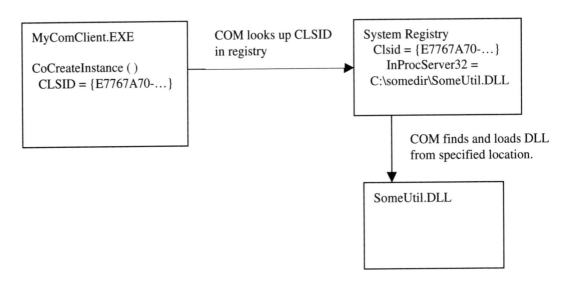

3. A DLL exposes all of its functions in a flat programming model, with no notion of hierarchy. Flat programming models are difficult to use, particularly when they get large. A DLL client can dynamically query for the presence of any function via GetProcAddress( ), but the hierarchy does not extend any deeper. Thus:

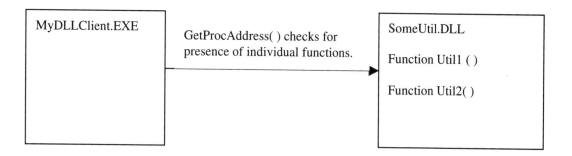

With COM, a DLL can contain more than one class of object, and each object can expose more than one interface. A client specifies the desired object class at creation time, and may then query for whatever interfaces it desires. This hierarchical programming model is much more efficient for logical division of functionality, and hence for shortening development time. Thus:

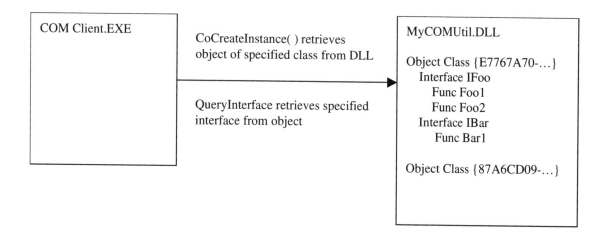

4. Versioning becomes much, much easier using COM because each new version of an interface has a different interface ID. A new release of a server can contain within it the code to support any previous versions, thereby eliminating the proliferation of DLLs for each version (VBRUN100.DLL, VBRUN200.DLL, etc.). You don't need to change the class ID, only the interface ID. Because a client app queries at runtime for the interfaces it wants, the server can load code for outdated features only if requested. Conversely, a new client that can use the latest features but finds an old server can gracefully degrade to use only those features supported by the server rather than crashing with an "undefined dynalink" error.

In the case shown below, a new server has just replaced an old one on a machine. The new server's installation program has changed the registry, pointing the CLSID of the old component to the new server DLL. An old client app creates an object, specifying the old CLSID and old interface ID. The object and interface are provided by the new server, and the old client is none the wiser. Thus:

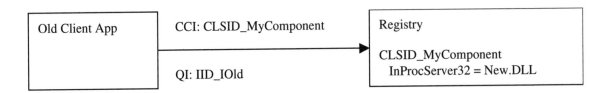

In the case shown below, a new client app finds itself on a machine that contains only the old version of the server, not the new one. The client creates an object of the same class ID, querying for the new interface, which the old server does not support. When the query fails, the client queries for the old interface, which the old server does support. The client gracefully degrades, perhaps graying out the menu items for the features that the old server does not support. Thus:

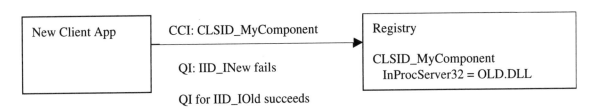

5. DLL functions by definition have to live in the same address space and on the same machine as the client app. Accessing components that live elsewhere requires different programming techniques, perhaps shared memory file maps and Win32 synchronization events to access a different address space on the same machine, and named pipes or RPC to access a different machine. You have to know at development time where your counterparty lives, choose a programming model accordingly, and rewrite everything if it changes.

If a COM client and object live in the same address space, the client gets a direct connection to the object, as shown here:

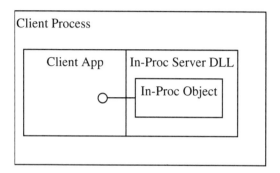

However, if the object lives in another address space or another machine (or, in the case of multiple threads, in a different apartment, see Chapter 6), COM will transparently set up a *proxy* on the client side, which connects through the *channel* to a *stub* on the server side. The client makes calls in its own address space; the object receives calls in its own address space. The proxy/stub mechanism takes care of all the nasty details of crossing the process or machine boundaries. Proxies and stubs are discussed in more detail in Chapter 3. Thus:

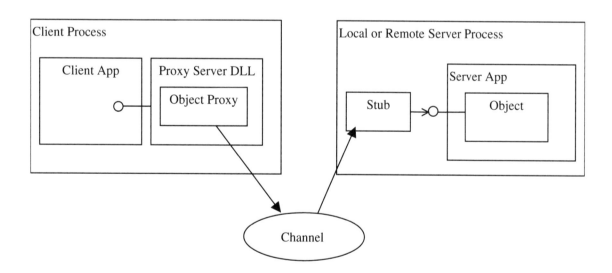

B. OBJECT CREATION FROM THE CLIENT'S PERSPECTIVE

1. A client application creates an object via the function **CoCreateInstance( )**. This tells COM to locate and wake up a registered server DLL or EXE and tell that server to create an object for you. You identify the object you want by means of its *CLSID*, a GUID used to identify the class. COM uses the CLSID to locate the server in the registry, as shown in the next section, beginning on the facing page.

When you call CoCreateInstance( ), you can specify whether you want to load the object from a *local server* (.EXE) or an *in-proc server* (.DLL). Most servers come in only one flavor or the other; it is rare to find both together. Combining the context flags as shown below causes COM to look for an in-proc server first, and use a local server only if unable to find an in-proc server. You will find the sample code for the app shown below in the directory \chap02\data3. Thus:

```
/*
CLSID of the object we want to create.  Supplied by the vendor who made
the server.
*/

static const CLSID CLSID_TimeData = { 0xe7767a70, 0xa409, 0x11ce,
    { 0xad, 0xf, 0x0, 0x60, 0x8c, 0x86, 0xb8, 0x9c } };


/*
User made menu selection telling us to create an object of the
specified type, using either an in-proc or a local server.  Tell COM to
find the server, wake it up, make it create an object, and give us back
a pointer to its IDataObject interface.
*/

LPDATAOBJECT lpd = NULL ;

case ID_DATAOBJECT_CREATE:
{
    HRESULT hr ;

    hr = CoCreateInstance (
        CLSID_TimeData,            // CLSID of desired object
        NULL,                      // outer wrapper, here none
        CLSCTX_LOCAL_SERVER |      // try in-proc server first; use
          CLSCTX_INPROC_SERVER,    // local server if unavailable
        IID_IDataObject,           // interface pointer desired
        (void **) &lpd) ;          // output variable

    return 0 ;
}
```

NOTE: I discuss the case of a remote server, one that lives on a different machine, in Chapter 7 (DCOM). It requires the new function CoCreateInstanceEx( ).

C. SERVER REGISTRATION

1. COM object servers must make entries in the system registry so that COM knows where to find them when the client calls CoCreateInstance( ). Most modern applications contain their own code for making these registry entries. To make it more obvious to you what's happening, however, most of the examples in the book provide .REG files for making these entries; in this case, \chap02\data3\data3.reg.

A server that wants to make its objects available via CoCreateInstance( ) must provide a LocalServer32 or an InProcServer32 entry in the registry's HKEY_CLASSES_ROOT\CLSID hive. Thus:

```
HKEY_CLASSES_ROOT
    CLSID
            <your object's class ID>
                    LocalServer32 = <full path to server .EXE>
                    InProcServer32 = <full path to server .DLL>
```

In the Data3 example, the entries are:

```
HKEY_CLASSES_ROOT
    CLSID
            {E7767A70-A409-11ce-AD0F-00608C86B89C}
                    LocalServer32 = c:\EssenceofCOM\chap02\data3\server\data3sv.exe
                    InProcServer32 = c:\EssenceofCOM\chap02\data3\inprocsv\data3ips.dll
```

You can view or edit them with the registry editor/viewer REGEDIT.EXE. Thus:

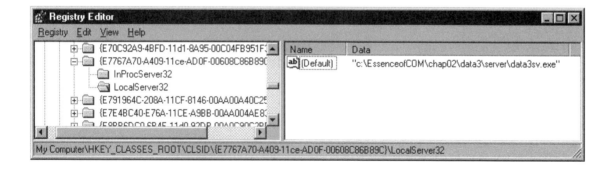

2. In addition to the required settings under the CLSID key, most servers choose to provide a human-readable name, known as a *Program ID* or ProgID, that identifies the class. This is a string, placed in the registry, that contains a key specifying the CLSID that applies to the class of object named by the ProgID. These are used in dialog boxes to provide human users with a list of recognizable objects to choose from, and are also used by clients such as scripting engines that can handle strings but not CLSIDs. A ProgID registry entry has the form

```
HKEY_CLASSES_ROOT
    <your app's human-readable name>
            CLSID = <your app's class ID>
```

In the Data3 example, these entries are:

```
HKEY_CLASSES_ROOT
    EssenceofCOM.Data3
            CLSID = {E7767A70-A409-11ce-AD0F-00608C86B89C}
```

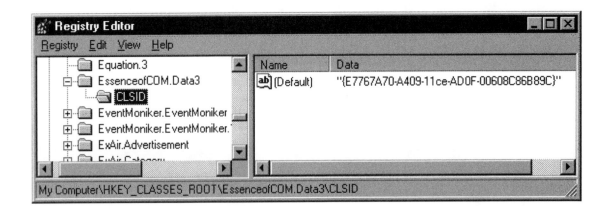

3. If you don't know the object's class ID but do know its ProgID, or perhaps have the user pick it from a list, you can fetch the class ID via the function **CLSIDFromProgID( )**. This function finds the specified key under HKEY_CLASSES_ROOT, looks for the CLSID subkey, reads the string value of the subkey, and converts it into a CLSID. It requires a wide character string, as do all COM functions and interface methods that take strings as their parameters. A wide character string is a string of 16-bit characters which uses the Unicode character set. For now, prepending the character 'L' to the string in quotes causes the compiler to treat the string as wide characters, whether the rest of your app uses wide characters or not. Thus:

```
case ID_DATAOBJECT_CREATEDLL:
{
    HRESULT hr ;

/*
Read class ID from registry key.
*/

    CLSID clsid ;
    hr = CLSIDFromProgID (L"EssenceofCOM.Data3", &clsid) ;

/*
Create object based on class ID read from registry.
*/

    hr = CoCreateInstance (clsid, ...) ;

    <rest of creation case>
}
```

D. THE CLASS FACTORY

1. When the client calls CoCreateInstance( ), COM goes to the registry, finds the server for the object's class, and loads that server. COM then gets from the server a *class factory*, an object that supports the *IClassFactory* interface. This interface is somewhat misnamed, as it manufactures objects rather than classes. The exact mechanism by which COM obtains the class factory is different for an EXE and a DLL, as described on the following pages.

In addition to IUnknown, the IClassFactory interface has only two methods. The method **IClassFactory::CreateInstance( )** is called by COM to create a new object and get a pointer to an interface on it. You will note that nowhere in the parameter list is the class of object that is to be manufactured. Each class of object therefore requires its own separate hard-wired class factory object. Thus:

```
STDMETHODIMP CTimeDataFactory::CreateInstance(LPUNKNOWN pUnkOuter,
    REFIID riid, LPVOID* ppvObj)
{

/*
Check for aggregation request. COM is asking us to create a new object
inside another object provided by COM.  This simple example doesn't
support this feature, and neither do most real-world apps.
*/
    if (pUnkOuter != NULL)
    {
      *ppvObj = NULL ;
      return CLASS_E_NOAGGREGATION ;
    }

/*
Create a new object of our hard-wired class.  Query the new object for
the interface requested by the caller.  If found, release our reference
on the object and return success code.
*/

    CTimeData * pTD = new CTimeData ( ) ;

    if (pTD->QueryInterface (riid, ppvObj) == S_OK)
    {
      pTD->Release ( ) ;
      return S_OK ;
    }

/*
The new object could not support the requested interface.  Delete the
newly created object and return an error code.
*/
    else
    {
      delete pTD ;
      return E_NOINTERFACE ;
    }
}
```

2. A client that creates and destroys many objects might want to keep the server running, ready for fast action, instead of frequently loading and unloading it. The client can get a pointer to the class factory itself via the API function **CoGetClassObject( )** (not shown), and call its **IClassFactory::LockServer( )** method. If your class factory implements the method, as does this one, you simply increment or decrement a lock count and refuse to shut down the server until all objects created by the server have been destroyed AND the lock count is zero. Many apps simply stub this one out. Thus:

```
STDMETHODIMP CTimeDataFactory::LockServer(BOOL bLock)
{

/*
Increment or decrement our server's lock count, based on the parameter
passed to this method, using a utility function that we write,
described later in this chapter.
*/

    if (bLock == TRUE)
    {
      MyOwnLockServer ( ) ;
    }


/*
In the case of a .EXE server, the unlocking utility function will
contain functionality that shuts down the server process.
*/


    else
    {
      MyOwnUnlockServer ( ) ;
    }

    return S_OK ;
}
```

3. When COM launches an EXE server app, it passes the string "-Embedding" on the server's command line. When a server finds this on its command line, it must register its class factory interface with COM via the function **CoRegisterClassObject( )**. This interface provides COM with the methods it needs to create new objects of the specified class. When the server app shuts down, it must unregister its class factory via the function **CoRevokeClassObject( )**.   The sequence of events is shown in the block diagram below. The code executed by the local server is shown on the facing page.

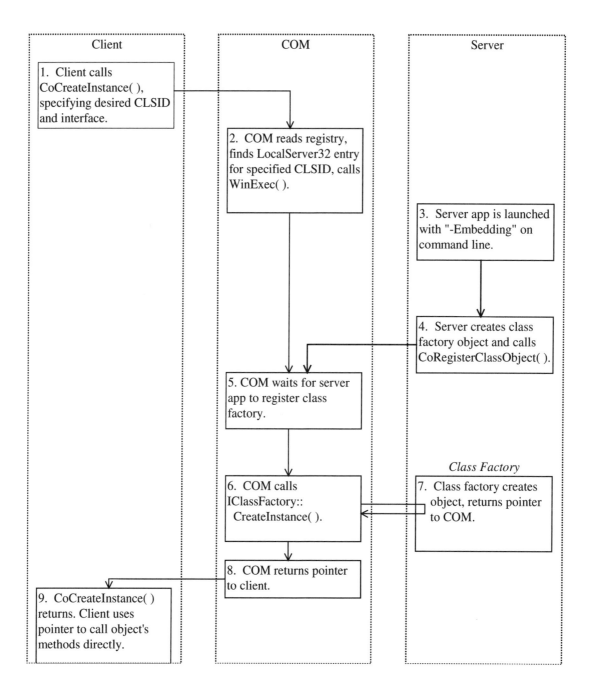

```
int WINAPI WinMain(HINSTANCE hInstance, HINSTANCE hPrevInstance,
    LPSTR lpCmdLine, int nCmdShow)
{

    < initialize, create windows, etc. >

/*
Check command line to see if launched as a COM server.  If so, register
the class factory for this app.
*/

    DWORD dwRegister ;

    if (strstr (lpCmdLine, "-Embedding"))
    {
      LPCLASSFACTORY pCF = new CTimeDataFactory ( ) ;

      CoRegisterClassObject(
            CLSID_TimeData,          // GUID of object mfd by this fy
            pCF,                     // ptr to IClassFactory object
            CLSCTX_LOCAL_SERVER,     // context, here a local server
            REGCLS_MULTIPLEUSE,      // more flags
            &dwRegister) ;           // output variable

    }

    <standard message loop >

/*
App going down, revoke down class factory
*/

    CoRevokeClassObject (dwRegister) ;


    < standard app shutdown >
}
```

Chapter 2   35   Object Servers

4. When your server is a DLL, you do not call CoRegisterClassObject( ) as you did for an EXE server. Instead, your server DLL must provide two named exported functions for COM to call. The first, **DllGetClassObject( )**, provides COM with the class factory object that creates objects of the specified class. This is the same class factory as we passed to CoRegisterClassObject( ) in the local server example previously shown. The sequence of events when an object is created from an in-proc server is shown in the following block diagram. The server's code is on the facing page.

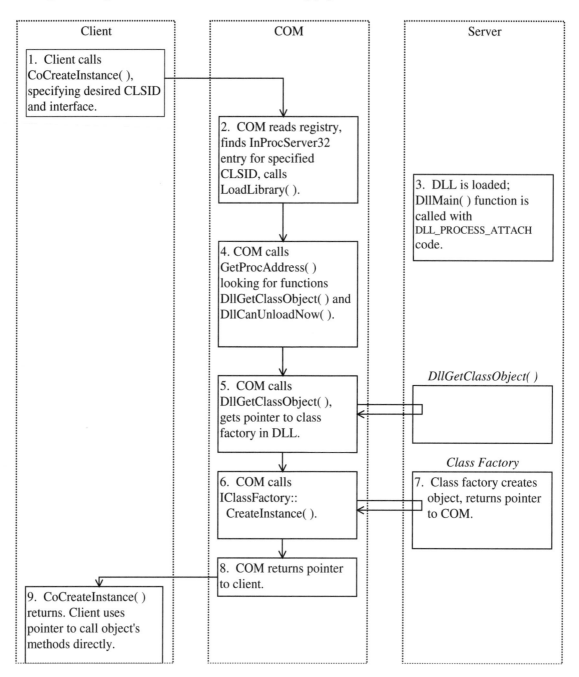

```
CTimeDataFactory cf ;   // IClassFactory implementation that
                        // manufactures this particular class of object.


STDAPI DllGetClassObject(REFCLSID rclsid, REFIID riid, LPVOID *ppv)
{
/*
Check to make sure that COM is asking for the CLSID that we support.
Maybe someone got the registry entry wrong.
*/
    if (rclsid !=  GUID_TimeData)
    {
      *ppv = NULL ;
      return E_FAIL ;
    }


/*
Take our hard-wired class factory and call QueryInterface( ) on it, on
behalf of the COM that called this function.
*/
    return cf.QueryInterface (riid, ppv) ;


}
```

5. A local server is responsible for shutting itself down, but an in-proc server will be unloaded by COM. It must provide a function called **DllCanUnloadNow( )**, which tells COM whether or not there are any outstanding references on this server's objects. Thus:

```
extern UINT g_LockCount ;

STDAPI DllCanUnloadNow(void)
{
/*
If no outstanding objects or lock counts, tell COM that it is now safe
to unload this DLL.  Otherwise, say it isn't.
*/
    if (g_LockCount == 0)
    {
      return S_OK ;
    }
    else
    {
      return S_FALSE  ;
    }
}
```

WARNING: The examples shown here have to be exported from the DLL via a .DEF file. The combination of STDAPI and __declspec(dllexport) in the function declaration does not work. The DLL will compile and link, but the function names will not be listed in the DLL's name table. COM's call to GetProcAddress( ) will therefore fail, and so will CoCreateInstance( ).

E. SERVER LIFETIME

1. A COM server must know how to manage its own lifetime. Generally a server wants to stay around as long as it has objects to service. Most COM servers manage this by maintaining a global variable representing the count of all the server's outstanding objects. The constructors and destructors of individual objects call utility functions that you write to increment and decrement this count. Thus:

```
/*
Object constructor. Call the helper function to increment the server's
global object count.
*/

CTimeData::CTimeData()
{
    < other object initialization >

    MyOwnLockServer ( ) ;
}



/*
Object destructor. Call the helper function to decrement the server's
global object count.
*/

CTimeData::~CTimeData(void)
{
    < other object cleanup >

    MyOwnUnlockServer ( ) ;
}
```

NOTE: Because, in the case of an EXE server, it is created and registered by the server app itself instead of by a client, the mere creation of a class factory should not lock the server, as is the case for other objects. If it did, the server would run forever. A class factory should only lock the server if explicitly requested to do so via the method IClassFactory::LockServer( ).

2. The utility functions provided by the server increment and decrement the server's global object count as appropriate. In the case of a .EXE server, as shown here, the utility function shuts the server down when its last object is destroyed. Thus:

```
int g_LockCount = 0 ;
HWND  hMainWnd ;

/*
Increment the server's global object count.
*/

void MyOwnLockServer ( )
{
    g_LockCount ++ ;
}

/*
Decrement the server's global object count. If it reaches zero, shut
down the server process.
*/

void MyOwnUnlockServer ( )
{
    g_LockCount -- ;

    if (g_LockCount == 0)
    {
      PostMessage (hMainWnd, WM_CLOSE, 0, 0) ;
    }
}
```

3. A DLL server does not provide shutdown code as does an .EXE server. Instead, a client application periodically calls the API function CoFreeUnusedLibraries( ) (not shown). COM then goes to each DLL server loaded into the client's process, calls the DllCanUnloadNow( ) function exported by the server, and unloads any DLL server that returns S_OK.

F. In-Proc and Out-of-Proc Servers

1. As explained previously, a COM object may live either inside or outside of its client's process. If a COM client and object live in the same address space, the client gets a direct connection to the object, as shown here:

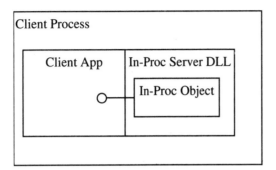

However, if the object lives in another address space or another machine (or, in the case of multiple threads, in a different apartment, see Chapter 6), COM will transparently set up a *proxy* on the client side, which connects through the *channel* to a *stub* on the server side. The client makes calls in its own address space; the object receives calls in its own address space. The proxy/stub mechanism takes care of all the nasty details of crossing the process or machine boundaries. Proxies and stubs are discussed in more detail in the Chapter 3. Thus:

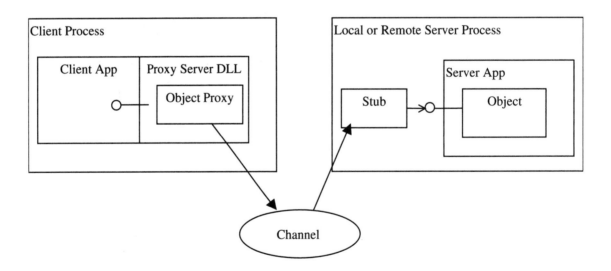

The process of transferring a call from one address space to another is known as *marshaling*. When a client makes a call, the proxy marshals the parameters through the channel to the stub. The stub makes the call into the object in the server's address space and marshals the results back through the channel to the proxy. This mechanism takes time, which is why in-proc calls are faster than out-of-proc calls, by a factor of about 100 to 1000. You can verify this yourself using the "Data Object — GetData Time Test" menu item on the data3 sample client application. Instructions for setting up and using this app are found at the end of this chapter.

2. There are three primary advantages of packaging your objects in DLLs, so that they can reside in the address space of their clients.

A. Speed: Because calls within the same process don't need to be marshaled via proxy and stub (except potentially in multithreaded situations, see Chapter 6), they can execute much faster than calls that require marshaling. A ballpark estimate is about 100 – 1000 times faster than out-of-proc calls.

B. Data Transparency: Not all data types can be marshaled across process boundaries. For example, an HDC in Windows NT is process relative. If you pass an HDC to another process and try to use it, it won't work. I have a customer who added COM relatively late in the lifetime of a C++-based product. He passes raw C++ object pointers as COM parameters from client to server and back again. While this isn't a great habit to form, this customer was adding COM relatively late in the lifetime of a product of which he only sold a few hundred units per year, and he didn't feel that it paid him to do anything more sophisticated. This works in-proc, but not out of proc.

C. COM+ on Windows 2000 provides useful runtime services, such as transactions, security, and synchronization. COM+ does these things by wrapping itself around your COM components in accordance with administrative entries that you make (think of the registry on steroids). COM+ can only do these things if your components live in DLLs. If they live in separate EXEs, COM+ can't get its arms around them to perform these useful actions. For more on COM+, consult my book *Understanding COM+* from Microsoft Press, ISBN 0-7536-0666-8.

3. OK, then, why would anyone ever want their server to live in a separate .EXE? There are at least five reasons that I've seen in real life.

A. If you need to service both 16-bit and 32-bit clients from the same binary server, that server must be a .EXE, it cannot be a DLL. Sixteen-bit apps cannot load 32-bit DLLs, and vice versa. While you and I probably wish all 16-bit apps would disappear tomorrow, they won't and we have to deal with it.

B. If you are adding COM to an existing .EXE, it may not pay you to rearchitect it. Microsoft Excel received COM support around 1994, with its source code base about 7 years old. While Excel would probably run more efficiently if it had been rearchitected to put its engine functionality in COM DLLs and its user interface in an EXE, Microsoft decided that the gain wouldn't be worth the major development cost and the possibility of breaking existing users. They were probably right.

C. If your server wants control over its own lifetime, it needs to live in a separate process from its client. For example, if your server is very expensive to launch, and you want to keep it running even when its last object is destroyed, to avoid the overhead of launching it the next time a client wants an object from it, you need it to run in a separate EXE.

D. If your server wants control over its own security context, it needs to live in a separate process from its client. For example, as we will see in the chapter on DCOM, a COM server may specify which users are allowed to make calls into it and which are not. This determination is made on a per-process basis, and it must be made before the first object is created within a process. If you write an EXE server, you have control over this, but if your server is a DLL, you don't. The security settings will have been made by the client before your object is created, and you won't be able to change them.

E. An object that throws an exception in its client app's process can kill the client app. An object in another address space cannot. Furthermore, an object running in its client's address space has full access to the memory space of the client app, and runs with the identity of the client app. A client that creates an in-proc object is trusting the object not to do anything bad.

Lab Exercises
Chapter 2
Basic COM Server

Directory: \EssenceOfCOM\chap02\data3

This sample application demonstrates basic server functionality in COM. It does not have type-along instructions, it is meant for you to run and then examine the code. It provides both in-proc and local servers for you to try.

1. You must first register the server EXE and DLL with COM. To do this, double click on the registry file "data3.reg" in the sample directory shown above. This file assumes that you have followed the directions in the sample code's root directory by unpacking the entire contents to your C: drive's root directory. If you have put it any other place, you will have to edit this file to point to your server's current location.

2. Now run the client app data3cl.exe, which you will find in the \client subdirectory. From the main menu, choose "Data Object — Create from .EXE server". A server window should appear. If not, you probably have the server registration wrong; go back and look again at the previous step. Now select "Data Object — GetData" from the main menu. The current time should appear in the client window. Now pick "Data Object — Release" from the main menu. The server window should disappear.

3. Try the same exercise choosing "Data Object — Create from .DLL server". You won't see a window; the DLL server doesn't pop one up, but the object should be created. The getting of the data and releasing the object should work similarly.

4. Now try a time test. Create an object either from an EXE server or from a DLL server. Then select "Data Object — GetData Time Test" from the main menu. Enter a number of bytes to transfer on each call and a number of calls to make. Ten thousand for each gives a reasonable test on most machines. You will find that it takes 5 – 10 seconds with an EXE server versus essentially nothing for a DLL server (although the latter is longer on Windows 95 due to an inefficient 16-bit based memory allocator). See how much faster in-proc is?

Chapter 3

Custom Interfaces

This page intentionally contains no text other than this sentence.

A. VTBL Interfaces Versus Dispatch Interfaces

1. When writing your own interfaces, why would you choose a VTBL-based interface rather than accessing all of your methods through an IDispatch interface as shown in the next chapter? The primary drawback of a VTBL-based interface is that an interpreted client, such as a Web browser, cannot use it. A VTBL interface has three main advantages:

A. The overhead of a VTBL function call is lower than that of a dispinterface function call. The client doesn't have to pack up all the parameters into a bunch of VARIANT structures. The server doesn't have to check the number of parameters or their types. All of this gets compiled away instead of being performed at runtime on every function call. I've found that the performance degradation of IDispatch versus VTBL is typically on the order of 100 microseconds per call, give or take. That's only significant if the client has a direct proxyless connection to the object; otherwise the marshaling overhead is greater. If you need the last smidgen of speed, you need a VTBL interface.

B. A method on a VTBL interface can support any type of parameter that you can describe in IDL (described on the next page), which means essentially anything. An IDispatch interface, on the other hand, can only support the types of parameters that are contained in a VARIANT structure. If you need other types of parameters, you will have to figure some workaround for passing these via a dispinterface method, costing performance and delaying ship dates. For example, the COM+ catalog administration interfaces support IDispatch in order to be accessible to scripting clients. Some of their methods need to deal with GUIDs for identifying applications and components. The IDispatch interface cannot pass a GUID directly, so all of these interfaces pass their GUIDs as strings. The object has to convert incoming strings into GUID before using them.

C. An object that exposes its functionality through VTBL interfaces can support more than one interface per object. However, an object may only support one IDispatch interface. This means losing the benefits of having multiple interfaces per object. For example, you can't version objects by interface ID any more (since it's always IDispatch), you have to version them by ProgID or CLSID. It's less clean and elegant than straight VTBL interfaces, which translates into being more difficult (and therefore longer, and more expensive) to develop and to use.

2. Which do you choose? In the end, much as I hate to say this, it's a marketing call. Anyone who is developing COM components for external sale will probably have to provide an IDispatch interface. With the explosive growth of the Web in just the few years since I wrote the first edition of this book, I find very few developers willing to close off this source of customers. The developers I see writing VTBL-only interfaces are doing it for internal use and not for external sale. In this case, the extra speed and richer parameter set often leads to the choice of a VTBL interface.

3. If you can't make up your mind, your objects can expose both a dispinterface and a VTBL interface. You can do this via the much-touted dual interface, which is a custom interface derived from IDispatch, allowing interpreted clients to use the dispinterface and compiled clients to use the VTBL interface. Dual interfaces are described beginning on page 60. This will mostly solve the performance problem for compiled clients, but not the other two discussed above.

Alternatively, you could have your object support the same functionality through an IDispatch interface and also a VTBL interface "side-by-side", instead of stacked on top of each other as is a dual interface. This would solve all the problems listed above, but at a great cost in development time and effort. Every developer I've ever observed at least considers this approach, but I've never seen anyone actually decide that it was cost-effective. They always decide that having two different mind-sets on the same object would turn them schizophrenic, and they're probably right.

B. ABSTRACT DEFINITION OF AN INTERFACE

1. Once you have made your design choices and decided what methods and parameters you want to have on an interface, you must write the abstract definition of the interface in *Interface Description Language* (IDL). IDL is a strongly typed language, syntactically somewhat similar to C++. It was originally developed to meet the needs of OSF DCE RPC programming, which uses an interface-proxy-stub mechanism similar to COM. This abstract definition is the canonical basis from which all other information about the interface flows.

Once you have written the .IDL file, you compile it with the Microsoft IDL compiler, which comes with VC++ and the Platform SDK. This compilation will produce the header files and code used for building the proxy and stub that marshals the interface's calls, and the type libraries necessary for development tools to implement and call your interface. This chapter discusses the former, and Chapter 5 discusses the latter.

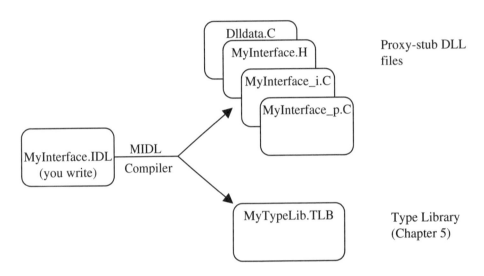

2. I've provided a sample program based on Eliza, the phony psychotherapist program that you probably first saw in artificial intelligence class. It exposes and uses an interface called IEliza, which contains a single method called Complain( ). The .IDL file describing the IEliza interface is shown on the facing page.

The keyword **import** tells the MIDL compiler to read in the specified file. In this case, the file "oaidl.idl" contains the definition of the HRESULT and LPWSTR data type.

Most of IDL consists of sets of *attributes* in square brackets, followed by blocks of IDL code describing the *items* to which those attributes apply. In the example on the facing page, the poorly-named attribute **object** indicates to the MIDL compiler that the following interface should be compiled according to the rules for a COM interface rather than an RPC interface. The attribute **uuid** indicates the universally unique ID that applies to the IDL item described in the following block of IDL code, in this case the IEliza interface.

The block of IDL code following the attributes uses the IDL keyword **interface**, which tells IDL that the block of code describes an interface. All interfaces must derive either directly from IUnknown, as does the IEliza interface shown here, or from other interfaces which in turn derive from IUnknown.

Each parameter in the definition of an interface method should contain direction attributes, such as **[in]** or **[out]**, as shown. A parameter marked [in] is marshaled from client to object, but not back. A parameter marked [out] is marshaled only from object to client. Parameters may also be marked [in, out], indicating that they are marshaled in both directions. The default direction for unmarked parameters is [in].

The MIDL compiler will use these attributes to determine the type of marshaling code to generate. These attributes will also be stored in the type library for the user of intelligent development environments.

The next block of .IDL code contains the keyword **library**. This tells the MIDL compiler to generate a type library containing the description of the IEliza interface. Note that the library has its own UUID, which is different from that of the interface. Type libraries are described in more detail in Chapter 5.

```
<file eliza.idl>

// Import definition of HRESULT and LPWSTR data types

import "oaidl.idl";

// Declaration of IEliza interface.
// The uuid is the interface ID.

[object, uuid(35FC0C40-C4FA-11ce-AD55-00608C86B89C)]

interface IEliza : IUnknown
{
    HRESULT  Complain ([in] LPWSTR pIn, [out] LPWSTR *pOut) ;
}


// Declaration of type library containing description
// of IEliza interface.

[uuid(35FC0C41-C4FA-11ce-AD55-00608C86B89C)]

library IElizaLib
{
    interface IEliza ;
}
```

NOTE: The definition of the IEliza interface must occur outside the library block, as shown above, or the MIDL compiler will not generate the desired proxy-stub files. You may see it moved inside the library block in other examples, where these files are not desired.

3. IDL supports primitive parameter types, such as char, short, long, float, double, and boolean. The only type you'll probably miss is 'int', which IDL doesn't support because it's not specific enough, potentially meaning short or long.

Other types of parameters take a little more work, but usually not much. Specifying interface pointers as method parameters in .IDL is quite easy. If you know the interface type at compile time, simply use it as a variable type. Just as in C++, the specified interface must have already been defined, often by including other files. In the example shown below, the method IRunningObjectTable::Register( ) requires a pointer to an IUnknown interface and another to an IMoniker interface. The attribute [unique] is discussed on the following pages. Thus:

```
interface IRunningObjectTable : IUnknown
{
    HRESULT Register (
        [in] DWORD grfFlags,
        [in, unique] IUnknown *punkObject,
        [in, unique] IMoniker *pmkObjectName,
        [out] DWORD *pdwRegister);

    <rest of interface definition omitted>
}
```

If you do not know the interface ID at compile time, you can use the attribute **iid_is** to instruct IDL to generate marshaling code that can accept an interface ID at runtime as another parameter to the same call. The method IUnknown::QueryInterface uses this technique. Thus:

```
interface IUnknown
{
    HRESULT QueryInterface(
        [in] REFIID riid,
        [out, iid_is(riid)] void **ppvObject) ;

    <rest of interface definition omitted>
}
```

4. Passing arrays in IDL is likewise simple. If you know the size of an array at runtime, simply put it in using square brackets, the same as in C++. Thus:

```
interface IWiseMonkeys : IUnknown
{
    SetSeeingState ( [in] long SeeingState [3]) ;

    < rest of interface omitted >
}
```

If you don't know the size of the array at compile time, you can use the attribute **size_is** to instruct IDL to generate marshaling code that can accept the array size at runtime as another parameter to the same call. Thus:

```
interface ICatRegister : IUnknown
{
    HRESULT UnRegisterCategories(
    [in] ULONG cCategories,
    [in, size_is(cCategories)] CATID rgcatid[]);

    < rest of interface omitted >
}
```

Passing a null-terminated string is a special case of array, denoted by the IDL attribute **string**. This tells IDL to obtain the array's size at runtime by looking for the NULL terminator at the end of the string. In the IEliza interface definition, the parameter type LPWSTR is actually typedefed in a header file as:

```
typedef [string] WCHAR  *LPWSTR ;
```

so the Complain method is actually compiled as:

```
HRESULT  Complain ([in] [string] WCHAR *pIn, [out] [string] WCHAR *pOut);
```

5. Writing the IDL description of pointers to other data types in IDL requires some thought. All pointers in IDL belong to one of three types: reference, unique, and full, in order of increasing power and (naturally) complexity.

The simplest type of pointer is a *reference pointer*, designated by the IDL attribute **ref**. A reference pointer is passed by a client to an object for the purpose of obtaining output. Think of them as the standard output pointers you are used to in C++, for example, the last parameter to the API function CreateThread( ), which is used for returning the resulting thread ID. All pointers declared as solely [out] must be of this type, for example, the output parameter pOut in the IEliza interface definition shown previously, or the output parameter in QueryInterface shown below. The ref attribute need not be included, and was not in this example, because the pointer type was implied by the [out] attribute. Pointers marked [in] and [in, out] may be of this type if you so desire. A reference pointer must always point to a valid storage location on the client. The value of the pointer itself may never be NULL (although the data to which it points may be), and must not change during the function call. It's simple, it's easy, it's what you are used to. Thus:

```
interface IUnknown
{
    HRESULT QueryInterface(
      [in] REFIID riid,

// pointer ppvObject is of type [ref], implied by the [out] attribute

      [out, iid_is(riid)] void **ppvObject) ;

    <rest of interface definition omitted>
}
```

6. The other two types of pointers, unique (denoted by IDL attribute **unique**) and full (denoted by the IDL attribute **ptr**, naturally), may be used for pointers marked with the [in] or [in, out]. They are very similar. A pointer of either type may have the value NULL, which a ref pointer may not. This allows you to design interfaces in which a caller may omit some parameters by passing NULL in their place. In the following interface definition, any of the rectangle pointers may be NULL. Thus:

```
interface IOleDocumentView : IUnknown
{
        HRESULT SetRectComplex(
                [in, unique] LPRECT prcView,
                [in, unique] LPRECT prcHScroll,
                [in, unique] LPRECT prcVScroll,
                [in, unique] LPRECT prcSizeBox);

    < rest of interface definition omitted >
}
```

Unique and full pointers also allow the object to change the value of the pointer. For example, using either type of pointer with the [in, out] attribute, a client may pass a memory block to an object and the object can reallocate the memory block and return the new block to the client. For example, in the following interface, the client could pass a valid rectangle pointer, or if it passed NULL, the object could allocate a new rectangle and return its value. The object would use the COM task memory allocator function **CoTaskMemAlloc( )** for allocating the memory, and the client would free it via the function **CoTaskMemFree( )**. Thus:

```
interface ICalcRect : IUnknown
{
        HRESULT UseOrCalculateRectangle (
            [in, out, unique] LPRECT *prcView);

    < rest of interface definition omitted >
}
```

The only difference between a unique pointer and a full pointer is that by marking a pointer unique, you are promising IDL that this is the only pointer referencing that memory location. That means that the marshaling code generated by IDL does not have to check the values of any other pointers passed in the call to see if they point at the same location, thereby making the marshaling code simpler and faster. Full pointers are used in the relatively few cases where this does not apply, for example, when using ring buffers. This situation doesn't arise often. At the time of this writing, there are exactly sixteen uses of full pointers in all the .IDL files shipped with the platform SDK. All the thousands of other pointers are either unique or reference.

Whenever an interface contains more then one level of pointer (whenever there is a parameter that comes back which is itself a pointer – the easy way to remember this is more than one asterisk), it is necessary to specify the type of the returned pointer via the **pointer_default** attribute. Thus:

```
[ object, uuid(00000000-0000-0000-C000-000000000046),
  pointer_default(unique) ]
interface IUnknown
{
    HRESULT QueryInterface([in] REFIID riid,
        [out, iid_is(riid)] void **ppvObject);
}
```

C. Standard Marshaling Via Proxy and Stub

1. As we have seen, COM sets up a proxy and a stub whenever a client calls a function (such as CoCreateInstance( )) or method (such as IUnknown::QueryInterface( )) that returns an interface pointer to an object that lives in a different process (Chapter 2), apartment (Chapter 6), or machine (Chapter 7) than the client. After the server returns the interface pointer to COM, but before COM returns the interface pointer to the client, COM creates the proxy and stub for the specified interface and returns to the client a pointer to the proxy. This process is called *marshaling the interface pointer*. Suppose a client calls the API function CoGetClassObject( ), which returns a pointer to the class factory that manufactures a specified class of object. If the class factory does not reside in the client's own apartment, COM will need to create a proxy and stub and return to the client a pointer to the proxy. In other words, COM needs to marshal the IClassFactory interface pointer into the client's address space.

How does COM accomplish this? A diagram is shown on the facing page. Steps 1 to 3 are contained in a low-level API function called CoMarshalInterface( ). Steps 5 to 7 are contained in another low-level API function called CoUnmarshalInterface( ). On the server side, the SCM first queries the object for the IMarshal interface(1). Every object has the right to control its own marshaling, though few of them actually choose to do so. An object that does so must support and implement this interface. If you care about it, see *Inside Distributed COM* by Guy Eddon and Henry Eddon, pp. 352-368.

If the object does not support custom marshaling, then COM performs its standard marshaling using proxy and stub. COM next goes to the registry (2) to obtain the CLSID of the DLL that provides the proxy and stub generator to the world. The location of this information in the registry is shown on the next page. COM then creates the stub in the server's address space and connects it to the object (3). Finally, COM goes to the stub and obtains a *marshaling packet* (4). This is a stream containing the data necessary for the proxy to locate the stub. The server-side SCM transfers the packet to the client side SCM (5) and drops out of the picture.

The client side SCM now uses the proxy/stub generator DLL to create the proxy object in the client's address space (6), then passes the marshaling packet to the proxy (7). The proxy and stub have intimate knowledge of each other, by which I mean that the proxy knows how to use the data in the marshaling packet create the channel and locate and connect to the stub (8). Finally, the client side SCM returns the proxy interface pointer to the client application (9). In this way, the proxy and stub are set up, and neither client nor server especially cares whether they're in the same apartment or not.

NOTE: You don't have to just let this happen behind the scenes. You can call CoMarshalInterface yourself, take the resulting marshaling packet, and store it, or transfer it to other parts of your program. Whoever passes that packet to CoUnmarshalInterface will create the proxy and be connected to the object. That's essentially what the running object table (see Chapter 9) does, and the global interface table (see Chapter 6) too.

NOTE: If you look at the marshaling packet in a binary editor, you will find that it starts with the ASCII characters "MEOW". Some say that stood for Microsoft Extended Object Wire format, but no one knows for sure. If you hear COM programmers seem to get into a cat fight, that might be what they are talking about.

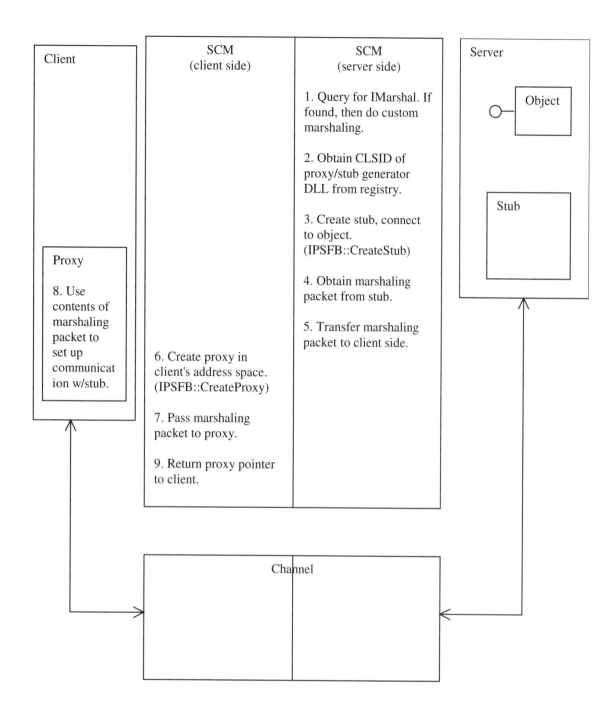

2. How does COM know where to find the marshaler DLL? It is up to the provider of the interface to provide the marshaler. It can live anywhere, but you must make registry entries so COM knows where to find it. The section of the registry in which it lives is:

HKEY_CLASSES_ROOT
   Interface
         <your IID>
                ProxyStubClsid32 = <CLSID of marshaler DLL.

In the registry screen shot below, the IClassFactory interface has the class ID {00000001-0000-0000-C000-000000000046}. Looking in the registry, we see that the proxy and stub for this interface are produced by the server whose class ID is {00000320-0000-0000-C000-000000000046}.

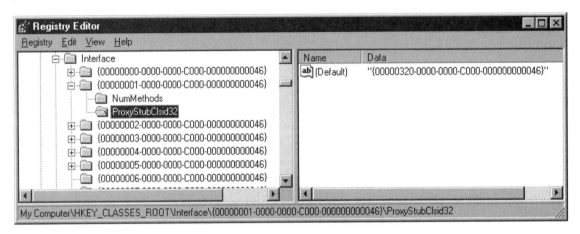

Looking at the CLSID section of the registry, we can see that the marshaler DLL that produces proxies and stubs for the IClassFactory interface is "ole32.dll".

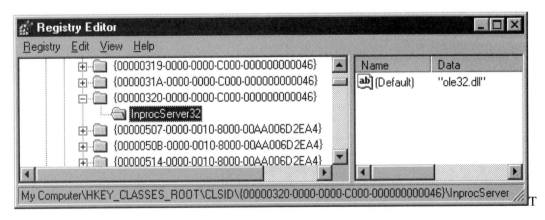

A marshaler DLL exports the barely documented interface *IPSFactoryBuffer*. Its member functions are:

CreateProxy( )   *// create client-side proxy for marshaling specified interface.*
CreateStub( )   *// create server-side stub for marshaling specified interface.*

3. Creating a marshaler DLL from IDL is fairly simple. As shown in the diagram below, we write the .IDL file and run MIDL over it. We take the output files and put them into a DLL project. We than add a .DEF file to export the required names and build these into a DLL. We make a few registry entries, and off we go. Sounds simple? It mostly is.

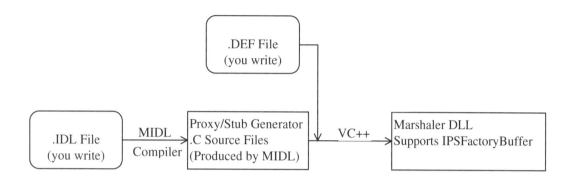

When we ran the MIDL compiler over our definition of the IEliza interface shown earlier, it produced 4 files, as listed in the following table:

File	Contents
ELIZA_I.C	Definitions of all UUIDs from the .IDL files, in this case, the IID of the IEliza interface.
ELIZA_P.C	Actual proxy/stub marshaling code. Look at it, shudder, and thank the stars you don't have to write it.
ELIZA.H	Header file containing C-language definition of IEliza interface.
DLLDATA.C	Contains standard COM DLL exported functions DllGetClassObject and DllCanUnloadNow. Also contains GetProxyDllInfo, used internally by COM. May also contain self-registration routines. All encoded in the form of macros.

4. You must also create and include in your project a .DEF file which tells the linker to export by name the functions DllGetClassObject( ), DllCanUnloadNow( ), and GetProxyDllInfo( ), as shown below. You do not have to write any code, all of it is in the proxy/stub code generated for you by MIDL. The first two you have seen before; the last one is new here. It provides the IPSFactoryBuffer interface to COM in the same way that DllGetClassObject( ) provided the IClassFactory interface. The DLL produced by building this project is the proxy/stub generator.

```
LIBRARY       ELIZAPRX
DESCRIPTION   IEliza Interface Proxy/Stub DLL


EXPORTS       DllGetClassObject       PRIVATE
              DllCanUnloadNow         PRIVATE
              DllRegisterServer       PRIVATE
              DllUnregisterServer     PRIVATE
              GetProxyDllInfo
```

5. To build these files into the marshaler DLL, make a new .DLL project in VC++ and add the three .C files and the .DEF file to it. You must also add the import library RPCRT4.LIB, which contains references to the operating system's RPC functions, to the linker input list. Also, if you define the constant REGISTER_PROXY_DLL, the DLLDATA.C file will put in the necessary exported functions for the marshaler DLL to support self-registration, a very nice feature. Thus:

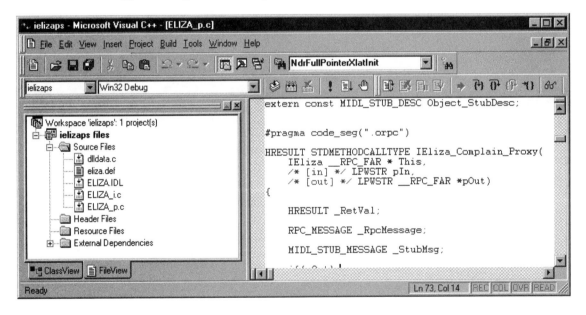

6. Now that we have our custom proxy/stub generator DLL, we need to tell COM where to look for it and how to use it. Once you have done this, COM will support standard marshaling for this interface for the use of any local or remote server. This is exactly the same mechanism as COM uses for its standard interfaces.

As you saw for the standard interfaces, we must make entries in the HKEY_CLASSES_ROOT\Interface section of the registry specifying the server that produces the proxy and stub for marshaling this interface. The required keys and values are:

```
HKEY_CLASSES_ROOT
  Interface
    <interface IID>
      BaseInterface = <IID of interface from which this one derives, IUnknown assumed if absent>
      NumMethods  = <Total # of methods in your interface, including any base interface(s)>
      ProxyStubClsid32 = <class ID of server providing IPSFactoryBuffer for this interface>
```

In our IEliza example, these entries are:

```
HKEY_CLASSES_ROOT
  Interface
    {35FC0C40-C4FA-11ce-AD55-00608C86B89C} = IEliza Custom Interface
    {35FC0C40-C4FA-11ce-AD55-00608C86B89C}\NumMethods = 4
    {35FC0C40-C4FA-11ce-AD55-00608C86B89C}\ProxyStubClsid32 =
      {35FC0C40-C4FA-11ce-AD55-00608C86B89C}  ;(sic)
```

Note that the interface ID and the proxy/stub server's class ID are identical. This is necessary when using MIDL to generate the proxy/stub code. They do not conflict because they are used in completely different contexts.

You also need to make the standard InProcServer32 entry in the CLSID section of the registry so that COM can find the IPSFactoryBuffer server. A human-readable app name with a CLSID key is not necessary. Note that the server's CLSID and the interface's IID are the same.

```
HKEY_CLASSES_ROOT
  CLSID
    {35FC0C40-C4FA-11ce-AD55-00608C86B89C} = IEliza Proxy/Stub Factory
    {35FC0C40-C4FA-11ce-AD55-00608C86B89C}\InProcServer32 =
      C:\EssenceOfOle\chap09\eliza\localsv\done\midl\elizaprx.dll
```

D. Standard Marshaling Via a Type Library

1. The foregoing wasn't hard to do and it was pretty flexible. The problem with it is that we need to provide a separate proxy/stub DLL to go along with our .EXE server; one more logistical headache. It would be cool if we could somehow describe the interface to COM with data at run time and have it roll a marshaler on the spot, instead of having to provide code, even code as easily generated as the proxy-stub marshaler.

It turns out that this isn't very hard to do. COM already has the requisite knowledge for runtime marshaling because it needs to marshal the parameters of Automation calls. We can tap into this same capability for custom interfaces by providing a type library to COM and telling COM to look there for marshaling information. The main drawback of this strategy is that it can only handle parameters of the types that Automation supports; that is, the types that can be held in a VARIANT structure.

2. To take advantage of type library marshaling in our Eliza server, we have to do a couple of things. I first modified the CEliza::Complain( ) method to use Automation-compatible BSTRs instead of standard string pointers, because COM's Automation marshaler only supports the former. I next added an .IDL file to the project to create a type library for it. This type library contains the description of the custom interface. In this example, I use a new interface called ITypeLibMarshaledEliza to prevent a conflict with the previous IEliza custom interface. The .IDL keyword **oleautomation** signals COM that this interface contains only parameters of the types supported by OLE automation. The sample code is in the directory \chap04\eliza\TypeLibMarshaled. The new .IDL file looks like this:

```
import "oaidl.idl" ;

[ uuid(088AFA02-DB7C-11d0-9121-00608C86B89C), oleautomation]

interface ITypeLibMarshaledEliza : IUnknown
{
    HRESULT Complain ([in] BSTR bstrIn, [out] BSTR *pbstrOut) ;
};

// declaration of coclass

[ uuid(088AFA01-DB7C-11d0-9121-00608C86B89C), version(1.0) ]

library TypeLibMarshaledElizaTlb
{
    [ uuid(088AFA00-DB7C-11d0-9121-00608C86B89C) ]

    coclass TypeLibMarshaledEliza
    {
      [default] interface ITypeLibMarshaledEliza ;
    };
};
```

3. To tell COM how to marshal our interface, we need to make registry entries describing it. We place the interface ID of our new custom interface in the \Interface section as before. The ProxyStubClsid32 key will always have the value "{00020424-0000-0000-C000-000000000046}", which is the class ID of COM's Automation marshaler.

We now add a new key called "TypeLib", which contains the GUID of the registered type library in which the description of this interface may be found. In this case, the value is "{088AFA01-DB7C-11d0-9121-00608C86B89C}", which as you will see on the preceding page, is the GUID of the type library itself. This type library must also be registered in the standard manner for type libraries, described in Chapter 5. In the supplied example, I bound the type library into my .EXE file as a resource so I wouldn't have the logistical hassle of two different files; so if you look in the .REG file in the sample directory, you will find that the registered type library path points back to the .EXE. Thus:

HKEY_CLASSES_ROOT
   Interface
      <interface IID>
         ProxyStubClsid32 = {00020424-0000-0000-C000-000000000046}
         TypeLib = <GUID of type library describing this interface>

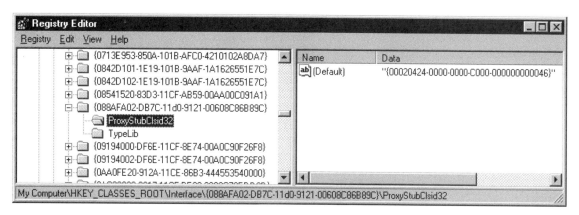

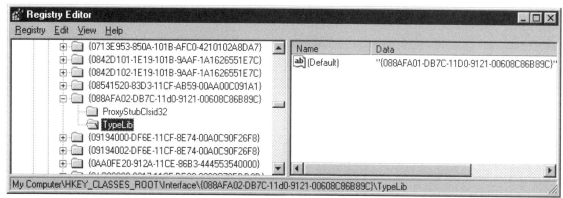

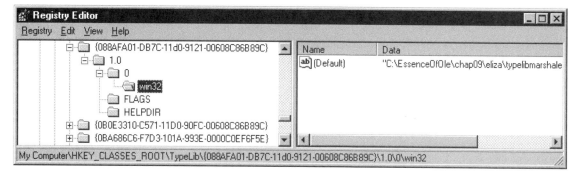

E. DUAL INTERFACES

1. A dual interface is an interface which supports the same functionality through both an IDispatch and also a VTBL interface. The former allows flexibility from an interpreted client; the latter allows speed from a compiled client. You do this by deriving your custom VTBL interface from IDispatch, rather than IUnknown, and specifying the IDL attribute **dual**. The IEliza provided via a dual interface would look like this:

```
[ uuid(98DA18B2-DB73-11d0-9121-00608C86B89C), dual]

interface IDualEliza : IDispatch
{
    [id(1)] HRESULT Complain ([in] BSTR In, [out] BSTR *pOut) ;
};
```

which means that the VTBL layout looks like this:

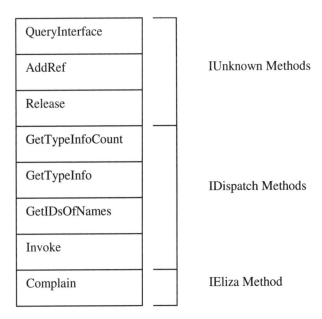

The VTBL interface receives its marshaling support via the type library mechanism shown on the previous pages. Its parameters must therefore be compatible with automation. You also must assign dispatch ID attributes to each of your interface's custom methods.

2. Dual interfaces are pound-for-pound the subject of more hype and more outrageous hype than any other feature of COM. In reality, they just aren't that important, neither in their presence nor in their absence. They don't cost much to put in, but neither do they buy your clients much additional functionality. When some evangelist gets misty-eyed over the glories of supporting both early binding and late binding, ask him, "Oh yeah? How does that make me any money?" The answer will be, "Not that often, and then not that much." But they should follow up by saying, "But they don't cost much to do, either."

Either your object requires an IDispatch interface for marketing reasons or it doesn't. If it doesn't, then you don't care about dual interfaces at all. The major client app that required an IDispatch used to be Visual Basic, but VB has known how to use a type library to call VTBL interfaces since 1995. The major application that requires runtime interpretation is a Web browser, which doesn't know what objects and what scripts it will be executing until the user surfs to a relevant page.

If you do need an IDispatch interface, then what about compiled clients? They can easily access your IDispatch with a wrapper class, which intelligent tools will generate in all of ten seconds. As discussed in the beginning of this chapter, using this wrapper class will cost some amount of run-time overhead compared to a straight VTBL call. **Eliminating this overhead while retaining compatibility with IDispatch clients is the sole advantage of a dual interface.** How much overhead? Ballpark value, a few hundred microseconds per call. This overhead is small enough that it gets swamped by the larger overhead of marshaling to another process or thread, so **you only collect this advantage in the case where the client has a direct (proxyless) connection to your object**.

3. OK, dual interfaces don't buy me much except the latest buzzword, what do they cost me? Again, the answer is not all that much. Adding a dual interface to your object requires very little extra work, it's almost free. In the ATL and VB, it actually is free; you would have to work to take it out. Because dual interfaces are marshaled at runtime using the automation marshaler and a type library, the VTBL portion of your interface will only be able to handle automation compatible parameters, which shouldn't be a big problem if you are already supporting an IDispatch. The main drawback is not in development, but in testing and support– since the timing of the two accesses is different, you have to QA them both for each release. When a client reports a bug, you have to find out which entry he's using, which he frequently won't know and which you'll have to train your support staff to ask. It looks cheap, but some of the costs are hidden. What do most programmers do? They use dual interfaces, because they fall out of most tools for free.

F. MULTIPLE INHERITANCE AND ERROR HANDLING

1. What do multiple inheritance and error handling have to do with each other? Nothing, except that implementing the latter was the first real-world example that I could think of for demonstrating the former. COM provides a mechanism for an object to return more detailed error information to its client than a simple HRESULT. In order to make use of this mechanism, an object must support the ISupportErrorInfo interface in addition to its others.

The easiest way for an object to support more than one interface is through multiple inheritance. You simply write a C++ class that lists both interface definitions in its inheritance table. The C++ compiler will construct a VTBL for each specified interface. Thus:

```
class  CEliza : public IEliza, public ISupportErrorInfo
{
    protected:
        ULONG            m_RefCount;


    public:
        CEliza  (void);
        ~CEliza (void);

    //IUnknown members

        STDMETHODIMP         QueryInterface(REFIID, LPVOID*);
        STDMETHODIMP_(ULONG) AddRef(void);
        STDMETHODIMP_(ULONG) Release(void);

    //IEliza members

        STDMETHODIMP    Complain (LPOLESTR, LPOLESTR *);

    // ISupportErrorInfo member

      STDMETHODIMP  InterfaceSupportsErrorInfo (REFIID riid);


};
```

2. The only GOTCHA! in this multiple inheritance operation is that every time you use the this pointer, you must cast it to specify which of the possible VTBLs it refers to. Don't worry, the compiler will remind you with an error if you forget. Thus:

```
STDMETHODIMP CEliza::QueryInterface(REFIID riid, LPVOID *ppv)
{

/*
Caller is querying for IEliza or IUnknown interface. Respond with a
pointer to the IEliza VTBL. IUnknown, as the common root of both
interfaces, is available through either VTBL.
*/

    if (riid == IID_IUnknown || riid == IID_IEliza)
    {
      *ppv = (IEliza *) this;
      AddRef( ) ;
      return NOERROR;
    }

/*
Caller is Querying for ISupportErrorInfo interface. Respond with a
pointer to that VTBL.
*/

    else if (riid == IID_ISupportErrorInfo)
    {
      *ppv = (ISupportErrorInfo *) this;
      AddRef( ) ;
      return NOERROR;
    }

/*
Caller is asking for unsupported interface. Respond with error HRESULT.
*/

    else
    {
      *ppv = NULL ;
      return E_NOINTERFACE ;
    }

}
```

3. In the beginning, COM interface methods reported errors by simply returning a DWORD HRESULT. It was easy; any language could do it. However, early adopters of COM quickly discovered that this wasn't enough; that they needed to pass back more detailed error information than this narrow channel allowed, so they started rolling their own solutions to this problem (see the EXCEPINFO structure in Chapter 4 for an example).

To avoid a Tower of Babel, Microsoft quickly developed a standardized way for an interface method to pass more detailed error information to its client. The lead architects of COM at the time were C++ gurus who wanted to throw C++ exceptions, but language independence was then and is now a major article of the COM faith. Rather than tie themselves to one specific language syntax, they decided to use a COM object to represent a COM method error. The object is called the error info object, and supports the *IErrorInfo* interface. Its methods are:

GetDescription	*// Returns a text description of the error.*
GetGUID	*// Returns the GUID of the interface that defined the error.*
GetHelpContext	*// Returns the Help context ID for the error.*
GetHelpFile	*// Returns the path of the Help file that describes the error.*
GetSource	*// Returns the name of the component that generated the error.*

Some writers call this an "exception object", or sometimes a "COM exception", but I won't use this nomenclature. It blurs the distinction between language-dependent native exceptions, such as C++ or Java language exceptions, and the language-independent COM mechanism.

A diagram of COM error handling is shown on the facing page. An object that wants to provide error information to its client creates an error info object and hands it to COM via the API function SetErrorInfo( ). A client that wants to retrieve that information does so via the API function GetErrorInfo( ). Each thread has its own separate error info slot, so the actions of one thread don't affect another. And COM takes care of remoting the error info object to the caller's process or machine if necessary.

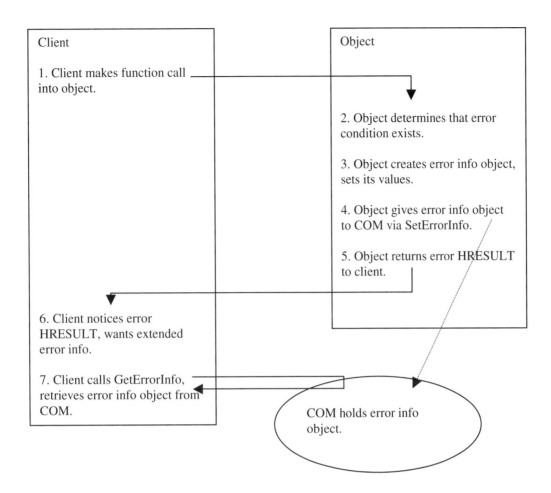

Client

1. Client makes function call
into object.

Object

2. Object determines that error
condition exists.

3. Object creates error info object,
sets its values.

4. Object gives error info object
to COM via SetErrorInfo.

5. Object returns error HRESULT
to client.

6. Client notices error
HRESULT, wants extended
error info.

7. Client calls GetErrorInfo,
retrieves error info object from
COM.

COM holds error info
object.

4. Where does the ISupportErrorInfo interface come in? It wasn't shown in the previous diagram. A client can always call GetErrorInfo( ), which will return an error code if no error info object is present. The designers provided the ISupportErrorInfo interface as a mechanism whereby a client can determine if an object ever provides error information — an object that doesn't support the interface is failing to say that it ever does. To determine an object's support of error information on a per-interface level, a client can call the method **ISupportErrorInfo::InterfaceSupportsErrorInfo( )**, passing the ID of the interface that the client wants to know about. The object will return S_OK if it provides error information for the specified interface. In this way, an object can signal its client that it supports error information on some interfaces but not on others. By using this interface, a client can determine if an object isn't providing error information because it never does, or simply because it doesn't feel like it right now.

```
/*
Caller is checking to see if we provide error information on the
specified interface. We only do this on the IEliza interface. If that's
the one he's asking for, then say yes, otherwise say no.
*/

STDMETHODIMP CEliza::InterfaceSupportsErrorInfo (REFIID riid)
{
    if (riid == IID_IEliza)
    {
      return S_OK ;
    }
    else
    {
      return S_FALSE ;
    }
}
```

NOTE: This is another one of the cases where COM uses the return value S_FALSE. It represents a funny intermediate value between success and failure, meaning essentially "Yes, I was able to successfully determine the answer to your question, and that answer is 'No'." Its value is 1, which means that the SUCCEEDED macro does not detect it. That's why I don't like that macro.

5. The error information code on the server side is shown below. In the provided sample code, the psychiatrist signals an error if the patient complains about his mother. COM provides a generic implementation of an error object via the function **CreateErrorInfo( )**. This returns an interface of type ICreateErrorInfo, which contains the methods needed to set the values of the error object's properties. You fill them out, query for the IErrorInfo interface, and pass it to **SetErrorInfo( )**. Thus:

```
STDMETHODIMP CEliza::Complain (LPOLESTR pIn, LPOLESTR *pOut)
{

/*
Check to see if caller is complaining about his mother. That's not
allowed, so create, populate, and set an error info object.
*/

    if (wcsstr (pIn, L"mother") != NULL)
    {
/*
Create generic COM error object.
*/

        ICreateErrorInfo *pCreateErrorInfo ;
        CreateErrorInfo (&pCreateErrorInfo) ;

/*
Populate the pieces we care about.
*/
        pCreateErrorInfo->SetDescription(L"No complaining about mother");
        pCreateErrorInfo->SetSource (L"Essence of COM ElizaIPS.DLL") ;

/*
Query for the IErrorInfo interface needed to set it into COM's
logical thread.
*/

        IErrorInfo *pErrorInfo ;
        pCreateErrorInfo->QueryInterface(IID_IErrorInfo,
              (void**)&pErrorInfo) ;

/*
Set it into COM's error context.
*/
        SetErrorInfo (0, pErrorInfo) ;

/*
Clean up.
*/
        pCreateErrorInfo->Release( ) ;
        pErrorInfo->Release ( ) ;
/*
Return error code.
*/
        return E_FAIL ;
    }
```

6. The client code below demonstrates querying for the ISupportErrorInfo interface and calling its **InterfaceSupportsErrorInfo( )** method. If this succeeds, the client then calls the API function **GetErrorInfo( )**, which returns an ErrorInfo object. The client displays some of its information to the user. Thus:

```
HRESULT hr ;
WCHAR *pwResponse, wComplaint [256]   ;

hr = pEliza->Complain (wComplaint, &pwResponse) ;

/*
If call fails for some reason, check to see if there is extended
error information available.
*/

    if (hr != S_OK)
    {

/*
Query for ISupportErrorInfo. If found, ask if the IEliza interface
provides said error information.
*/
        ISupportErrorInfo *pSEI ;
        if (pEliza->QueryInterface (IID_ISupportErrorInfo,
            (void **)&pSEI) == S_OK)
        {
            if (pSEI->InterfaceSupportsErrorInfo (IID_IEliza) == S_OK)
            {
/*
Get error info object
*/
                IErrorInfo *pEI ;
                GetErrorInfo (0, &pEI) ;
/*
Get strings from error info and show to user.
*/

                BSTR pDesc ;
                BSTR pSrc ;

                pEI->GetDescription (&pDesc) ;
                pEI->GetSource (&pSrc) ;

                <display and cleanup code omitted>

                pEI->Release ( ) ;
            }
            pSEI->Release( ) ;
        }
    }
```

This chapter contains more sample apps than the others. They are arranged as follows:

```
\EssenceOfCOM
    \chap03
        \Eliza
                \client              client app for all IEliza samples
                \dual                IEliza through a dual interface
                \inprocsv            in-proc server for IEliza interface
                \localsv             local server for IEliza interface, standard marshaling
                \typelibmarshaled    IEliza marshaled via a type library
```

Because of the number and interrelatedness of these apps, this chapter does not contain a prefabricated lab exercise. Instead, this section contains detailed instructions for getting the sample code up and running, and provides suggestions for experiments you might like to make with it.

1. First you must register all the servers. The root directory \Eliza contains three registry files. Examine their contents until you feel comfortable with them, and run them all.

2. Run the client app. Use the "Eliza" menu to create an object from any of the servers. The Local, Type Library Marshaled, and Dual servers open in a separate window; the In-Proc server doesn't. Enter a complaint into the "Outgoing Text" box and click "Send".

3. The in-proc server will return an error if the complaint contains the word "mother" in all lower case letters. The other servers do not demonstrate this capability.

This page intentionally contains no text other than this sentence.

Chapter 4

Automation

A. Concepts and Definitions

1. *Automation* (originally known as OLE Automation, another MINFU) is a mechanism by which COM objects can expose their functionality for the use of interpreted clients, such as scripting languages, rather than compiled clients. It was originally conceived and developed as a way for Microsoft Office applications such as Excel to expose their internal macro functionality to external tools such as Visual Basic for Applications. Application vendors could thus reap the advantages of macro programming without having to develop and maintain the tools to do it, and customers could use whatever tools they liked and were familiar with for programming all of their applications.

The architecture of automation was dictated by the need to accommodate Microsoft Visual Basic for Applications. At the time automation was being designed (late 1992-early 1993), VB could not produce compiled .EXE programs, but could only run in an interpreted fashion. While VB has since acquired (version 4, fall 1995) the ability to produce compiled applications that use VTBL interfaces, the explosion of the World Wide Web has vastly increased the use of scripting languages, and thus the importance of automation, both on the client side and the server side, far beyond anything VB would ever have produced.

When a COM interface client is compiled during development, the compiler reads the source code, resolves the names of methods into their VTBL entries by consulting interface definitions in header files or type libraries, and generates object code for pushing the requisite parameters onto the stack and jumping to the address held by the corresponding entry in the interface's VTBL. The compilation process can take a long time, but once it's done, running the binary code is relatively quick. An interpreted client, on the other hand, does not do the work of resolving human-readable source code into machine code until it actually runs. This is a much more flexible approach, as it can handle code not known at development time, say, scripts on a web page, but it's slower because the resolution process takes place in real time when the program is executing.

A COM object has its own internal methods. Instead of exposing each of them as an entry in the VTBL of a specific custom interface, an automation object exposes all of its functionality through a single standard interface called IDispatch. Any call to any internal method on the object proceeds through this one interface. The developer of a scripting language can thus provide hardwired support for IDispatch, thereby being able to work with any object it encounters.

The IDispatch interface looks deceptively simple. Its methods are:

IDispatch::Invoke	*// Access property or method exposed by the object.*
IDispatch::GetIDsOfNames	*// Maps a single member name and an optional set of argument names*
	// to a set of integer DISPIDs for use by IDispatch::Invoke().
IDispatch::GetTypeInfo	*// Get type information describing an automation object.*
IDispatch::GetTypeInfoCount	*//Find out whether an automation object provides type information.*

2. When a client wants to call an internal method on an automation object, it calls the object's IDispatch::Invoke( ). Every internal method is identified by a *dispatch ID*, an integer constant. This ID is passed as the first parameter to IDispatch::Invoke( ). Any parameters that the internal method may require are passed in an array of structures as another parameter to IDispatch::Invoke( ). When you call the method IDispatch::Invoke( ), you are in essence saying, "Hey, Mr. Object, do thing number 1 (or 2, or 3, etc.) and here's the data for it." The server's implementation of the Invoke( ) method looks at the dispatch ID and executes the internal method specified by that ID.

How does the client know which number to ask for? That's what the method IDispatch::GetIDsOfNames( ) is for. The client will call that first, essentially saying, "Hey, Mr. Object, when I want you to do the thing whose name is 'DoSomething' (or whatever the method name is in the script being interpreted), what number do I ask for?" The object responds, "Let's see, 'DoSomething', that would be number 3." The client then calls IDispatch::Invoke( ), saying, "OK, do thing #3, please."

Suppose we have scripting code like this:

```
Dim foo as object
Set foo = CreateObject ("MyObjectsProgID")      // create an object
Call foo.SayHello                               // call a method on it
```

The script interpreter, when it reads those lines, will perform operations very much like this:

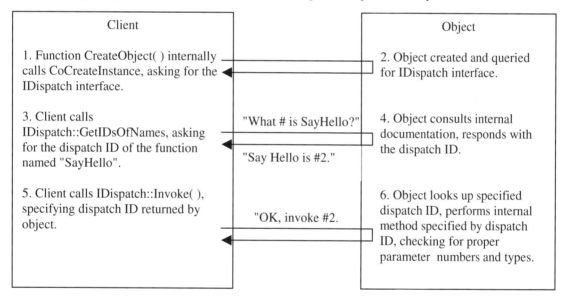

3. The sole advantage of exposing an object's functionality through IDispatch is that the object will then be usable by interpreted clients. With the explosive growth of the Web in the past few years, very few vendors are willing to forego this potential customer base, which means that support for automation is almost universal for objects sold commercially. The benefit is decisive, but what are the costs?

A. An interpreted client is slower at runtime than a compiled client would be. The interpreter needs to do a lot of thinking at runtime. Invoking an internal method on an object takes two roundtrips to the object, one to get the dispatch ID, and the next to actually invoke the method. On the client side, packing up the parameters to call IDispatch::Invoke can be complex and takes more time than for a compiled client. On the server side, checking that a client has passed the correct number and type of parameters, and converting the passed types if necessary and possible, takes time as well. How much time? It varies widely depending on the object; a ballpark estimate is a few hundred microseconds per call. This is much lower than the inter-machine, inter-process, or even inter-thread marshaling overhead, so you really only notice it when the client has a direct connection to the object. Of course, you probably went to great trouble to arrange to have a direct connection to the object because you wanted the maximum speed. If you need both maximum speed and also the flexibility for interpreted clients, consider exposing an object's internal methods through both an IDispatch interface and also a VTBL interface.

B. The IDispatch interface severely restricts the types of parameters that can be passed to an object's method. IDispatch only supports the types of parameters that can be packaged in a VARIANT structure, described later in this chapter. Essentially, IDispatch method parameters can contain numbers, strings, and COM objects, and arrays of all of these types. They cannot contain anything else, for example, structures such as GUIDs. This sometimes leads to funny workarounds. For example, the architects of the system-provided object that administers the COM+ catalog in Windows 2000 wanted to make sure that it was accessible to interpreted clients, so it supports IDispatch. However, the catalog requires GUIDs, which IDispatch does not support. The designers of the catalog therefore decreed that the GUIDs they require will be passed in the form of a string, which IDispatch does support. The client has to create a GUID and convert it to a string, and the object has to convert the string back to a GUID, all because the IDispatch that connects them won't deal with a GUID directly.

C. The third cost is not so much a disadvantage as simply an architectural reality. Since automation objects expose all of their internal methods via the IDispatch interface, it follows that they can really only expose one interface per object. (They can certainly contain more, but interpreted clients won't be able to use them.) This means that your object design has to be deep rather than wide. You have essentially lost the notion of objects and interfaces as separate entities. Since there can only be one interface per object, interfaces and objects are more or less the same thing.

Suppose you had an object that represented a customer. A VTBL-based design might expose three interfaces from the main object; one for address information, another for phone information, and another for buying history. I call this a wide design. However, a scripting client won't be able to use those interfaces. You could mash all of this information into a single IDispatch interface, but that's terrible from a modularity standpoint. Instead, you would make each collection of information be a sub-object exposing its own IDispatch. The outer object would expose one IDispatch, and each of the three sub-objects would be accessed as a property of the outer object.

4. Although all automation objects are accessed through the same IDispatch interface, it is clear that the same dispatch ID may mean different things to different objects. A dispatch ID of 1 may instruct one object to save all of its data carefully to disk; whereas to another object, the same dispatch ID may mean to format its hard drive and everyone else's on the network without asking for confirmation. The meaning of the set of IDs accessed through an IDispatch interface to which an object responds is called a *dispinterface*. It is conceptually similar to a custom interface, except the dispinterface's VTBL does not vary from one object to another. It is the interpretation of the data supplied to the IDispatch::Invoke( ) method that makes it custom. Making sure you have the right methods and parameters for the dispinterface you are using is the primary challenge of automation programming.

An automation object may expose properties as well as methods. A property is a single data value accessed by a call to IDispatch::Invoke( ). The difference between methods and properties is solely an abstraction of the programming language that uses automation.

The sample program provided with this chapter provides a single object that has one method, called SayHello, that takes no parameters, and one property, of type BSTR (a VB string, length-prefixed and Unicode), named HelloMessage. Its .IDL file description would look like this:

```
//  A dispinterface is a custom set of methods and properties accessed
//  via the IDispatch interface mechanism.

    [ uuid(6CED2902-A1DD-11cf-8A33-00AA00A58097)]

    dispinterface IDHello
    {

//  properties and methods contained in the dispinterface with their
//  dispatch ids and types.

    properties:
            [id(1)] BSTR HelloMessage;

    methods:
            [id(2)] void SayHello();
    };
```

B. BASIC CLIENT FUNCTIONALITY

1. Building an automation client is conceptually simple, although the exact syntax of the methods can be tricky. To ease the task of the application programmer, you probably want to encapsulate the client's interface to the automation object in a C++ wrapper, in this example called **CHelloDriver**. This also makes it much easier to supply dummy or test data while the server is still under development. In Chapter 10, we will see how automated tools can generate this wrapper class for us.

In the following examples, we want to create a dedicated client app that manipulates the simple automation server described on the previous page. The server object displays a text string in a window on the screen. The object exposes a single method called "SayHello( )", which draws the object's current string in an edit control. It also exposes that current string as a property named "HelloMessage", whose value clients may set and get. In this example, we pretend we knew all this from reading the documentation provided by the vendor that sold us the server. The source code for this example is in the directory \chap04\helloau\hlodrv32. The client app's WinMain( ) looks like this:

```
extern BOOL WINAPI HelloDlgProc (HWND, UINT, WPARAM, LPARAM) ;

/*
Client   object   that   encapsulates   the   interface   to   the   server's
automation object.
*/

CHelloDriver chd ;

int WINAPI WinMain(HINSTANCE hInst, HINSTANCE hPrevInstance,
    LPSTR lpCmdLine, int nCmdShow)
{
    MSG msg ;
    OleInitialize (NULL) ;

/*
Try to connect to the automation object.  If unsuccessful, terminate
app.
*/
    if (chd.Create( ) == FALSE)
    {
      MessageBox (NULL, "Can't hook up hellodrv", "Error", 0) ;
      return -1 ;
    }

/*
Connection made to automation object.  Pop up dialog box that will call
object's methods in response to dialog box's controls.
*/

    DialogBox (hInst, MAKEINTRESOURCE(IDD_DIALOG1), NULL,
      HelloDlgProc);

    OleUninitialize ( ) ;
    return msg.wParam;
}
```

2. The class **CHelloDriver** is the client's wrapper for the automation object exposed by the server. It looks like this:

```
/*
Wrapper class for the client side of the Hello automation object.
*/

class CHelloDriver
{
    private:
      LPDISPATCH m_pDisp ;            // IDispatch interface from server
      DISPID m_dSayHelloId ;          // Say hello method ID
      DISPID m_dHelloPropID ;         // string set/get ID

    public:
      CHelloDriver( ) ;
      ~CHelloDriver( ) ;

      BOOL Create(LPSTR) ;            // set up dispatch with server
      HRESULT SetString (LPOLESTR) ;// tell server what string to use
      HRESULT GetString (LPOLESTR) ;// ask what string server is using
      HRESULT SayHowdy(void) ;        // tell server to output its string
      HRESULT BadSetString (void) ; // intentional error for demo
} ;


/*
Class destructor.   If we have a pointer to an IDispatch interface,
release it.
*/

CHelloDriver::~CHelloDriver( )
{
    if (m_pDisp)
    {
      m_pDisp->Release( );
    }
    return ;
}
```

3. The client must first create an object of the appropriate class and get a pointer to the object's IDispatch interface. We do exactly the same thing as we did in Chapter 2, call the API function **CoCreateInstance( )**. The only difference is that this time we ask for the IDispatch interface pointer. Thus:

```
BOOL CHelloDriver::Create ( )
{
    HRESULT hr ;

    CLSID clsid ;

    < read class ID from the registry >


/*
Try to create an instance of the Hello object and get a pointer to its
IDispatch interface.
*/

    hr = CoCreateInstance (
      clsid,                     // class ID of object
      NULL,                      //
      CLSCTX_LOCAL_SERVER,       // context
      IID_IDispatch,             // type of interface ptr wanted
      (LPVOID *) &m_pDisp) ;     // output variable

    if (!SUCCEEDED(hr))
    {
      return FALSE ;
    }
```

4. The IDispatch interface provides access to all the methods and properties exposed by the automation object. Each method or property is identified by a DWORD *dispatch ID*, which we will need to access via the method IDispatch::Invoke( ). The vendor might have given us a header file or type library with those IDs predefined, but maybe was too lazy or wanted to reserve the right to change them later. Since we don't have them at compile time, we must query the object for them at run time via the method **IDispatch::GetIDsOfNames( )**. This is a somewhat misnamed method, as it provides the ID of only a single method or property at a time. The designers gave it a plural name because it can also get the IDs of any named parameters (dealt with later) that a single method might support. Note that as for all strings in COM, the names provided to this method must always use wide (Unicode) characters, even if neither client nor server are wide character apps. Thus:

```
/*
Get the ID numbers associated with the names in the IDispatch
interface. SayHello( ) is a method.
*/

    WCHAR *Name = L"SayHello" ;

    hr = m_pDisp->GetIDsOfNames (
      IID_NULL,                           // reserved
      &Name,                              // Array of names to get IDs for
      1,                                  // # of names in the array
      LOCALE_SYSTEM_DEFAULT,              // System locale
      &m_dSayHelloId) ;                   // Array of IDs to fill on output

    if (hr)
    {
      return FALSE ;
    }


/*
HelloMessage is a property.
*/
    Name = L"HelloMessage" ;

    hr = m_pDisp->GetIDsOfNames (
      IID_NULL,                           // reserved
      &Name,                              // Array of names to get IDs for
      1,                                  // # of names in the array
      LOCALE_SYSTEM_DEFAULT,              // System locale
      &m_dHelloPropID) ;                  // Array of IDs to fill on output

    if (hr)
    {
      return FALSE ;
    }

    return TRUE ;
}
```

This page intentionally contains no text other than this sentence.

5. A method is called in an automation object via the method **IDispatch::Invoke( )**, specifying the dispatch ID of the object's method that you want to call. We also specify a flag that tells the server that what we are doing is calling a method on the object, as opposed to getting or setting a property. The arguments required by the object's method are passed in a structure of type **DISPPARAMS**, which is defined thus:

```
typedef struct  tagDISPPARAMS
{
    VARIANTARG *rgvarg;         // array of VARIANT structs holding args
    DISPID __*rgdispidNamedArgs;   // array of DISPIDs naming args
    UINT cArgs;                 // number of VARIANTS in array
    UINT cNamedArgs;            // number of names in array
}   DISPPARAMS;
```

All parameters in automation are passed in VARIANT structures, which are described in more detail on the next page. The DISPPARAMS structure is a holder for VARIANTs and the data that describes their use, containing pointers to two arrays and the counts of the items in each array. In this example, the object's method does not require any arguments, so we set both pointers in the DISPPARAMS to NULL and both counts to zero. Thus:

```
/*
Invoke the server's SayHello( ) method.
*/

HRESULT CHelloDriver::SayHowdy(void)
{
    HRESULT hr ;
    EXCEPINFO ei ;
    UINT uiErr ;
    DISPPARAMS dispparamsNoArgs = {NULL, NULL, 0, 0};

    hr = m_pDisp->Invoke (
      m_dSayHelloId,                // ID of function to call
      IID_NULL,                     // reserved
      LOCALE_SYSTEM_DEFAULT,        // system locale
      DISPATCH_METHOD,              // we are calling a method
      &dispparamsNoArgs,            // no parameters are being passed
      NULL,                         // no return value expected
      &ei,                          // exception information
      &uiErr ) ;                    // error information

    return hr ;
}
```

6. The value of a property is fetched via the same IDispatch::Invoke( ) method with slightly different parameters. We pass the dispatch ID of the property that we want to get and the flag that says that what we are doing is getting the value of a property. We declare a structure of type **VARIANT** and pass it as the sixth parameter; the server will place the property's value into it.

All parameters and return values in automation are passed by means of VARIANT structures, the definition of which is shown on the facing page. Used extensively throughout VB, a VARIANT is a structure containing a self-describing union supporting 13 different data types which COM knows how to marshal both by value and by reference. You can pass essentially any type of single-variable value, including arrays (via the SAFEARRAY type). You can pass pointers to IDispatch interfaces directly, and pointers to any other interface by passing the object's root IUnknown interface and then querying it at the destination for the desired interface.

Strings in automation are always passed in the form of a BSTR, again a type of data used in VB. You can use it in C++ as if it were a regular null-terminated string; however, you must allocate it via the function SysAllocString( ) and free it via the function **SysFreeString( )**. Thus:

```
HRESULT CHelloDriver::GetString (LPOLESTR pOut)
{
    HRESULT hr ;
    VARIANT var ;          // holder for return value
    EXCEPINFO ei ;
    UINT uiErr ;
    DISPPARAMS dispparamsNoArgs = {NULL, NULL, 0, 0};

    var.vt = VT_EMPTY ;

/*
Try to get the string from the object.
*/

    hr = m_pDisp->Invoke (
        m_dHelloPropID,           // ID of property
        IID_NULL,                 // reserved
        LOCALE_SYSTEM_DEFAULT,    // system locale
        DISPATCH_PROPERTYGET,     // flag
        &dispparamsNoArgs,        // no parameters passed
        &var,                     // holder for returned value
        &ei,                      // exception info
        &uiErr ) ;                // error info

/*
If string was successfully retrieved, it is in the buffer pointed to by
the variant's bstrVal element.  Copy it into our local buffer and free
the string.
*/
    if (SUCCEEDED(hr))
    {
      wcscpy (pOut, var.bstrVal) ;
      SysFreeString (var.bstrVal) ;
    }
    return hr ;
}
```

```
typedef struct tagVARIANT VARIANTARG;
typedef struct tagVARIANT VARIANT;

typedef struct tagVARIANT
{
    VARTYPE vt;
    unsigned short wReserved1;
    unsigned short wReserved2;
    unsigned short wReserved3;

    union
    {
        short        iVal;                /* VT_I2                */
        long         lVal;                /* VT_I4                */
        float        fltVal;              /* VT_R4                */
        double       dblVal;              /* VT_R8                */
        VARIANT_BOOL bool;                /* VT_BOOL              */
        SCODE        scode;               /* VT_ERROR             */
        CY           cyVal;               /* VT_CY                */

        DATE         date;                /* VT_DATE              */
        BSTR         bstrVal;             /* VT_BSTR              */
        IUnknown     FAR* punkVal;        /* VT_UNKNOWN           */
        IDispatch    FAR* pdispVal;       /* VT_DISPATCH          */


        short        FAR* piVal;          /* VT_BYREF|VT_I2       */
        long         FAR* plVal;          /* VT_BYREF|VT_I4       */
        float        FAR* pfltVal;        /* VT_BYREF|VT_R4       */
        double       FAR* pdblVal;        /* VT_BYREF|VT_R8       */
        VARIANT_BOOL FAR* pbool;          /* VT_BYREF|VT_BOOL     */
        SCODE        FAR* pscode;         /* VT_BYREF|VT_ERROR    */
        CY           FAR* pcyVal;         /* VT_BYREF|VT_CY       */
        DATE         FAR* pdate;          /* VT_BYREF|VT_DATE     */
        BSTR         FAR* pbstrVal;       /* VT_BYREF|VT_BSTR     */
        IUnknown FAR* FAR* ppunkVal;      /* VT_BYREF|VT_UNKNOWN  */
        IDispatch FAR* FAR* ppdispVal;    /* VT_BYREF|VT_DISPATCH */


        SAFEARRAY    FAR* parray;         /* VT_ARRAY|*           */
        VARIANT      FAR* pvarVal;        /* VT_BYREF|VT_VARIANT  */

        void         FAR* byref;          /* Generic ByRef        */
    };
} ;
```

7. Setting a property is slightly more complicated. We use the same IDispatch::Invoke( ) method, passing the dispatch ID of the property that we want to set. We also pass a flag saying that what we are doing is setting a property.

The trick in setting a property is packaging up the parameters in the DISPPARAMS structure. The DISPPARAMS structure, as previously shown, has an element called `rgvarg` which points to an array of VARIANTS containing the parameters that are passed to the method. It also has an element called `cArgs`, which contains the number of VARIANTS in the array, in this case one. We allocate a VARIANT and initialize it to default values via the function **VariantInit( )**. We use the function **SysAllocString( )** to allocate a BSTR containing the string we want to pass, place it in the VARIANT, and set the VARIANT's `vt` element to the flag **VT_BSTR**, indicating that this VARIANT contains a BSTR so that COM will know how to marshal it. Finally, we set `rgvargs` to point to the VARIANT. Similar footwork is required when calling a method that requires parameters.

You would think this would be all we have to do, but it isn't. Parameters in automation can be passed either by position, as in a compiled language, or by name. In a DISPPARAMS structure, the element `rgdispidNamedArgs` is a pointer to an array of dispatch IDs specifying the name of each argument in the `rgvargs` array, and the element `cNamedArgs` is the number of elements in the array. For historical reasons, when setting a property, it is necessary to provide an ID for the VARIANT containing the property's value, and the ID must have the reserved value **DISPID_PROPERTYPUT** (-3). The element `rgdispidNamedArgs` must point at an integer whose value is this, and the count of named arguments must be set to 1. Hey, I didn't design it. A working code example is shown on the facing page.

```
HRESULT CHelloDriver::SetString(LPOLESTR cp)
{
    HRESULT hr ;                DISPPARAMS dp ;
    VARIANTARG vString ;        EXCEPINFO ei ;
    UINT uiErr ;                DISPID dPutID ;
/*
Allocate a string from the system memory allocator.  Place it into the
element of a VARIANT structure, and set the flags.
*/

    BSTR bstr = SysAllocString (cp) ;
    VariantInit (&vString) ;
    vString.vt = VT_BSTR ;
    vString.bstrVal = bstr ;


/*
Set up the DISPPARAMS structure.  Point to the array of VARIANTs that
contains the parameters, and set the count in the array (here only 1).
*/

    dp.rgvarg = &vString ;          // variant array containing params
    dp.cArgs = 1 ;                  // # of elements in the array

/*
Now set the elements that identify the parameter passed to the method.
*/

    dPutID = DISPID_PROPERTYPUT ;   // use SET property function
    dp.rgdispidNamedArgs = &dPutID ;  // needs it by reference
    dp.cNamedArgs = 1 ;             // number of elements

/*
Invoke the function.
*/
    hr = m_pDisp->Invoke (
      m_dHelloPropID,               // ID of property
      IID_NULL,                     // reserved
      LOCALE_SYSTEM_DEFAULT,        // system locale
      DISPATCH_PROPERTYPUT,         // set value of property
      &dp,                          // array of parameters to pass
      NULL,                         // no return value expected
      &ei,                          // exception info
      &uiErr ) ;                    // error info
/*
If function was successful, recipient should free string; otherwise we
have to.
*/
    if (!SUCCEEDED(hr))
    {
      SysFreeString (bstr) ;
    }
    return hr ;
}
```

C. BASIC SERVER FUNCTIONALITY

1. An automation object must provide the *IDispatch* interface, which is the means whereby the client invokes the methods and accesses the properties of the object. The server may be either an in-proc (DLL) or local (.EXE) server.

Exposing an automation object means writing your own dispinterface. Consider a very simple automation object used in the client example. It exposes a single method called "SayHello( )", which draws a text string in a window on the screen. It also exposes a single property called "HelloMessage", which is the string drawn on the screen when the SayHello( ) method is invoked. We want to expose these features to other apps, which means wrapping them in an IDispatch interface. The source code for this example is in the directory \chap04\helloau\hello32. We would call it CHelloDispatch, and its header file would look like this:

```
#include <windows.h>

class CHelloDispatch : public IDispatch
{
 public:

/*
Data members
*/

    BSTR m_bstrHelloMsg;              // HelloMessage property
    ULONG m_RefCount;                 // Reference count

 /*
 Class constructor and destructor
 */

    CHelloDispatch();
    ~CHelloDispatch();

 /*
 IUnknown methods
 */

    STDMETHODIMP QueryInterface (REFIID riid, void FAR* FAR* ppv);
    STDMETHODIMP_(ULONG) AddRef (void);
    STDMETHODIMP_(ULONG) Release (void);

/*
IDispatch methods
*/

    STDMETHODIMP GetTypeInfoCount(UINT *pctinfo) ;
    STDMETHODIMP GetTypeInfo(UINT, LCID, ITypeInfo **pptinfo) ;
    STDMETHODIMP GetIDsOfNames(REFIID, LPOLESTR *, UINT, LCID,DISPID*);
    STDMETHODIMP Invoke(DISPID, REFIID, LCID lcid, WORD, DISPPARAMS *,
      VARIANT *, EXCEPINFO *, UINT *) ;

};
```

2. Now we have to implement the methods of the IDispatch interface. As before, some can be stubbed out completely, and some others are trivial. The methods **GetTypeInfoCount( )** and **GetTypeInfo( )** are optional, and can be stubbed out, thus:

```
STDMETHODIMP CHelloDispatch::GetTypeInfoCount(UINT *pNtypeInfo)
{
    *pNtypeInfo = 0;
    return E_NOTIMPL ;
}


STDMETHODIMP CHelloDispatch::GetTypeInfo(UINT itinfo, LCID lcid,
    ITypeInfo **pptinfo)
{
    *pptinfo = NULL ;
    return E_NOTIMPL ;
}
```

The method **GetIDsOfNames( )** is fairly simple. We are passed the name of a property or method, and simply return the dispatch ID to which it refers. If we do not support a member with that name, we return an error code. Note that the names are always passed in wide character strings. Thus:

```
STDMETHODIMP CHelloDispatch::GetIDsOfNames(REFIID riid,
    LPOLESTR *pNames, UINT cNames, LCID lcid, DISPID *pDispID)
{
    if (_wcsicmp (*pNames, L"SayHello") == 0)
    {
      *pDispID = 2 ;
      return NOERROR ;
    }
    else if (_wcsicmp (*pNames, L"HelloMessage") == 0)
    {
      *pDispID = 1 ;
      return NOERROR ;
    }

    return DISP_E_UNKNOWNNAME ;
}
```

3. As usual, there is one interface method that requires a significant amount of programming, and in this case it's the **Invoke( )** method. This method is passed the ID of the property or method being accessed, and the data that has been marshaled from the caller in an array of self-describing VARIANT structures. The method figures out what to do and does it.

Unlike the normal implementation of a VTBL-based interface, you cannot assume that the compiler has checked for the correct number and type of parameters. The main drawback of automation's late-bound architecture is that such checking must be done at runtime. If an error is found, we return the appropriate error code and hope the client has some mechanism to present the error to the user/programmer so it can be corrected. Thus:

```
STDMETHODIMP CHelloDispatch::Invoke(DISPID dispidMember, REFIID riid,
    LCID lcid, WORD wFlags, DISPPARAMS *pDispParams,
    VARIANT *pVarResult, EXCEPINFO *pexcepinfo, UINT *puArgErr)
{
/*
Caller wants to get or set the HelloMessage property.
*/
    if (dispidMember == 1)
    {
/*
Caller wants to get the HelloMessage property.
*/
        if (wFlags & DISPATCH_PROPERTYGET)
        {
/*
Check that the caller hasn't passed us any parameters.  That would be
an error.
*/
            if (pDispParams->cArgs != 0)
            {
                return DISP_E_BADPARAMCOUNT ;
            }
/*
Allocate a string containing it, and place it in the VARIANT used for
the return value.
*/
            pVarResult->vt = VT_BSTR ;
            pVarResult->bstrVal = SysAllocString(m_bstrHelloMsg) ;
        }
```

<continued on facing page>

```
/*
Caller wants to set the HelloMessage property.
*/
      else if (wFlags & DISPATCH_PROPERTYPUT)
      {
/*
Check parameter count and type.  If either is incorrect, return
appropriate error code.
*/
            if (pDispParams->cArgs != 1)
            {
                  return DISP_E_BADPARAMCOUNT ;
            }
            if (pDispParams->rgvarg[0].vt != VT_BSTR)
            {
                  return DISP_E_BADVARTYPE ;
            }
/*
Copy the new value from the array of VARIANTS holding the calling
parameters.
*/
            SysReAllocString(&m_bstrHelloMsg,
                  pDispParams-> rgvarg->bstrVal);
      }
      return NOERROR ;
   }
/*
Caller wants to call the SayHello( ) method.
*/

   else if (dispidMember == 2)
   {
/*
Check that there are no parameters.  If not, return an error code.
*/
      if (pDispParams->cArgs != 0)
      {
            return DISP_E_BADPARAMCOUNT ;
      }

/*
Put the current HelloMessage property into the edit control and beep to
signal the user.
*/
      MessageBeep (0) ;
      SetDlgItemText(hMainWnd, IDC_HELLOAREA, m_bstrHelloMsg);
      return NOERROR ;
   }

   return DISP_E_MEMBERNOTFOUND ;
}
```

Lab Exercises
Chapter 4
Automation Client

Directory: \EssenceOfCOM\chap04\helloau\hlodrv32\templ

In this lab, we'll create the automation client discussed in the first part of this chapter. All of the interesting code will take place in the file HELLODRV.CPP.

1. To develop and test the client, it is necessary to have a server to interact with. Go to the root directory of this example and run the registry file HELLO32.REG. This will make the necessary entries in the system registry to connect the server HELLO32.EXE in the \helloau\hello32\done directory as the automation server for the object whose human-readable name is "EssenceofCOM.HelloAutomation". If the root directory you are using for your samples is anything other than C:\, you will need to edit the .REG file to make the LocalServer32 entry point to the exact path location of the server file.

2. The method CHelloDriver::Create( ) is the place where the connection is first made between the automation client and the object provided by the server. The first thing the client needs to do is create the automation object by calling the API function CoCreateInstance( ). The class ID of the object has already been read from the registry for you and may be found in the variable "clsid". The interface that you need returned is IID_IDispatch. Store the returned object pointer in the member variable "m_pDisp". You should build and run your app at this point. The server should appear, but none of the automation methods should work because you have not yet gotten the dispatch IDs needed to identify them. If the server does not come up, you probably have the registry path wrong.

3. Having gotten the IDispatch interface, we need to get the IDs within it that correspond to the named dispatch elements via the method IDispatch::GetIDsOfNames( ). You will have to do this twice, once for the property "HelloMessage" and once for the method "SayHello". Store the IDs in the member variables "m_dHelloPropID" and "m_dSayHelloId" respectively. Remember that the strings you pass to GetIDsOfNames( ) must always be a wide character string, even if your app is not a wide character app.

4. The first actual invocation of the automation object's method takes place in the method CHelloDriver::SayHowdy( ). Use the method IDispatch::Invoke( ) to call the automation object's SayHello( ) method. Pass an empty parameter array to the function and expect no return value.

5. Next implement the CHelloDriver::GetString( ) method. This uses the IDispatch interface to get the value of the automation object's HelloMessage property. You must allocate and initialize a VARIANT structure to receive the return value. The code to put it into the dialog box's edit control has already been written for you.

6. Finally, implement the CHelloDriver::SetString( ) method. You must now allocate a VARIANT to hold the input parameters, and a DISPPARAMS structure to hold the variant and other flags. Initialize them and set their values as shown in the text. Use the IDispatch::Invoke( ) method to set the value of the automation object's HelloMessage property.

EXTRA CREDIT: Examine the CHelloDriver::BadSetString( ) method until you feel comfortable with the processing of the EXCEPINFO structure. The first time you select the "Help" button in the dialog box, WinHelp will probably not be able to find the specified file. You will have to locate it yourself, in the directory \helloau\hello32\help. The operating system will then remember where it lives, so subsequent calls to WinHelp will find it.

Lab Exercises
Chapter 4
Automation Server

Directory: \EssenceOfCOM\chap04\helloau\hello32\templ

1. Now that your client is working, you have something to test the server with. Before starting to work on the server, you must change the entries in the registry so that the client will use the new server that you are developing rather than the finished one supplied in the \done directory. You can do this either by editing the .REG file to point to the new server's path (in the directory \templ\windebug) and reregistering the whole thing, or by using the registry editor and changing only the path itself.

2. The server app is a small one. All the interesting code takes place in the file HELLO.CPP. As you are already conversant with the concepts, the class factory registration has been done for you, as have the two trivial methods of the IDispatch interface. First, you must implement the method IDispatch::GetIDsOfNames( ). Compare the name supplied by the caller with the names "HelloMessage" and "SayHello". The ID for the former is 1, and that of the latter is 2. Note that the caller always supplies these names in a wide character string, even though it might not be a wide character app and you might not be either.

3. Now you must implement the IDispatch::Invoke( ) method. Since it's complex, we'll do it a piece at a time. First, let's handle the property get case. Check the wFlags element for DISPATCH_PROPERTYGET. If found, the caller is trying to get the HelloMessage property. Set the vt element of the pVarResult parameter to the proper value to indicate a string. Use the function SysAllocString( ) to allocate a new BSTR containing the string in the member variable m_bstrHelloMsg. Place this BSTR in the return variant and return the success code. Test with your client; you should now be able to get the value of this property.

4. Next, let's implement the set operation. Check the wFlags element for DISPATCH_PROPERTYPUT. If found, the caller is trying to set the HelloMessage property. Check the vt element of the supplied variant to make sure it contains a BSTR. If so, use the function SysReAllocString( ) to reset the value of the member variable m_bstrHelloMsg to the new value supplied in the VARIANT. Return success or failure code. The SayHello( ) method has been implemented for you so you will be able to see the results.

EXTRA CREDIT: Finally, let's implement the EXCEPINFO structure. Use the function VariantChangeType( ) to attempt to coerce the passed parameter into a BSTR. If this function doesn't succeed, then fill out the fields of the EXCEPINFO structure passed in the parameter list. Your app comes with a help file called "hello32.hlp". The context for the topic inside it that explains this error is 1. Return the error code DISP_E_EXCEPTION to indicate to the client that extended error information can be found in the EXCEPINFO structure.

This page intentionally contains no text other than this sentence.

Chapter 5

Type Libraries

A. CONCEPTS AND DEFINITIONS

1. Any COM server can greatly enhance its usability by providing self-description information for the use of intelligent tools that program it, such as VB, VC, or VJ. You will never be able to sell an object server that doesn't provide one. You can think of a type library as a binary, machine-readable software manual, or as a language-independent header file. A type library can contain information describing:

The types of objects the server supports

Each object's methods with their parameters and types

Each object's properties with their types

Enumerated constant values

References to specific items of on-line documentation

2. A *type library* is a collection of static data structures provided by the object vendor and accessed via the *ITypeLib* interface. A type library is a container for one or more *type infos*. A type info is a set of static data structures provided by the object vendor that contains information about a single object, interface, or class, accessed via the *ITypeInfo* interface. I always remember the difference by thinking of a library as a container for books. The type library is a container for type infos. Thus:

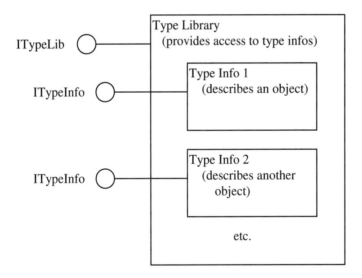

WARNING: A type library and its contents are nothing but a fancy software manual. They are not generated by runtime examination of an object's binary code; they contain whatever descriptive information the author decided to put in them and are only as good as their contents. What's the first law of computer science? Garbage in, garbage out. If the library contains misinformation, you are, as we say here in Boston, "scrod."

3. Type libraries are used for a great many purposes, such as the following. I'm sure you'll think of more.

Instead of having to write the CHelloDriver wrapper class shown in Chapter 4 for accessing the methods and properties of a dispatch object, you can have Visual C++ read a type library describing the particular IDispatch interface and automatically generate the wrapper class for you. VC will regenerate it if the type library changes. This is shown in Chapter 11.

When writing an automation server, you can actually use the type library to implement the IDispatch::GetIDsOfNames( ) and IDispatch::Invoke( ) methods. You don't have to write them manually as shown in the preceding chapter. That's actually the strategy used by the ATL, as you will see in examining the source code.

Development environments such as VB and VJ cannot use C++ header files to find out about an interface's methods or properties. In order to use a VTBL interface, these tools require a type library describing the interface. Think of the type library as a language-independent header file.

A type library makes it possible for intelligent development environments such as VB to provide user interface support, such as Intellisense and auto-completion, that makes a developer's life much easier. Some developers look down their noses at this (REAL programmers don't need any of this nonsense), but this attitude generally lasts for about 5 minutes after they try it. Time to market is the number one constraint in development today, and anything that saves a programmer time flipping through paper manuals is a great feature. This is shown in Chapter 13.

When you write your own custom interfaces, you usually have to provide the code that marshals the call from client to server and back again. If you have a type library that describes your custom interface, and if that custom interface uses only parameter types supported by automation, you can avoid having to write any marshaling code. You can simply make a few registry entries which tell the operating system to perform the marshaling at runtime based on the information in the type library. This is shown in Chapter 3.

When you use an ActiveX control in a script, the script host needs to find out the events that the control fires in order to properly resolve the incoming IDispatch calls announcing the events with the script procedures to be executed. IDispatch::GetIDsOfNames doesn't work in this case because it's going in the wrong direction. As described on page 102, a control contains its own type library bound inside it as a resource. This allows the browser to discover the control's events at runtime.

COM+, the Windows 2000 runtime system, needs a type library in order to apply many of its prefabricated features to components. For example, the Queued Component Recorder (see my book *Understanding COM+* from Microsoft Press, or my article in the June 1999 MSJ) needs a type library to know the methods and properties of the interface for which it records calls. Many other COM+ features, such as the event system (see my article in the September 1999 MSJ) require type libraries as well.

B. BUILDING TYPE LIBRARIES

1. A type library is produced by the MIDL compiler when it compiles an .IDL file containing the **library** directive. You may also see type libraries built from files using ODL, an older version of IDL. A type library is identified with a UUID in the same manner as an interface or a class, specified in the library attributes as shown below. The library will contain type infos describing the elements placed inside the curly braces of the library directive. In this case the library contains only one type info, the one describing the IEliza interface. The actual definition of the interface is placed outside the library directive in this case so the MIDL compiler will generate the necessary code for a proxy/stub marshaler DLL. The single statement "interface IEliza" inside the library curly braces is enough to include the interface description in the type library. Thus:

```
<file eliza.idl>

// Import definition of HRESULT and LPWSTR data types

import "oaidl.idl";

// Declaration of IEliza interface.
// The uuid is the interface ID.

[object, uuid(35FC0C40-C4FA-11ce-AD55-00608C86B89C), version (1.0)]

interface IEliza : IUnknown
{
    HRESULT  Complain ([in] LPWSTR pIn, [out] LPWSTR *pOut) ;
}


// Declaration of type library containing description
// of IEliza interface.

[uuid(35FC0C41-C4FA-11ce-AD55-00608C86B89C) , version (1.0)]]

library IElizaLib
{
    interface IEliza ;
}
```

2. You generally include the .IDL file in your VC project. When you build the project, VC runs the MIDL compiler to generate the type library, generally a separate file having the extension .TLB. Thus:

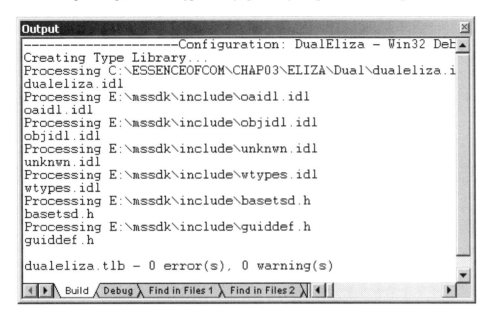

```
Output                                                          ×
--------------------Configuration: DualEliza - Win32 Deb ▲
Creating Type Library...
Processing C:\ESSENCEOFCOM\CHAP03\ELIZA\Dual\dualeliza.i
dualeliza.idl
Processing E:\mssdk\include\oaidl.idl
oaidl.idl
Processing E:\mssdk\include\objidl.idl
objidl.idl
Processing E:\mssdk\include\unknwn.idl
unknwn.idl
Processing E:\mssdk\include\wtypes.idl
wtypes.idl
Processing E:\mssdk\include\basetsd.h
basetsd.h
Processing E:\mssdk\include\guiddef.h
guiddef.h

dualeliza.tlb - 0 error(s), 0 warning(s)                     ▼
◄ ► \ Build ∧ Debug ∧ Find in Files 1 ∧ Find in Files 2 ∧ ◄ |     ►
```

3. Not every development environment uses IDL. For example, VB and VJ do not go through this intermediate step, but instead write their type libraries directly to disk. This functionality is available to anyone via the API function **CreateTypeLib( )** and its descendents. You can use this to roll your own type library on the fly if you need to.

C. TYPES OF OBJECTS DESCRIBED IN TYPE LIBRARIES

1. A type library may contain type infos describing interfaces, as shown on several previous occasions. The interface declaration may appear either inside the library braces or outside of them. If the former, then MIDL compiler does not generate proxy-stub files, which is generally not the desired behavior.

A type library may also describe a dispinterface, which is a set of meanings for dispatch IDs. The dispinterface from the automation server in Chapter 4 is shown below. The keyword **dispinterface** identifies a set of methods and properties accessed through the IDispatch interface. The keyword **methods** identifies the set of methods, and the keyword **properties** the set of properties (in case you couldn't guess). The attribute **id** denotes the dispatch ID of the method or property. Thus:

```
[uuid(6CED2901-A1DD-11cf-8A33-00AA00A58097), version(1.0)]

library hello32
{

// Standard types incorporated by reference.

    importlib("stdole32.tlb");

// A dispinterface is a custom set of methods and properties accessed
// via the IDispatch interface mechanism.

    [ uuid(6CED2902-A1DD-11cf-8A33-00AA00A58097)]
    dispinterface IDHello
    {

// properties and methods contained in the dispinterface with their
// dispatch ids and types.

    properties:
            [id(1)] BSTR HelloMessage;

    methods:
            [id(2)] void SayHello();
    };

    <rest omitted>
}
```

2. A type library may also contain a type info describing a **coclass**, which denotes an object that is creatable through a class factory. The **uuid** attribute specifies the CLSID of the identified class. The type library is saying that you should be able to call CoCreateInstance( ) specifying this CLSID to create an instance of this class. The interface definitions inside the coclass block specify the interfaces that the object supports. There are two in the example shown below. Only one can be the default interface, which tells VB (and other apps that have trouble with the distinction between objects and interfaces) which interface to identify with the object until otherwise specified by the programmer. Thus:

```
// Generated .IDL file (by the OLE/COM Object Viewer)
//
// typelib filename: EssenceOfComVbObject.dll

[
  uuid(B494CF4F-4DD0-446F-8EB8-2E9EB0CA0806),
  version(1.0)
]
library EssenceOfComVbObject
{
    < interface definitions omitted >

    [uuid(AD9A90C6-E507-45F5-BAFE-793AE5346CB9), version(1.0)]

    coclass Class1
    {
        [default] interface _Class1;
        interface ITypeLibMarshaledEliza;
    };
};
```

3. Type can also contain enumerations, which are lists of allowed constants to be used as parameters in a function call. For example, COM+ contains an interface called IContextState, whose definition is:

```
[ odl, uuid(3C05E54B-A42A-11D2-AFC4-00C04F8EE1C4)]

interface IContextState : IUnknown {
    HRESULT _stdcall SetDeactivateOnReturn(VARIANT_BOOL bDeactivate);
    HRESULT _stdcall GetDeactivateOnReturn([out] VARIANT_BOOL* pbDeactivate);
    HRESULT _stdcall SetMyTransactionVote(tagTransactionVote txVote);
    HRESULT _stdcall GetMyTransactionVote([out] tagTransactionVote* ptxVote);
};
```

The last two methods require as their parameter a member of the enumeration named tagTransactionVote. This is an enumeration that restricts the numerical values that can be passed to these methods. The definition of that enumeration in IDL is:

```
typedef enum {
    TxCommit = 0,
    TxAbort = 1
} tagTransactionVote;
```

A type library can also contain the definition of structures. For example:

```
typedef struct tagCAppStatistics
{
        unsigned long m_cTotalCalls;
        unsigned long m_cTotalInstances;
        unsigned long m_cTotalClasses;
        unsigned long m_cCallsPerSecond;
} CAppStatistics;
```

A type library can also contain typedefs. Thus:

```
typedef [public]
CAppStatistics APPSTATISTICS;
```

4. The type libraries we have seen so far have listed only the types and names of an object's properties, methods, and parameters. This isn't anywhere near enough to be able to program it intelligently. A type info may provide a *help string*, a small string provided within the type info itself. The attribute **helpstring** denotes this string, as shown below. The string that you want to display is placed inside the parentheses in quotes. A development environment that wants to display the string can retrieve it via the ITypeLib and ITypeInfo interfaces as shown in the latter part of this chapter.

A help string is generally displayed in a cramped location inside a development environment, so there is a fairly low limit on the amount of explanation it can usefully provide, perhaps a dozen words or so. To provide a more detailed explanation of a property or method, you can place references in the type library to specific topics within your object's on-line help file (which you must provide anyway if you expect anyone to buy it). A smart development environment will provide the programmer with a button that launches WinHelp (via the API function WinHelp( )) and jumps directly to the specified topic. You specify the help file that contains the help topics via the attribute **helpfile**, containing the name of the help file in parentheses. This attribute must appear only once in the library's attributes section. Any attributes section within the library may contain the attribute **helpcontext**, which specifies the context integer of the topic within the specified help file that (you hope) explains the item. The development environment retrieves these elements via the ITypeLib and ITypeInfo interfaces as shown in the latter part of this chapter. Thus:

```
// Help file for library specified here.

[ uuid(6CED2901-A1DD-11cf-8A33-00AA00A58097), version(1.0),
    helpfile ("Hello32.hlp") ]

library hello32
{
    importlib("stdole32.tlb");

// Help string explaining this type info specified here.

    [ uuid(6CED2902-A1DD-11cf-8A33-00AA00A58097),
      helpstring ("IDispatch for Hello32 Object") ]

    dispinterface IDHello
    {

// Help string explaining this property and help context of further
// explanation specified here.

    properties:
            [id(1), helpstring ("Displayed message"), helpcontext(1)]
                    BSTR HelloMessage;

    <rest of file omitted>
```

D. DEPLOYING AND REGISTERING TYPE LIBRARIES

1. An object may deploy its type libraries in several ways. You can ship a separate file with your application. This is especially good if your type library is large and infrequently used. Microsoft Excel, for example, comes with a type library file named "xl5en32.olb", which is 223 Kbytes long. Most end users have no interest in it, only the minority who actually install the programming package.

Most COM developers instead choose to bind the type library into the object's server as a resource, thereby making your server self-contained. You can't forget to bring it along. Most intelligent programming environments, such as VB, VJ, and the ATL, automatically use this mechanism. To bind the type library as a resource, add a **TYPELIB** directive to your .RC file, specifying the name of the type library you want included. **The resource id of the type library within your .EXE or .DLL must be 1, as shown here, or the system's type library access functions will have difficulty finding it.**

```
<.RC file>

//////////////////////////////////////////////////////////////////
//////
//
// TYPELIB
//

1           TYPELIB DISCARDABLE      "hello32.tlb"
```

You may find that you need the type library both bound into the object server and also standing alone as a separate file. For example, when using type library marshaling in distributed COM, the type library needs to be installed on both client and server machines. You probably don't want to install the actual object server on the client machine just for its type library, but at the same time, you'd like it self-contained on the server machine. In this case, you would produce both, deploying the standalone type library on the client machine and the object server with its bound-in type library on the server machine.

2. However you decide to distribute your type library files, you must make entries in the system registry so that client applications and development tools can find the correct type library for your object. The registry does not contain the type library itself; rather, it contains a reference to the file in which the type library can be found. First, under the automation object's CLSID key, you must place the subkey "TYPELIB" with a value of the uuid which identifies the type library in which the type info describing the specific automation object can be found. Thus:

```
HKEY_CLASSES_ROOT
  CLSID
    <your app's clsid>
      TYPELIB=<uuid of your object's type library>
```

In the hello32 example from Chapter 4, these entries are:

```
HKEY_CLASSES_ROOT
  CLSID
    {6CED2900-A1DD-11cf-8A33-00AA00A58097}
      TYPELIB={6CED2901-A1DD-11cf-8A33-00AA00A58097}
```

The TYPELIB section of the registry contains an entry for every type library registered on the system. The entry structure provides the capability of specifying different type libraries for different version numbers, language IDs, and 16- or 32-bit servers. Since the type library frequently contains references to an object's on-line help files, the registry entry structure also contains an entry specifying the directory in which these may be found. These entries can be easily made via the API function **RegisterTypeLib( )**, and removed via the function **UnRegisterTypeLib( )** (not shown). The resulting registry entries will look like this:

```
HKEY_CLASSES_ROOT
  TYPELIB
    <type library uuid> >
      <version> = <human-readable name of your type library
        <language id, 0 == any language>
          Win32 = <your type library file name>
          HelpDir = <directory containing help files>
```

In the hello32 example, these entries are:

```
HKEY_CLASSES_ROOT
  TYPELIB
    {6CED2901-A1DD-11cf-8A33-00AA00A58097}
      1.0 = Automation Hello 1.0 Type Library
        0
          Win32 = c:\EssenceOfCOM\chap04\helloau\hello32\done\hello32.tlb
          HelpDir = c:\EssenceOfCOM\chap04\helloau\hello32\help
```

E. READING TYPE LIBRARIES

1. Writers of programming tools, spy programs, or other apps that require the definitions of objects and interfaces need to be able to open the type libraries and read their contents. This section discusses the services and interfaces provided by the operating system for this purpose. The code shown in this section comes from a sample browser program that you will find in the directory \Chap05\TypeLibraryBrowser. The user interface of the application looks like this:

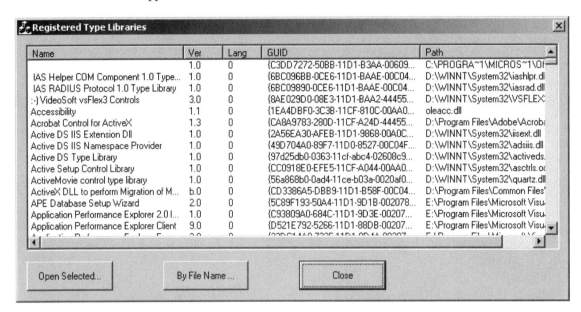

2. There are two ways to open a type library. You can call the API function **LoadTypeLib( )**, specifying the file that contains the type library. This opens and reads the type library, returning an interface of type *ITypeLib*, which provides access to the type library's information. Thus:

```
extern ITypeLibPtr m_pTypeLib ;

void CTypeLibraryBrowserDlg::OnByFileName()
{
/*
Display dialog box allowing user to choose type library files.
*/
    CFileDialog dlg  (TRUE)  ;
    dlg.m_ofn.lpstrFilter = "Possible Type Libraries (*.tlb, *.dll,"
      "*.exe)\0*.tlb;*.dll;*.exe\0" ;

    if (dlg.DoModal ( ) == IDOK)
    {
/*
Open type library file selected by user.
*/
        LoadTypeLib (A2W(dlg.GetPathName ( )), &m_pTypeLib);

        <display code omitted>
    }
}
```

3. Alternatively, you can open a type library via the function **LoadRegTypeLib( )**, specifying the UUID of the desired type library. This function looks up the type library in the registry based on the supplied UUID, version numbers, and locale; then internally delegates to LoadTypeLib( ). Thus:

```
extern ITypeLibPtr m_pTypeLib ;

void CTypeLibraryBrowserDlg::OnOpenSelected()
{

/*
Convert type library ID from registry string.
Convert version and locale from registry string.
*/
    UUID TypeLibID ;    CString strLocale ;
    unsigned short wVerMajor, wVerMinor  ;

    < conversion code omitted >

/*
Open type library based on registry information.
*/

    LoadRegTypeLib (
      TypeLibID,              // Type library UUID
      wVerMajor,              // major version
      wVerMinor,              // minor version
      atoi (strLocale) ,      // locale ID
      &m_pTypeLib ) ;         // output variable

      <display code omitted>
    }
}
```

4. The functions for opening a type library return the ITypeLib interface, which is implemented by the operating system. It contains the methods that you need to read the data structures inside the type library. Its methods are:

ITypeLib::FindName	*// Finds name of a type description in a type library.*
ITypeLib::GetDocumentation	*// Get library's documentation strings.*
ITypeLib::GetLibAttr	*// Get attributes of library.*
ITypeLib::GetTypeComp	*// Get pointer to the ITypeComp for compiling a type library.*
ITypeLib::GetTypeInfo	*// Get a type description from the library.*
ITypeLib::GetTypeInfoCount	*// Get the number of type descriptions in the library.*
ITypeLib::GetTypeInfoType	*// Get the type (function or variable) of a type description in the lib.*
ITypeLib::GetTypeInfoOfGuid	*// Get type description corresponding to the specified GUID.*
ITypeLib::IsName	*// Does lib contain member of this name?*
ITypeLib::ReleaseTLibAttr	*// Release TLIBATTR structure obtained from ITypeLib::GetLibAttr.*

NOTE: Type libraries can contain custom attributes that you define yourself via the [custom] attribute in IDL. You can read these attributes via the ITypeLib2 interface, which you obtain by querying the ITypeLib interface.

The main thing that you do with a type library is to look at the type infos that it contains. The method **ITypeLib::GetTypeInfoCount( )** will tell you how many of them the type library contains. The method **ITypeLib::GetDocumentation( )** will retrieve descriptive information about a type info: its name, a short descriptive help string, the name of the on-line help file in which more detailed information may be found, and the help context (an index value) within that file. It returns its information in the form of BSTRs, which you must release via the function SysFreeString( ). This information is used to compile the list of type infos, shown in the list box on the left side of the screen shot below. The code used to accomplish it is shown on the facing page. Thus:

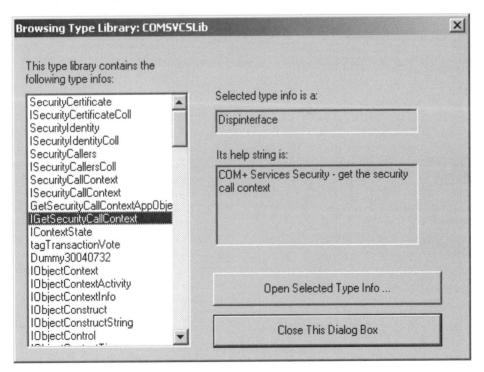

```
/*
User clicked button to open a type library.
*/

extern ITypeLibPtr m_pTypeLib ;

BOOL CDisplayTypeLibDlg::OnInitDialog()
{
    CDialog::OnInitDialog();
    USES_CONVERSION ;

/*
Get the name of the type library. Passing -1 to GetDocumentation
obtains information about the type library itself. Put it in the dialog
box's title bar. The name comes in a BSTRING which we must free.
*/

    BSTR bstrTypeLibName ;
    _bstr_t Title = "Browsing Type Library: " ;

    m_pTypeLib->GetDocumentation (-1, &bstrTypeLibName, NULL,
      NULL, NULL) ;

    Title += bstrTypeLibName ;
    SetWindowText ((char *) Title) ;
    SysFreeString (bstrTypeLibName) ;

/*
Find out how many type infos this type library contains.
*/
    int i ;
    int TypeInfoCount = m_pTypeLib->GetTypeInfoCount();

/*
For each type info in the library, get its name and add it to the type
list control in the dialog box. A type info is identified by a zero-
based ordinal. The name comes in a BSTRING which we must free.
*/
    BSTR bstrName;

    for(i = 0; i < TypeInfoCount; i++)
    {
      m_pTypeLib->GetDocumentation(i, &bstrName, NULL, NULL, NULL);

      m_List.AddString (W2A(bstrName)) ;
      SysFreeString(bstrName);
    }

    return TRUE;
}
```

5. You can find the type of item described by a type info (interface, coclass, etc.) via the method **ITypeLib::GetTypeInfoType( )**. When the user of the sample program clicks on a particular type info, as shown in the preceding diagram, I call this method to display the type info type in the edit control on the right side of the box. I use the method **ITypeLib::GetDocumentation( )** to get the help string, if any, provided by the type library author and display it below the type info type. Thus:

```
void CDisplayTypeLibDlg::OnSelchangeList1()
{

    USES_CONVERSION ;

    static char * TypeKind[] = {
     "Enum",              /* TKIND_ENUM */
     "Struct",            /* TKIND_RECORD, actually means 'structure' */
     "Module",            /* TKIND_MODULE */
     "Interface",         /* TKIND_INTERFACE */
     "Dispinterface",     /* TKIND_DISPATCH */
     "Coclass",           /* TKIND_COCLASS */
     "Typedef",           /* TKIND_ALIAS, actually means 'typedef' */
     "Union",      };     /* TKIND_UNION */


    m_CurSel = m_List.GetCurSel ( ) ;

    if (m_CurSel != LB_ERR)
    {
      m_btnOpenThisTypLib.EnableWindow (TRUE) ;

/*
Get type info type. Convert to string, display to user.
*/
      TYPEKIND tk ;
      m_pTypeLib->GetTypeInfoType (m_CurSel, &tk) ;
      m_EditTypeInfoType.SetWindowText (TypeKind [tk]) ;



/*
Get selected type info's help string. Display to user.
*/
      BSTR bstrDocString ;
      m_pTypeLib->GetDocumentation (m_CurSel, NULL, &bstrDocString,
            NULL, NULL) ;
      m_EditTypeInfoHelpString.SetWindowText (W2A(bstrDocString)) ;
      SysFreeString (bstrDocString) ;
    }
}
```

6. There's not all that much interesting information at the type library level. You will get bored here fairly quickly and want to get down to the type info level, where the interesting descriptions of objects and interfaces live. You open a type info via the method **ITypeLib::GetTypeInfo( )**, specifying the ordinal number of the desired type info inside the type library. If you don't want to go through the trouble of enumerating the type infos, and if you know the GUID of the object or interface whose type info you want, you can obtain it directly via the method **ITypeLib::GetTypeInfoOfGuid( )** (not shown). The sample application does the former when the user clicks the "Open Selected Type Info..." button. Thus:

```
/*
User clicked the "Open Selected Type Info" button.
*/

extern ITypeInfoPtr m_pTypeInfo ;

void CDisplayTypeLibDlg::OnOpenThisTypeInfo()
{

/*
Open the type info that the user has selected.
*/

    m_pTypeLib->GetTypeInfo (m_CurSel, &m_pTypeInfo) ;

    <display code omitted>

}
```

7. A type info is a set of static data structures that describes a single object or interface. You read a type info's information via the ITypeInfo interface, which is implemented by the operating system. It has the following methods:

ITypeInfo::AddressOfMember	*// Get address of static functions or variables.*
ITypeInfo::CreateInstance	*// Create a new instance of a component object class (coclass).*
ITypeInfo::GetContainingTypeLib	*// Get type library containing the type info.*
ITypeInfo::GetDllEntry	*// Get entry point for a function in a DLL.*
ITypeInfo::GetDocumentation	*// Get documentation string describing type info.*
ITypeInfo::GetFuncDesc	*// Get description of a function, in a FUNCDESC structure.*
ITypeInfo::GetIDsOfNames	*// Map between names and IDs.*
ITypeInfo::GetMops	*// Get marshaling information.*
ITypeInfo::GetNames	*// Map between IDs and names.*
ITypeInfo::GetRefTypeInfo	*// Get type descriptions referenced by other type descriptions.*
ITypeInfo::GetTypeAttr	*// Get attributes of a type, in a TYPEATTR structure.*
ITypeInfo::GetTypeComp	*// Get ITypeComp interface for a type, used for compilers .*
ITypeInfo::GetRefTypeOfImplType	*// Get description of the specified interface types.*
ITypeInfo::GetVarDesc	*// Get description of a variable, in a VARDESC structure.*
ITypeInfo::Invoke	*// Invokes a method or accesses a property of a described object.*
ITypeInfo::ReleaseFuncDesc	*// Releases a FUNCDESC previously returned by ITI::GetFuncDesc.*
ITypeInfo::ReleaseTypeAttr	*// Releases a TYPEATTR previously returned by ITI::GetTypeAttr.*
ITypeInfo::ReleaseVarDesc	*// Releases a VARDESC previously returned by ITI::GetVarDesc.*

NOTE: Type infos can contain custom attributes that you define yourself via the [custom] attribute in IDL. You can read these attributes via the ITypeInfo2 interface, which you obtain by querying the ITypeInfo interface.

8. One of the dialog boxes from the sample program that displays information about an individual type info is shown below. The program contains separate display forms for interfaces, coclasses, and enums. Thus:

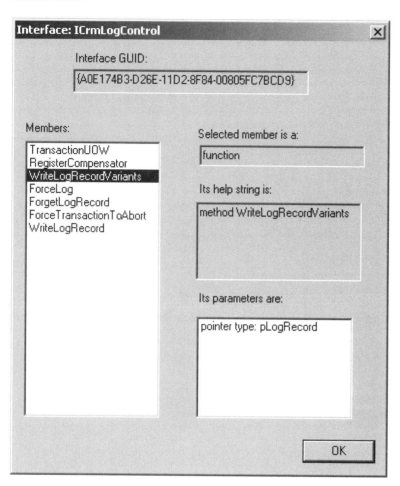

9. A type info contains global information about the object that it describes, such as GUID, locale, and version, in a structure called a **TYPEATTR**. This structure is defined as follows:

```
typedef struct FARSTRUCT tagTYPEATTR
{
    GUID guid;                         // GUID of the type info
    LCID lcid;                         // locale of names and doc strings
    unsigned long dwReserved;          // reserved
    MEMBERID memidConstructor;         // ID of constructor
    MEMBERID memidDestructor;          // ID of destructor
    char FAR* lpstrSchema;             // reserved
    unsigned long cbSizeInstance;      // size of an instance of this type
    TYPEKIND typekind;                 // kind of this type info
    unsigned short cFuncs;             // number of functions
    unsigned short cVars;              // number of variables/data members
    unsigned short cImplTypes;         // number of implemented interfaces
    unsigned short cbSizeVft;          // size of this type's VTBL
    unsigned short cbAlignment;        // byte-alignment for this type
    unsigned short wTypeFlags;         // flags
    unsigned short wMajorVerNum;       // major version number
    unsigned short wMinorVerNum;       // minor version number
    TYPEDESC tdescAlias;               // type this type is an alias for
    IDLDESC idldescType;               // IDL attributes of the type

} TYPEATTR, FAR* LPTYPEATTR;
```

You get it via the method **ITypeInfo::GetTypeAttr( )**. This allocates and returns a structure, which you must later release via the method **ITypeInfo::ReleaseTypeAttr( )**. Thus:

```
/*
Get TYPEATTR structure.
*/
    TYPEATTR *pTA ;
    m_pTypeInfo->GetTypeAttr (&pTA) ;

/*
Get GUID of interface from TYPEATTR. Convert to string, place in
edit control.
*/

    LPOLESTR pstrGuid ;
    StringFromCLSID (pTA->guid, &pstrGuid) ;
    m_edGUID.SetWindowText (W2A(pstrGuid)) ;
    CoTaskMemFree (pstrGuid) ;

    < functions and variables enumerated on facing page >
/*
Free TYPEATTR.
*/

    m_pTypeInfo->ReleaseTypeAttr (pTA) ;
}
```

10. The most interesting thing to see in a type is its list of member functions and variables. These are presented by the **FUNCDESC** and **VARDESC** structures, respectively. We fetch them via the methods **ITypeInfo::GetFuncDesc( )** and **ITypeInfo::GetVarDesc( )**. The structures are allocated dynamically and need to be released via the methods **ITypeInfo::ReleaseFuncDesc( )** and **ITypeInfo::ReleaseVarDesc( )**. The member ID item that each contains is necessary for getting the documentation names for the item via the method **ITypeInfo::GetDocumentation( )**. It also represents the item's automation dispatch ID. Thus:

```
< code excerpted from previous page>

int i ;
FUNCDESC *pFuncDesc ; VARDESC *pVarDesc ;
BSTR bstrName ;

/*
For each function in the TYPEATTR, get its description in a FUNCDESC.
Use the member id from the funcdesc to get the function's name from the
type info. Place the name into the list box, then release the string
and the funcdesc.
*/
    for (i = 0 ; i < pTA->cFuncs ; i ++)
    {
        m_pTypeInfo->GetFuncDesc(i, &pFuncDesc) ;
        m_pTypeInfo->GetDocumentation(pFuncDesc->memid, &bstrName, NULL,
            NULL, NULL);

        _bstr_t MemName = bstrName ;
        m_ListMembers.AddString ((char *) MemName) ;
        SysFreeString(bstrName);
        m_pTypeInfo->ReleaseFuncDesc(pFuncDesc);
    }

/*
For each variable in the TYPEATTR, get its description in a VARDESC.
Use the member ID from the vardesc to get the variable's name from the
type info. Place the name into the list box, then release the string
and the vardesc.
*/
    for (i = 0 ; i < pTA->cVars ; i ++)
    {
        m_pTypeInfo->GetVarDesc(i, &pVarDesc) ;
        m_pTypeInfo->GetDocumentation(pVarDesc->memid, &bstrName, NULL,
            NULL, NULL);

        _bstr_t MemName = bstrName ;
        m_ListMembers.AddString ((char *) MemName) ;
        SysFreeString(bstrName);
        m_pTypeInfo->ReleaseVarDesc(pVarDesc);
    }
```

11. The FUNCDESC and VARDESC contain many interesting entries, such as the type of a variable, and the number and types of parameters in a function. In the interest of space, I'm not going to write any more in this text about picking these things apart. You will, however, find this information in the sample browser program.

```
typedef struct tagFUNCDESC
{
    MEMBERID memid;             // function member ID
    SCODE FAR* lprgscode;       // legal SCODES for the function
    ELEMDESC FAR* lprgelemdescParam;    // array of param types
    FUNCKIND funckind;          // is fn virtual, static,or dispatch-only
    INVOKEKIND invkind;         // is fn method, prop-get or prop-set
    CALLCONV callconv;          // function's calling convention
    short cParams;              // total number of parameters
    short cParamsOpt;           // number of optional parameters
    short oVft;                 // offset in virtual function table
    short cScodes;              // count of permitted Scodes
    ELEMDESC elemdescFunc;      // return type of the function
    unsigned short wFuncFlags;// flags
}
FUNCDESC;

typedef struct FARSTRUCT tagVARDESC
{
    MEMBERID memid;             // member ID
    char FAR* lpstrSchema;      // reserved
    union
    {
      unsigned long oInst;      // offset of variable within the instance
      VARIANT FAR* lpvarValue;  // value of the constant

    }UNION_NAME(u);
    ELEMDESC elemdescVar;       // Variable data, in a VARIANT
    unsigned short wVarFlags;  // Flags
    VARKIND varkind;            // kind of variable
} VARDESC, FAR* LPVARDESC;
```

Lab Exercises
Chapter 5
Type Library Browser

Directory: EssenceOfCOM\Chap05\TypeLibraryBrowser.

1. This sample program is very easy to use. Simply run the executable TypeLibraryBrowser.exe. It will display a list of all the registered type libraries on the system. Either select one and click "Open Selected...", or click "By File Name..." and use the resulting dialog box to surf to whatever type library file you want to view.

2. You will next see a dialog box displaying all the type infos in the type library you have selected. Click on an entry in the list box to see type library level information (its type and help string) about that type info. Click "Open Selected Type Info..." to examine it in more detail.

3. You will see a new dialog box whose exact structure depends on the type info that you have selected. The box for displaying interfaces and dispinterfaces was shown in the text. There are different dialog boxes for displaying coclasses and enums.

This page intentionally contains no text other than this sentence.

Chapter 6

Threads and COM

A. CONCEPTS AND DEFINITIONS

1. Using COM in multithreaded applications generates more *FUD* (Fear, Uncertainty, and Doubt) among programmers than any other area of COM. If you are writing a COM object server, might different objects in your server be called from different threads? Might one object's methods be called from different threads? Do you have to worry about serializing access to the object server's global functions and data? To each object's member functions and data? To anything?

And what about writing a client app that uses COM objects? Can your client app access the same object from two threads without screwing everything up? Can it access two different objects from the same server from two different threads? What if some classes of object work differently than others? What if an object's behavior changes from one version to the next?

Don't worry. As with most topics in COM, the reality isn't nearly as bad as the anticipation. The 'C' in COM stands for "Component". To require a client to have intimate knowledge of the internals of the objects that it wants to use, or to have an object need to care about the internals of its clients, would violate the most fundamental principle in all of COM — that it is a binary standard, so you don't need or want to know anything about the other guy except that he follows it too. If you follow a few simple rules, COM will take care of the gory details of threading. It works according to the following principles:

A. Each thread in a client app chooses a set of rules to follow for its handling of objects, from doing nothing at all with them to going completely crazy with them. The thread tells COM the rules that it intends to follow when it initializes COM via the function CoInitialize( ) or CoInitializeEx( ).

B. An object server chooses a set of rules to follow for its handling of threads, from not knowing anything at all about threads to going completely crazy with them. The server tells COM the rules that it intends to follow, either by making registry entries for a .DLL server, or when it calls CoInitialize( ) or CoInitializeEx( ) for an .EXE server.

C. Whenever a client thread creates or connects to an object, COM compares the rules that each party has said that it follows. If they have promised to play by the same rules, then COM sets up a direct connection between the two and gets out of the way. If they are different, then COM sets up marshaling proxies between the two parties so that each sees only the threading rules that it has told COM it knows how to handle. The latter case costs some performance, but allows parties following dissimilar threading rules to work together seamlessly without croaking.

The beauty of how COM handles threads is that neither client nor server need to know or care about the model used by its counterparty. Each follows the rules of the model with which it was written, and COM intercedes and mediates between them to the extent necessary to make it work. It's not a matter of getting it to work at all, but getting it to work optimally.

2. The main obstacle to understanding COM threading is nomenclature. I know more potential COM programmers that have run for the hills over the buzzwords "threading model", "apartment and free threading", or "single-threaded versus multi-threaded apartments" than anything else in all of Windows.

The problem is that there are two competing sets of nomenclature in current use, even within Microsoft. Both describe the same thing, but from different standpoints. The older of the two takes a thread-centric point of view. Its names derive from the registry entries that a DLL component makes to tell COM about the threading rules that it follows. In this nomenclature, a "threading model" is a set of rules that a client or an object follows. Available threading models are "single", "apartment", "free", and "both".

The newer nomenclature takes its names from the logical segregation of objects that COM performs internally. This nomenclature uses an object-centric point of view, saying that every object lives in exactly one "apartment", a logical container that determines its threading behavior. The different types of apartments that an object may choose to occupy include "single threaded", "multi-threaded", and "neutral".

The nomenclature is even more confusing because Microsoft can't make up their minds which one to use. At the time of this writing, the tools teams seem to be using the older nomenclature, while the MTS and COM+ teams use the newer. When I wrote my first MSJ article (Feb '97) on COM threading, I used the older nomenclature and the editors changed it to the newer one. When I wrote the follow-on article six months later, still using the older nomenclature, they let it stand. My favorite example of this confusion is the flag that you pass to the function CoInitializeEx( ), which initializes COM on a thread. Your choices are COINIT_APARTMENTTHREADED, which uses the older nomenclature to describe the behavior it requires, and COINIT_MULTITHREADED, which uses the newer. Microsoft can't even keep its nomenclature consistent within two values of a flag to the same function call. No wonder the rest of us have trouble.

I've pretty much switched over to the newer nomenclature, despite a rabid (even for me) tirade against it in the previous edition of this book. I found that the older nomenclature worked well as long as you were only differentiating between single versus apartment threaded, and I could stretch it to cover free threading if I had to. But I couldn't extend it to cover the neutral apartment introduced in Windows 2000; it broke down completely. I'll use the newer one throughout this book, while noting parenthetically what the older nomenclature would call a situation. Don't be surprised if you find the newer nomenclature confusing, especially at first. For example, your process will usually contain multiple single-threaded apartments, but only a single multi-threaded apartment. And just try to aurally distinguish the terms "MTA" and "NTA" in a heated design review (and what other kind is there?), or on the phone with someone who speaks with an accent.

WARNING: Even more than for other chapters in this book, follow this one through from beginning to end. Even if you only care about the multi-threaded apartment ("free threading model"), don't jump straight there. Read the entire chapter, or you'll get lost.

B. THREADING APARTMENTS

1. To understand threading in COM, you need to understand the concept of an *apartment*, which is a logical container within a process for objects that share the same thread access requirements. COM automatically assigns an object to one and only one apartment at the time of the object's creation. The object remains in that apartment throughout its lifetime. Calls made by a client thread to objects in its own apartment, which means that the object and the thread have promised to follow the same threading rules, proceed directly. Calls made by a client thread to objects in other apartments, which means that the thread and the object are playing by different threading rules, proceed through a proxy/stub mechanism similar to that used between processes. This inter-apartment marshaling ensures that each side sees only the threading behavior that it has told COM it knows how to handle.

COM supports three types of apartments, corresponding to the different types of threading access allowed by objects, as shown on the facing page. Every thread that wants to use COM must initialize COM by calling the API function CoInitializeEx( ), passing either the flag COINIT_APARTMENTTHREADED or COINIT_MULTITHREADED (calling CoInitialize( ) or OleInitialize( ) implies to the former). A thread that does this is said to have *entered an apartment*, in which it will remain until it calls CoUninitialize or terminates.

When a thread, say T1, calls CoInitializeEx( ) and passes the COINIT_APARTMENTTHREADED flag, T1 is said to have created and entered a new *single-threaded apartment*, or STA. Think of an STA as a small studio apartment with room for only one thread, although it can contain any number of objects. All objects in an STA will receive their calls only on the thread that created the apartment, in this case T1. A process can contain any number of STAs. If threads T2 and T3 each call CoInitializeEx( ) and pass the COINIT_APARTMENTTHREADED flag, then each of these will create and enter a new STA.

The programmer of an object specifies that the object must live in an STA when he wants to ensure that all calls to the object are made from the same thread. This means that the developer of an object that lives in an STA does not have to write serialization code to protect the object's instance data against concurrent access by multiple threads. COM routes all incoming calls from other threads to the STA thread's message queue. A COM call actually gets made on an STA object only when the STA thread retrieves and dispatches the relevant message from its queue. This is ideal for user interface programming, because the programmer knows that an incoming COM call won't interrupt him in the midst of handling a Windows message.

Since STA objects are always called from the same thread, they are said to have *thread affinity*. A developer can therefore use thread local storage to keep track of an object's internal data. Components developed with Visual Basic 6 and the MFC use this technique and therefore must live in an STA.

STA components are fine for single-desktop user interface programming, but the STA architecture imposes performance penalties in distributed situations. Suppose you have a DCOM server accessed by clients on other machines. When the remote client calls a method on an object, the server machine receives that call on a random RPC thread from a pool that exists for this purpose. This receiving thread then makes the call locally to the actual object. If the object lived in an STA, the receiving thread would have to marshal the call to the STA thread and wait for that thread to service it, a terrible performance drag, severely limiting the scalability of the server. The desired STA thread might be busy servicing other objects, or, worse, blocked while waiting on some synchronization event. It would be much more efficient if the object didn't care which thread it received its call on. The call could proceed directly from the receiving thread and not waste time with any of this message queuing nonsense.

COM provides the *multi-threaded apartment*, or MTA, to solve exactly this problem. A process contains only one MTA. A thread that calls CoInitializeEx and passes the COINIT_MULTITHREADED flag is said to have entered the process's lone MTA. Think of it as a bunkroom that can sleep any number of threads if they don't mind being cozy. All objects created in the MTA can receive calls on any MTA thread. If our receiving thread and object both lived in the MTA, the call could proceed directly from the receiving thread, without wasting time or being vulnerable to bottlenecks. This is a good choice for worker components that don't have any user interface components.

The drawback to writing an MTA object is that, because it can receive a call from any MTA thread at any time, you must write serialization code to ensure that concurrent accesses from different MTA threads do not cause any damage. An STA object gets its serialization from its built-in thread affinity, but that's too high a price to pay in high-performance, non-user-interface situations. Prior to Windows 2000, this requirement forced developers to write some extremely difficult code, which is why relatively few of these MTA objects exist. In Windows 2000, programmers can obtain this serialization transparently from the operating system.

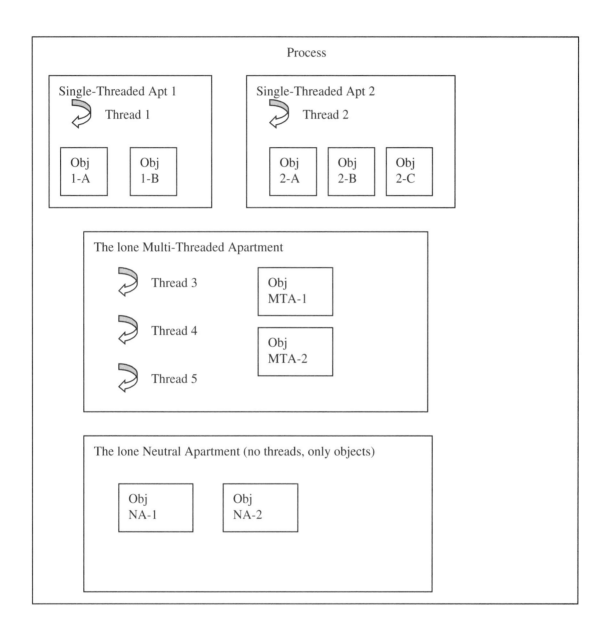

2. How does COM know which apartment to create an object in? The relatively unusual case of a local server is discussed later in this chapter. In the much more common case of a DLL server, the developer of a component specifies the type of apartment its objects can live in by adding the named value ThreadingModel to the component's InProcServer32 registry entry. Thus:

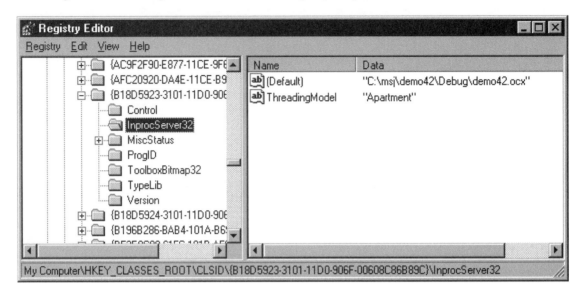

Here's where the nomenclature first gets confusing. An entry of "Apartment" tells COM to create an object in an STA where it can have an intimate relationship with the STA's single thread. An entry of "Free" tells COM to create the object in the process's lone MTA, where it can party with anyone in the bunkroom, accepting calls on any thread that lives in the MTA. The "Both" entry is misnamed; it really should be called "Either". It tells COM that the object doesn't give a hoot which apartment it lives in: it is equally at home in an intimate studio with one thread or in the bunkroom with everyone. An object with this ThreadingModel entry is always created in the apartment of its creating thread. An entry of "Neutral" tells COM to create the object in the neutral apartment. Thus:

ThreadingModel Entry	Apartment Type
Single or absent	First STA created in the process
Apartment	Any STA in the process
Free	Process's lone MTA
Both	Creating thread's apartment, regardless of type
Neutral	Process's lone Neutral apartment

3. If a client thread creates an object and the object's ThreadingModel entry allows it to live in the client thread's apartment, for example, an STA thread creates an object whose ThreadingModel entry is "Apartment" or "Both", everything's fine. The client thread gets a direct connection to the object. But what happens when a client thread creates an object that needs to live in a different type of apartment than the thread? For example, what happens if an STA thread creates an object marked as "Free", which needs to live in the MTA? An object is always created in the apartment that its ThreadingModel entry specifies. If that is not the same apartment as the thread that is creating the object, then the thread doesn't get a direct connection; instead it gets an inter-thread marshaling proxy. For example:

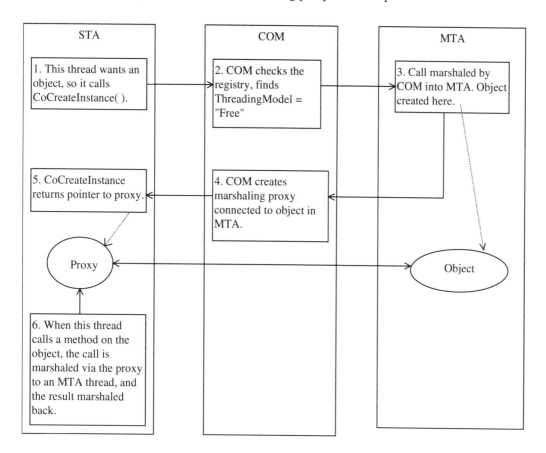

4. You might think that placing an object in the MTA solves all your performance problems. It doesn't, because inter-apartment accesses are still slow. An STA calling an MTA object is expensive, because making a call across apartment boundaries requires the use of a thread-switching proxy. The apartments still don't like each other.

To solve this performance problem, Windows 2000 provides a new type of apartment called the *neutral apartment* (NA), or sometimes the thread neutral apartment (TNA). Do not call it the NTA; life's already confusing enough without trying to distinguish M(as in 'Mike')TA from N(as in 'Nancy')TA by ear. Unlike the STA or MTA, the NA contains no threads, only objects (which is why I refer to it as the NA, to emphasize the fact that there's no 'T' in it). An object with the registry entry ThreadingModel=Neutral is always created in the NA, regardless of the apartment occupied by the thread that creates it. The creating thread always receives a lightweight proxy. When a thread makes a call to an NA object using this proxy, the call proceeds without changing threads, which makes it much faster than a standard thread-switching proxy. This means that an object in the NA always receives its call on the thread of its caller, regardless of type. If an STA thread calls an NA object, the call is received on the STA thread. If an MTA thread calls an NA object, the call is received on the MTA thread.

NA objects require serialization code in the same manner as do MTA threads. Fortunately, Windows 2000 also provides the capability of obtaining automatic synchronization from the operating system. I discuss this problem a little more later in this chapter.

It is up to COM to figure out at creation time which apartment the object will live in and which type of connection to the object, direct or marshaled, and if the latter, heavyweight or lightweight (thread switching or not) its creator will receive. If an object is created in the same apartment as the thread that creates it, the thread gets a direct connection to the object, which is very fast. If the object is created in a different apartment, the thread gets a proxy/stub connection, heavyweight in the case of STA or MTA, lightweight in the case of NA. Thus:

ThreadingModel Registry Entry	Creating thread in any STA	Creating thread in lone MTA
"Apartment"	Creator's STA (direct)	Special-case STA (standard proxy)
"Free"	MTA (standard proxy)	MTA (direct)
"Both"	Creator's STA (direct)	MTA (direct)
"Neutral"	Neutral (lightweight proxy)	Neutral (lightweight proxy)

Because objects that live in the NA can be accessed efficiently from both an STA or the MTA, I think that Neutral will eventually replace Free and Both as component types. Apart from legacy components that you don't want to rewrite, I can't think of any reason that you'd want to use the MTA. Objects that require thread affinity, especially those using windows for user interface work, will still need to live in an STA.

This page intentionally contains no text other than this sentence.

C. SINGLE-THREADED APARTMENT EXAMPLE

1. A client thread that wants to live in a single-threaded apartment is simple to write. The thread must create and enter an STA by calling the function CoInitialize( ) when it starts up. The first STA created in the process is special, because this is where legacy components (those with no knowledge of threads whatsoever, ThreadingModel = "Single" or absent) go. Accordingly, the first thread to initialize COM must also be the last thread to uninitialize COM, to keep this apartment alive.

An STA thread must have a message loop and service it frequently. COM objects in an STA receive their inter-apartment calls through this message loop, by COM posting private messages to hidden windows. If you fail to get and dispatch the messages that appear in a thread's message queue, objects in that thread's apartment will not receive incoming inter-apartment calls. You probably don't have to change your code a bit. The normal message loop you've been using in your main thread has been doing exactly this since day one, and you haven't heard a thing about COM and window messages. They've always been there; you just haven't had any reason to notice. If your STA thread creates windows, you'll have to do it anyway. Just make sure you don't plan a design using an STA thread that doesn't check a message queue. A sample STA thread would look something like this:

```
DWORD WINAPI ThreadProc (LPVOID lpv)
{
/*
Initialize COM on this thread.
*/
    CoInitialize (NULL) ;

    <other initialization>
/*
Acquire and dispatch messages for this thread until a WM_QUIT message
is received.
*/
    MSG msg ;
    while (GetMessage(&msg, NULL, NULL, NULL))
    {
      TranslateMessage(&msg);
      DispatchMessage(&msg);
    }

/*
Shut down COM in this thread.
*/
    CoUninitialize( ) ;
    return 0 ;
}
```

2. Writing COM object servers that live in STAs works well with threads that handle user interfaces. In the screen shot below, the control on the Web page is a COM server that lives in STAs, being marked with ThreadingModel=Apartment. Directions for running the sample code appear at the end of this chapter. Each Internet Explorer window is a separate thread of the same process (not a separate process, though it looks like that). The control simply reports the thread on which it lives. Since each thread is an STA thread, and the control is marked ThreadingModel = "Apartment", each control lives in the STA of the thread that created it. No marshaling, no bottlenecks. Each thread accesses its control directly. Life is good.

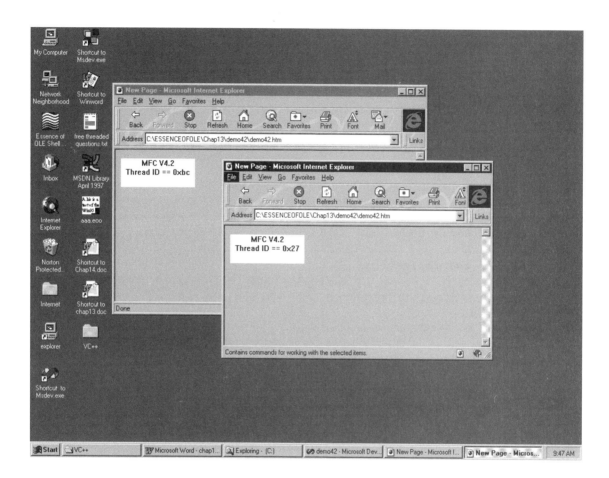

3. OK, what's the catch? The objects receive all their calls on the same thread, so they don't have to serialize access to their own instance variables. That makes your life much easier. However, two objects from the same server can live in two different STAs in the same process. What happens if each object receives a call from its own thread, and they both try to access global data from that call? For example, every server must maintain a global object count so it knows when to shut itself down (for an .EXE server) or how to respond to DllCanUnloadNow( ) (for a .DLL server). The usual way of doing this is with a global variable that is incremented in an object's constructor and decremented in its destructor. Thus:

```
int g_ObjectCount = 0 ;

CSomeObj::CSomeObj ( )
{
    g_ObjectCount ++ ;
}

CSomeObj::~CSomeObj ( )
{
    g_ObjectCount -- ;
}
```

The problem is that the increment and decrement operations shown above are not thread-safe in their accesses to the global variable g_ObjectCount. The assembler listing of the increment statement above usually looks something like this:

```
mov ax, [g_ObjectCount]      ; move global variable into register
add ax, 1                    ; increment contents of register
mov [g_ObjectCount], ax      ; move new value to global variable
```

Suppose that Thread A starts the above sequence near the end of its timeslice. It executes the first two statements, then gets swapped out before it can execute the third. Thread B now gets swapped in and executes all three statements. Eventually, Thread A will get swapped back in, execute the third statement, and overwrite the value stored in g_ObjectCount by Thread B. An operation that was safe in the non-threaded case is now fatal when objects can be called from multiple threads. Therefore, unless a control server identifies itself as knowing how to handle itself in a multithreaded environment, COM creates all of that server's objects on a single thread, thereby ensuring that this can't happen.

4. A server whose objects can live in separate STAs is promising COM that the server has serialized access to all of its global data, such as its object count, to whatever extent it needs to ensure that it is safe in this type of situation.. It does not need to serialize access to its individual object's member variables and functions, because COM promises that each object will always be called from the same thread. The objects do need to serialize access to the server's global variables and functions, as different objects may try to access these from different threads. This also applies to class statics, which are just a politically correct form of global.

Consider the code listing on the previous page that we used as an example of conflict potential. It isn't hard to write code that makes sure that different threads never conflict over the same global variable. Consider the example below. The API functions **InterlockedIncrement( )** and **InterlockedDecrement( )** are thread-safe functions for accessing a variable. The quickest, easiest, and cheapest way of serializing access to more complicated operations is with a critical section, as shown later in this chapter. Thus:

```
int g_ObjectCount = 0 ;

/*
Object constructed. Perform a thread-safe increment of the server's
global object count.
*/

CSomeObj::CSomeObj ( )
{
    InterlockedIncrement (&g_ObjectCount) ;
}

/*
Object destroyed. Perform a thread-safe decrement of the server's
global object count.
*/

CSomeObj::~CSomeObj ( )
{
    InterlockedDecrement (&g_ObjectCount) ;
}
```

NOTE: An object that doesn't do even this amount of serialization can still be made safe for a multithreading environment by marking it ThreadingModel="Single" (or leaving out the ThreadingModel registry entry entirely). In this case, all objects of that class will be created in the same STA, the first one created in the process, sometimes known as the *legacy STA*. All the inter-apartment marshaling really slows the system down, though, so don't write any new code that does this.

D. MULTI-THREADED APARTMENT EXAMPLE

1. This section describes the operation of the *multi-threaded apartment*, known as the "free threading model" in the older nomenclature. An object that lives in the MTA may be called from any MTA thread at any time. It is up to the object to serialize access to its methods and instance data to whatever extent it requires to keep incoming calls from conflicting. Removing the thread affinity of the STA can greatly improve performance in certain cases. The cost is that you have to write code to handle serialization and race conditions that COM would handle for you if you stayed in an STA.

Living in the MTA makes us a profit over living in an STA in any situation where an object needs to be accessed regularly by more than one thread. Suppose you have a DCOM server app accessed by remote clients. When the remote client calls a method on an object, the server machine receives that call on a random thread from a pool that exists for this purpose. This receiving thread then makes the call locally to the actual object. If the object lived in an STA, the receiving thread would have to post a message to the STA thread's message queue and wait for the STA thread to get around to servicing it. This is done transparently, so you don't have to write code for it as explained in a few pages, but it's an unnecessary performance drag. The desired STA thread might be busy servicing other objects, or worse, blocked while waiting on some synchronization event. It would be much more efficient if the object didn't care which thread it received its call on. The call could proceed directly from the receiving thread and not waste time with any of this message queuing nonsense.

Living in the MTA incurs a cost over living in the STA if most of your object's clients are going to be STA threads. Remember, COM sets up marshaling proxies when client and server live in different apartments. Why does COM do this when the MTA object has stated that it can be called from any thread at any time, that it has already serialized its methods to whatever extent they require? The reason has to do with callbacks from the object to its client. It is a relatively rare case where an object is purely a server and its container purely a client. It is much more common for each side to call methods on interfaces provided by the other. For example, a container calls methods on a control by calling IDispatch::Invoke( ) on an interface provided by the control. A control fires an event to its container by calling IDispatch::Invoke( ) on an interface provided by its container. Each side is the server of one interface and the client of another. While an MTA object has indicated its willingness to accept method calls from any MTA thread, an STA object is expecting its callback methods to be called only from the STA thread. By marking itself as "Free", an object is indicating that it doesn't have the discipline to do this. The object is saying, "You can call me from any thread at any time, but I reserve the right to call you back from any thread at any time." Since an STA container can't handle that, COM creates the free control in the MTA and marshals all calls to or from an STA. So if your object is MTA and your clients STA, you'll have spent lots of extra time and money slowing your clients down. Not smart. However, if you expect a mix of clients for your objects, your in-proc server can live in the neutral apartment instead. In this case, both types of clients can have almost the speed of a direct connection and STA clients will have the thread safety they need.

You don't want to use an MTA object to deal with any sort of user interface. If a user interface thread depended on the state of an MTA object, the state of the object could change while the thread was in the middle of processing a message. STA objects won't do this, as incoming calls arrive through a thread's message queue. The container app used as a sample for this section puts user interface threads in the MTA solely so you can see the results of the various options. A real world app wouldn't do this.

Your object can't live in the MTA if it requires any kind of thread affinity, for example, if your object uses thread local storage to remember its state from one call to the next. The MFC supports only the STAs because it makes extensive use of thread local storage, as does VB through version 6. The ATL, described in the Chapter 12, does offer a choice of threading models for servers you create with it.

If you want your MTA client or server to run on Windows 95, you will have to write an installation program to make sure that the DCOM service pack, which contains support for the free threading model, is installed on your customer's machine. Not all customers will allow this.

2. An MTA client thread follows different rules than an STA client thread. An MTA must call the API function **CoInitializeEx( )**, passing a value of **COINIT_MULTITHREADED** as its second parameter, thereby entering the process's lone MTA. Once it does this, the thread may call any COM function or object method from any thread at any time. Previous writings, including some of mine, have stated that this only needs to happen one thread per process. This was true in NT 4.0, but is not true in Windows 2000. You need to make this function call from every thread that wants to use the MTA.

When the MTA client thread creates an object, COM detects via registry entries any object that cannot live in this apartment, for example, those marked with ThreadingModel="Apartment". For these objects, COM transparently sets up proxies and stubs to serialize access to their methods in the way that the objects are expecting. Your client thread does not have to think about the threading model used by any of the objects that it creates. The client simply tells COM which rules it is following and then follows them. COM checks the rules that the object says it follows, and transparently intercedes between client and object to the extent, if any, needed to make them work together properly.

The MTA is not supported in native Windows 95, though it is in all later versions of Windows. To make sure that inattentive programmers don't mistakenly write code that requires MTA functions not available on that OS, the relevant functions are conditionally compiled out of the current edition (6.0) of VC. To gain access to these functions, you must either define the constant **_WIN32_DCOM** in your project, or define the constant **_WIN32_WINNT** to a value ox 0x400 or greater. In the samples supplied with this book, I defined the former constant in my project settings to make sure it applied everywhere.

A sample MTA thread would look something like this:

```
#define WIN32_DCOM

DWORD WINAPI MTAThreadProc (LPVOID lpv)
{

/*
Initialize COM on this thread. Enter the MTA.
*/

    CoInitializeEx (NULL, COINIT_MULTITHREADED) ;

/*
Do whatever work you need. A message loop is not necessary for correct
functioning of incoming calls as it is in an STA thread.
*/

    <code omitted>

/*
Uninitialize COM in this thread.
*/
    CoUninitialize ( ) ;
    return 0 ;
}
```

3. An MTA object has to serialize its own methods to whatever extent they need. It is up to the programmer to determine what that extent is and to write the code that makes it happen. Consider the sample object's implementation of IUnknown, shown on the facing page. The QueryInterface( ) method doesn't need any serialization. It is completely reentrant; everything is done on the stack.

In the STA object shown previously, I used InterlockedIncrement( ) and InterlockedDecrement( ) in the object's constructor and destructor, because I had to serialize access to globals. Now I need to serialize access to my object's instance data as well, such as its internal reference count. AddRef( ) is pretty simple; I just use the function InterlockedIncrement( ). Release( ) is a little trickier; no harder to write the code for but you do have to think about threads. Suppose thread A and thread B each have a pointer to this object, whose reference count is 2. Suppose A, near the end of its timeslice, calls Release( ), which executes the InterlockedDecrement( ), returning a reference count of 1 and assigning it to the variable `retval`. Suppose thread A has now exhausted its timeslice and gets swapped out before it can execute the test for zero on the next line. Now suppose that thread B gets swapped in, calls Release( ), and because it has a new timeslice manages to execute the entire Release( ) method. The reference count is decremented to zero and the object destructed. Now suppose thread A gets swapped in, and goes to test for zero. The test will fail, because the reference count wasn't zero when thread A decremented it. Control passes to the last line, where the current reference count is returned. If we didn't use a stack variable, but instead returned `m_RefCount`, as in most of the examples in this book, we would be returning a garbage value because the object would have already been destructed and its member variables meaningless. Worse, if we put any real code after the test in Release( ), that did real things with member variables instead of just returning the reference count, it would probably croak on us. The things that you have to do aren't very hard, but writing an MTA object forces you to think in ways an STA object didn't.

```
/*
The QueryInterface() method does everything on the stack. It is thread
safe as is.
*/

HRESULT CTimeData::QueryInterface(REFIID riid, LPVOID FAR *ppv)
{
    if (riid == IID_IUnknown || riid == IID_IDataObject)
    {
        *ppv = (LPVOID)this;
        AddRef();
        return S_OK ;
    }
    else
    {
      *ppv = NULL;
      return  E_NOINTERFACE ;
    }
}


/*
AddRef() uses InterlockedIncrement()to serialize access to the member
variable m_RefCount, thereby making themselves thread-safe.
*/

STDMETHODIMP_(ULONG) CTimeData::AddRef(void)
{
    return InterlockedIncrement (&m_RefCount) ;
}



/*
Release needs to not only call InterlockedDecrement( ), but also to
refrain from using its member variables afterwards, in order to make
itself thread-safe.
*/

STDMETHODIMP_(ULONG) CTimeData::Release(void)
{
    UINT retval = InterlockedDecrement (&m_RefCount) ;

    if (retval == 0)
    {
        delete this;
    }
    return retval ;
}
```

4. What other types of serialization might we have to do? The answer for this example is in the methods IDataObject::DAdvise and DUnadvise( ), shown on the facing page. These methods are used to establish a callback circuit so the object can advise the client when its data changes. The client provides an object that supports the IAdviseSink interface, and the object calls the method IAdviseSink::OnDataChange( ) to notify the client when the data changes.

My data object as written only supports one connection at a time. A request for a second connection will fail until the first one is released. Since these methods access internal member variables, I need to write code to make sure that only one thread uses them at a time. I do this with a critical section that I set up as member variable of my object's class as shown below. Each method calls EnterCriticalSection( ) at its beginning and LeaveCriticalSection( ) at its end. If one thread gets swapped out in the middle of one of these methods, and another thread gets swapped in and calls one of them, the second thread will block until the first one finishes.

You may wonder why I am working directly with the IAdviseSink interface instead of following the standard practice of delegating these operations to a data advise holder, an object created by the API function CreateDataAdviseHolder( ). I don't do that in this example because IDataAdviseHolder, even though it is a standard interface, does not seem to have a marshaler in my operating system (NT 4.0, service pack 2). I could write and install a marshaler for it, which would take under an hour, but I thought it was better to show how to run with the OS as shipped.

```
class CTimeData : public IDataObject
{

    public:
       long             m_RefCount ;
       LPADVISESINK     m_pAdvSink ;
       CRITICAL_SECTION m_csDAdvise ;

    <rest of class declaration omitted>
}

CTimeData::CTimeData()
{
    InitializeCriticalSection (&m_csDAdvise) ;

    <rest of initialization omitted>
}
CTimeData::~CTimeData(void)
{
    DeleteCriticalSection (&m_csDAdvise) ;

    <rest of cleanup omitted>
}
```

NOTE: As part of COM+, Windows 2000 provides the capability of obtaining this serialization service from the operating system. Instead of writing all of this nasty code, you simply check a box in the COM+ Explorer and say, "Synchronize me, please." This only works with configured components in Windows 2000. See the Spring 1999 issue of my ThunderClap newsletter on my Web site, www.rollthunder.com, for an explanation and example.

```
STDMETHODIMP CTimeData::DAdvise (FORMATETC FAR* lpfe, DWORD dw,
     LPADVISESINK lpas, DWORD *lpdw)
{
    HRESULT hr, retval = S_OK ;

/*
Wait on the critical section so that no other threads making this
method call can interrupt this operation.
*/
    EnterCriticalSection (&m_csDAdvise) ;

    if (m_pAdvSink == NULL)
    {
      <set up callback circuit>
    }
/*
Leave the critical section.
*/
    LeaveCriticalSection (&m_csDAdvise) ;
    return  hr ;
}

STDMETHODIMP CTimeData::DUnadvise  (DWORD dw)
{
/*
Wait on the critical section so that no other threads making this
method call can interrupt this operation.
*/
    EnterCriticalSection (&m_csDAdvise) ;


    <perform cleanup>

/*
Leave the critical section.
*/
    LeaveCriticalSection (&m_csDAdvise) ;
    return S_OK ;
}
```

WARNING: Making a COM call while holding a synchronization lock has the potential, in certain circumstances, to create a deadlock condition. You will find this situation discussed and examples of solutions provided in the Spring 1999 issue of my *ThunderClap* newsletter on my Web site, www.rollthunder.com.

E. INTER-APARTMENT OBJECT MARSHALING

1. Since each object lives in exactly one threading apartment, interface references are apartment-relative. By this I mean that the type of reference a thread is allowed to use to access an interface depends on the apartment of the thread and of the object. For example, an STA thread that created an object in its own STA would get a direct pointer to it. If the STA thread simply handed that direct pointer to any other thread through a global variable, and the other thread called a method on it, chaos could result, because that direct pointer was only legal for access within that STA. The object was expecting a call only on its STA thread, and when you carried that naked pointer across apartment boundaries, you violated the expectations of an STA object.

Suppose that we need to provide object references across apartment boundaries. For example, suppose an STA thread wants one of its objects to be called (logically, not physically) from an MTA thread. The two threads somehow need to cooperate to construct a pointer that the MTA thread can legally use to access the STA object. They do that by going through the marshaling process of constructing a proxy and stub, as shown earlier in this chapter. There are two ways of accomplishing this. In the first, the two threads exchange a marshaling packet directly. The owner of the object calls the gloriously-named API function **CoMarshalInterThreadInterfaceInStream( )**, passing the interface pointer to be marshaled. The function internally creates a stream and calls CoMarshalInterface( ), returning the marshaling packet in this stream. Thus:

```
IDispatch *pMyApartmentDisp ;
IStream *g_pStream ;

/*
Create stream for marshaling IDispatch to search thread.
*/
    hr = CoMarshalInterThreadInterfaceInStream(
        IID_IDispatch,      // ID of interface to marshal
        pMyApartmentDisp,   // interface ptr to marshal
        &g_pStream) ;       // output variable
```

The owner of the object somehow gets this marshaling packet to the recipient thread, perhaps through a global variable. It's legal to pass a marshaling packet in this manner, that's what they were created for. The recipient thread calls the almost-as-coolly-named API function CoGetInterfaceAndReleaseStream( ), passing the received marshaling packet. Internally, this calls CoUnmarshalInterface( ), reading the marshaling packet, setting up proxy and stub if necessary, and returning an interface pointer that the recipient thread may legally use. Thus:

```
extern IStream *g_pStream ;
IDispatch *pOtherApartmentDisp ;

/*
Use stream pointer to create IDispatch the I can call from
this thread.
*/
    hr = CoGetInterfaceAndReleaseStream(
        g_pStream,          // stream containing marshaling info
        IID_IDispatch,      // interface desired
        (void **) & pOtherApartmentDisp) ;  // output variable
```

2. If the sender and recipient threads don't want the overhead of figuring out their own sharing mechanism, they can use the *global interface table* provided by COM. This is an object, provided by the operating system, that allows threads to swap interfaces in a friendly manner. It essentially abstracts away the details shown on the previous page. The global interface table supports (you guessed it) the IGlobalInterfaceTable interface. Its methods are:

RegisterInterfaceInGlobal   *// Place interface in table, allowing access from any apt in process.*
RevokeInterfaceFromGlobal *// Remove interface from table.*
GetInterfaceFromGlobal   *// Obtain interface pointer that is legal in the calling thread's apt.*

The sending thread creates the global interface table and calls RegisterInterfaceInGlobal( ) to place its interface pointer in the global interface table. It gets in return a DWORD that identifies the interface. It makes that DWORD available to the recipient process in any way it so desires (shown here with a global variable). Thus:

```
IGlobalInterfaceTable *pThisThreadGIT ;
IDispatch *pMyApartmentDisp ;
DWORD g_dwThisInterfaceCookie ;


/*
Create global interface table.
*/
        CoCreateInstance(CLSID_StdGlobalInterfaceTable, NULL,
            CLSCTX_INPROC_SERVER, IID_IGlobalInterfaceTable,
            (void **)&pGIT)

/*
Register my interface in the GIT. Place ID cookie in global DWORD.
*/
        pThisThreadGIT ->RegisterInterfaceInGlobal (
            pMyApartmentDisp,          // interface to marshal
            IID_IDispatch,             // ID of interface to marshal
            & dwThisInterfaceCookie) ;    // output variable
```

The recipient thread then calls the method GetInterfaceFromGlobal( ), passing the cookie. Thus:

```
IGlobalInterfaceTable *pOtherThreadGIT ;
IDispatch *pOtherApartmentDisp ;
DWORD g_dwThisInterfaceCookie ;

<creation of GIT omitted, looks just like the previous case above>

/*
Use the cookie to fetch the desired interface from the GIT, and create
a legal pointer for the calling thread.
*/

        pOtherThreadGIT->GetInterfaceFromGlobal (
            g_dwThisInterfaceCookie,   // cookie ID'ing interface in GIT
            IID_IDispatch,             // ID of desired interface
            &pOtherApartmentDisp) ;    // output variable
```

F. THREADING AND .EXE SERVERS

1. COM reaches into a .DLL server via the function DllGetClassObject( ) and pulls out a class factory whenever it needs one. In an .EXE, it is up to your code to register class factories when it first starts up, maintain a global object count, and revoke the class factories and shut itself down when the object count reaches zero. This causes a multithreaded .EXE server to have timing and concurrency problems that a .DLL server doesn't. Fortunately, COM now contains auxiliary functions that make it easy to handle these situations, once you know where they are.

An .EXE server does not tell COM which threading model it supports by making registry entries, as did a .DLL server. Instead, it signals this to COM in the same way as a client app, by calling CoCreateInstanceEx( ), passing the flag **COINIT_MULTITHREADED** to support the free threading model or **COINIT_APARTMENTTHREADED** for the apartment model. When the server does the former, it is saying to COM that any objects that it provides to COM, including class factories, may be called from any thread; that the objects have already been internally serialized to whatever extent they require.

The first timing problem comes when the EXE server registers its class factory. A single-threaded server could call CoRegisterClassObject( ) at whatever point in its initialization it felt like doing so. The server didn't have to worry about receiving incoming calls to IClassFactory::CreateInstance( ) until it checked its message loop, since that was necessary for receiving the call. A free threaded server doesn't have this luxury. It might receive calls to create objects at any instant after it registers its class factory. An apartment server may have a similar problem if the main thread creates auxiliary threads and the auxiliary threads register class factories. An object might get created and try to run before the server app had completed its own initialization. You could make registering the class factory your last piece of initialization, but that would needlessly tie your hands. And what about the fairly common case where .EXE server registers more than one class factory? At best, you would have to do a complicated timing dance to make sure everything happened in the right order. There has to be a better way.

This is an easy problem to solve. You create and register the class factories as before, but you add the flag **REGCLS_SUSPENDED** to the fourth parameter of CoRegisterClassObject( ). This registers the class factory with COM but leaves it in a suspended state, in which COM will not accepts incoming requests for that class factory. When your server has finished all its initialization, it tells COM that its class factories are open for business by calling the new API function **CoResumeClassObjects( )**. This allows all of your registered class factories to accept incoming calls. This code is shown on the facing page.

NOTE: In the sample code provided with this book, I use the same local server app to demonstrate both the free and apartment threading models. I have registered two different class IDs, one for each model. In the LocalServer32 entry of the apartment model server class ID, I have appended the string "-Apt" to the server's command line. When the server's WinMain( ) starts running, the first thing it does is to check its command line for this flag. If present, the server initializes itself to use the apartment threading model; otherwise it initializes itself to use the free threading model. Make sure that you understand that I did this for my own convenience in not having to write two server apps. It is not a standard part of COM, as is the "-Embedding" command line switch that tells a server app that it was launched by COM. While non-standard, you could certainly use this technique yourself if you wanted to have a switch-hitting local server.

```
int WINAPI WinMain(HINSTANCE hInstance, HINSTANCE hPrevInstance,
    LPSTR lpCmdLine, int nCmdShow)
{

    MSG msg;    WNDCLASS  wc;
    HRESULT hr ;

/*
Check which threading model the client wants us to support. This is my
own addition to the LocalServer32 key for convenience in the
demonstration app, not part of COM. Initialize COM accordingly.
*/

    BOOL bApartment ;

    if (strstr (lpCmdLine, "-Apt"))
    {
      bApartment = TRUE ;
      ClsidToRegister = GUID_ApartmentThreadedTimeDataLocal ;
      hr = CoInitializeEx (NULL, COINIT_APARTMENTTHREADED) ;
    }
    else
    {
      ClsidToRegister = GUID_FreeThreadedTimeDataLocal ;
      bApartment = FALSE ;
      hr = CoInitializeEx (NULL, COINIT_MULTITHREADED) ;
    }
/*
Check command line to see if launched as a COM server.  If so, register
the class factory for this app, but leave it in a suspended state.
*/

    DWORD dwRegister ;  BOOL bRegister = FALSE ;

    if (strstr (lpCmdLine, "-Embedding"))
    {
      LPCLASSFACTORY pCF = new CClassFactory ( ) ;

      hr = CoRegisterClassObject(
             ClsidToRegister, pCF,
             CLSCTX_LOCAL_SERVER,
             REGCLS_MULTIPLEUSE | REGCLS_SUSPENDED,
             &dwRegister) ;
    }
/*
Resume class objects, telling COM that all the class factories in this
process are now open for business.
*/
    CoResumeClassObjects ( ) ;

    < rest of WinMain >
}
```

2. The next problem comes in shutting down your local server. Your server app has probably controlled its lifetime with your own utility functions, which I call LockThisObjectsServer( ) and UnlockThisObjectsServer( ). You call these in the constructor and destructor of each object, as shown below, and also in your class factory's LockServer( ) method.

The problem is one of thread-safe timing. When the last object on an .EXE server is destroyed, it usually starts the sequence of events that leads to the server shutdown, calling CoRevokeClassObject( ) and posting itself a WM_QUIT message, or perhaps WM_CLOSE if it has a main window. In a single threaded server, you never had to worry about a call to CreateInstance( ) coming in during this shutdown, because you just wouldn't service the message loop until you had revoked the class factory. This strategy doesn't work at all with a free threaded server and would require a complicated timing dance with an apartment model server having class factories on multiple threads. What happens if just after decrementing the server's global object count to zero and starting the server's shutdown code, but before the call to CoRevokeClassObject( ), a call comes into the class factory on another thread? It would try to create a new object on a server that was in the process of shutting itself down. At best, you'd have to write complicated code for aborting the shutdown; at worst, you'd croak.

COM has added two new API functions for solving this problem, **CoAddRefServerProcess( )** and **CoReleaseServerProcess( )**. These functions manipulate a global per-process reference count maintained by COM. They are serialized relative to each other, so you don't have to worry about them colliding. The important new feature is that when CoReleaseServerProcess( ) decrements this reference count to 0, COM immediately suspends all activity on all of your server app's registered class factories, by internally calling the API function **CoSuspendClassObjects( )**. When CoReleaseServerProcess( ) returns 0, you know that the object just destructed was the last one in your process and your server can safely initiate the shutdown – your class factories are already suspended; they won't be getting any incoming calls. If a client app now attempts to create an object of the class manufactured by your server, COM will launch another instance of it.

I've wrapped these functions into the utility locking and unlocking functions on the facing page. The critical section csShutdown is present only for serializing access to the server's global flag bShuttingDownNow. It has nothing to do with CoAddRefServerProcess( ) or CoReleaseServerProcess( ), which have their own internal serialization.

```
CTimeData::CTimeData()
{
    m_RefCount = 1 ;
    InterlockedIncrement (&g_ObjectCount) ;
/*
New object created, call utility function to lock server
*/
    LockThisObjectsServer( ) ;
}


CTimeData::~CTimeData(void)
{
    InterlockedDecrement (&g_ObjectCount) ;
    InvalidateRect (hMainWnd, NULL, TRUE) ;
/*
Object destroyed. Call utility function to lock server.
*/
    UnlockThisObjectsServer ( ) ;
}
```

```
extern CRITICAL_SECTION csShutdown ;
extern BOOL bShuttingDownNow ;

/*
Caller wants to lock the server. Call the API function that increments
COM's per-process reference count.
*/

void LockThisObjectsServer ( )
{
    CoAddRefServerProcess( ) ;
}

/*
Caller wants to unlock the server.
*/

void UnlockThisObjectsServer ( )
{

/*
Enter the critical section that serializes access to the global flag
bShuttingDownNow.
*/
    EnterCriticalSection (&csShutdown) ;

/*
Call the API function that decrements COM's per-process reference
count.
*/

    if (CoReleaseServerProcess( ) == 0)
    {
/*
Post a WM_CLOSE message to tell the main window to destroy itself, and
set the global state flag that says that shutdown is underway.
*/
        PostMessage (hMainWnd, WM_CLOSE, 0, 0) ;
        bShuttingDownNow = TRUE ;
    }

/*
Leave the critical section allowing other threads to access the global
flag bShuttingDownNow.
*/
    LeaveCriticalSection (&csShutdown) ;
}
```

3. This leaves us with one more hole to plug. Suppose client A creates an object from a local server. The server's process reference count is 1. Now suppose client B calls CoCreateInstance( ) to create another object, and the call reaches the first line of your class factory's CreateInstance( ) method before getting swapped out. Now suppose client A gets swapped in and calls Release( ) on its object, destroying it and decrementing the server's reference count to 0, thereby starting server shutdown. The creation of client B's object has started, but has not yet reached the point where it would keep the server alive. Eventually client A's thread will get swapped out, client B's will get swapped in, and try to create an object in a dying server. This is a problem.

It has always been possible to detect this situation and have the class factory fail the object's creation. The problem was that then the client wouldn't get the object that he wanted because of a simple timing problem. If the client tried it again a few seconds later, the original server would have been shut down, COM would launch a new instance, and the client would have his object.

Windows NT 4.0 added a new error code called **CO_E_SERVER_STOPPING**. When the method IClassFactory::CreateInstance( ) returns this error code, it tells COM that the object whose creation has been requested cannot be created because the server is in the process of shutting down. COM then launches a new instance of the server and creates the object from the new instance. Thus:

```
STDMETHODIMP CClassFactory::CreateInstance(LPUNKNOWN pUnkOuter,
    REFIID riid, LPVOID* ppvObj)
{
    HRESULT retval ;
/*
Wait on critical section that gates access to bShuttingDownNow.
*/

    EnterCriticalSection (&csShutdown) ;

/*
If shutdown flag set, then fail creation with the error code that tells
COM to launch another instance of the server to create the object.
*/
    if (bShuttingDownNow)
    {
      retval = CO_E_SERVER_STOPPING ;
    }

/*
Otherwise, create the object, which will increment the server process's
reference count.
*/
    else
    {
      <code omitted>
    }

    LeaveCriticalSection (&csShutdown) ;
    return retval ;
}
```

NOTE: If you want to try this, comment out all the other code in CreateInstance( ) and have it just return CO_E_SERVER_STOPPING. You will see COM launch instance after instance after instance of your server, trying to get one to work. Make sure you have saved your files in all your other apps first.

G. ThreadingModel = "Both"

1. An object can avoid any marshaling, providing direct connections to all clients, by setting the "ThreadingModel" registry value to "Both". This entry is misnamed, it really should be called "Either". An object marked in this manner always resides in the apartment of the thread that creates it, and the creating thread always receives a direction connection. After its creation, the object is either in an STA or in the MTA, and is subject to all the rights and responsibilities of that particular apartment.

An object that supports this model is saying that a) it will accept calls to any method on any object from any thread at any time, as would an MTA object, and b) that the object will ensure that any callbacks it might make to its client are made only on the thread on which the object received the callback interface, as would an STA object. The object is promising to be both robust and civilized.

Supporting both threading models has a reputation for being difficult. Like most such reputations for difficulty in COM, it's far greater than it deserves. If you look through your registry, you will find that such servers as the VBScript engine, class ID {B54F3741-5B07-11CF-A4B0-00AA004A55E8}, support both threading models, although you'll also find that they are currently a small minority. As previously stated, the serialization code necessary to live in the MTA is tricky and tedious, so you don't do it unless it will make you some money. Having incurred that cost, it doesn't usually cost much more to go ahead and support both models.

To write an "either" object, you have to follow the disciplines that both the STA and MTA require of their adherents. You must serialize access to your object's instance data and ruthlessly avoid thread affinity as if it lived solely in the MTA, because sometimes it will. And you must also make sure that your object serializes its global data and makes callbacks into its client only from the thread on which it received the callback object, as if it lived solely in an STA, because sometimes it will.

Suppose we've done the first part, writing an MTA object. What other things do we still have to do to upgrade to support for both models? Maybe not much. If all your callbacks are synchronous, you don't have to write any additional code. Your object can make callbacks into its client from within any of your object's methods called by the client. An STA client will always make that call on the right thread (or be responsible for the consequences if it doesn't), and an MTA client won't care. However, if your object makes asynchronous callbacks to its client from other threads, you must set up marshaling so that every callback interface method is called on the thread from which it came, whether the callback interface needs it or not.

2. Objects that live in either type of apartment have to decide whether or not to support the free threaded marshaler. The free threaded marshaler is a piece of code that allows your STA clients to avoid creating marshaling proxies in certain situations where they don't need them. **WARNING: supporting the free threaded marshaler is a great way to get terrible, hard to reproduce, seemingly random crashes. Never add it to objects marked single, free, or apartment. It will properly perform its functions of avoiding marshaling proxies, but that isn't what your object's clients need. Read this page thoroughly. Better yet, just don't do it.**

Suppose STA thread A creates an object from a server marked as ThreadingModel = "Both". The object is created in thread A's STA and the thread receives a direct, unmarshaled connection to the object. Now suppose that thread A gives a pointer to this object to STA thread B so thread B can do some useful work with it. Knowing nothing about the object but simply following the rules of the cross-apartment object marshaling, thread A calls CoMarshalInterThreadInterfaceInStream( ) and passes the resulting stream to thread B. Thread B calls CoGetInterfaceAndReleaseStream( ) and gets a proxy pointer to the object, which marshals all calls back to thread A to be made and then marshals the results back to thread B.

Since the object supports both threading models, setting up this proxy looks like it ought to be unnecessary. The vendor of the object has gone to great trouble to write it in such a manner that thread B could call it directly if only it knew that. So the vendor goes one step further, by putting a free threaded marshaler in its object. The free threaded marshaler causes the pointer that thread B receives from CoGetInterfaceAndReleaseStream( ) to be a direct connection instead of a proxy.

When threads go through the marshal/unmarshal process as described above, COM marshals the interface as described in Chapter 3. COM first queries the object for the IMarshal interface to see if the object wants to do custom marshaling. Our examples so far haven't done that, so COM set up standard marshaling proxies. The free threaded marshaler is an object supplied by COM that implements the IMarshal interface. All it does is pass a direct pointer to the interface in the marshaling packet and unpack that direct pointer on the other side. It thus overrides COM's standard marshaling mechanism. In this manner, when the threads call their marshaling functions as described above, thread B winds up with a direct connection to the object, not with a proxy.

Doing this, however, opens you up to tricky race conditions having to do with callbacks. The problem is that the object still resides in Thread A's STA, even though Thread B has a direct connection to it. Suppose Thread A sets up a callback circuit with the object. Suppose Thread B now calls a method on the object which causes the object to make a callback into its client. Since Thread B has a direct connection, the method call is made on Thread B, so the callback will also be made on Thread B. However, the client was expecting this code to be called only from Thread A. Sometimes you'll get away with that, sometimes you won't, which isn't exactly the platinum standard for code reliability. At best, it will be a very frustrating bug to reproduce and track down. If your object didn't support the free threaded marshaler, Thread B would have gotten a proxy instead of a direct connection, and the potential bug would have been avoided. I'd suggest only using the free threaded marshaler if your object is purely an engine; if it doesn't support any callbacks to its client. Otherwise, the effort it takes to plug this hole isn't worth the performance improvement for the small percentage of cases that it helps.

Adding free threaded marshaler support is temptingly easy. The API function **CoCreateFreeThreadedMarshaler( )** creates the free threaded marshaler, which supports the IMarshal interface. You can create it in your object's constructor, as shown on the facing page, or you can wait and create it only when someone queries for it. Whichever you do, don't forget to release it in your object's destructor. You then connect the free threaded marshaler into your control via aggregation, as described in the Appendix. To do this, all you have to do is modify your QueryInterface( ) method to delegate requests for IMarshal to the free threaded marshaler. But think twice before you put this in a product. Or three times. That's why I'm not going to show the code for it.

Lab Exercises
Chapter 6
Threading and COM

Directory: \EssenceOfCOM\chap06\demo40

1. Register the control demo40.ocx. Open the file Demo40.htm using Microsoft Internet Explorer. You may need to adjust the security settings to allow the control to be created. Pick "File – New Window" from the main menu, which creates another IE window containing the same page. Note that the controls on the two pages are reporting that they are owned by the same thread, indicating that they both live in the same STA, the legacy STA.

Directory: \EssenceOfCOM\chap06\demo42

2. Register the control demo42.ocx. Open the file Demo42.htm using Microsoft Internet Explorer. You may need to adjust the security settings to allow the control to be created. Pick "File – New Window" from the main menu, which creates another IE window containing the same page. Note that the controls on the two pages now report that they are owned by different threads, indicating that they live in different STAs.

Directory: \EssenceofCOM\chap06\data6

3. Register the sample servers by running the registry script data6.reg. Run the client app \client\data6cl.exe. Select one of the windows labeled "MTA thread". Create an object using the main menu, observe the thread on which the object receives its calls. Release and repeat for the other object types. Select the window labeled "STA thread" and repeat. Try a time test to get a feeling for the magnitude of inter-apartment call marshaling.

This page intentionally contains no text other than this sentence.

Chapter 7

Distributed COM (DCOM)

A. Concepts and Definitions

1. COM's initial release occurred at the OLE 2.0 conference in the spring of 1993 as the underlying plumbing used for the second version of object linking and embedding. Once developers got over the fundamental shift in mindset (and recovered from the conference's terrible presentation; Microsoft evangelists who were there still cringed at the memory of that conference 4 years later), they saw that COM was a pretty cool idea. Naturally, they immediately started asking for more features. And the big feature that everyone asked for, besides support for COM on multiple threads, was "Hey, when am I going to be able to use COM in a distributed system? When am I going to be able to have my client on one machine and my server and object on another machine?"

It sounded like a cool idea, but it turned out to be much harder to implement than Microsoft originally thought. Microsoft included a 16-bit pre-beta version of Distributed OLE (as it was called at the time) with the SDK at COM's initial release. But it turned out that extending COM from one machine to another posed new classes of problems that single desktop COM did not. For example, security and authentication become major issues when one machine attempts to create objects and call methods on another – how do you know that the caller really is who he says he is, and that he's allowed to do the things he's trying to do? Encryption becomes an issue – what happens if someone is running a network sniffer program while you are sending sensitive data? Multithreading becomes an issue – how do you keep one badly-behaved program from hanging your entire distributed network? You would expect such capabilities to be supplied by any distributed operating system worthy of the name. That excluded 16-bit Windows. Extending COM to multiple machines would have to wait for 32-bit Windows.

Windows NT 3.1 shipped in August of 1993, but didn't manage to support COM except in the 16-bit subsystem. All of Microsoft's COM programmers had to work full-time on getting COM into it, which they finished in October of 1994 in NT 3.5 (version 2 to the rest of the world). Then they had to work full-time on making 32-bit COM work correctly, for the release of NT 3.51 (version 3, ditto) and Windows 95 a year later. Only in late 1995 was Microsoft's COM team turned loose to work on DCOM. It first shipped as an integral organic part of Windows NT v4.0 (the version number finally makes sense) in the fall of 1996. A service pack that allowed it to run on Windows 95, albeit poorly, came out the following spring, and it was part of Windows 98 out of the box.

2. Consider the model of COM shown in the diagram below. A client application creates an object, and receives an in-process proxy. The proxy connects through a channel to the stub on the server side. This is one of the major, you might argue THE major, strength of COM – neither client nor server needs to know or particularly care whether its counterparty is on the same machine or a different machine. While initially the server lived in another process on the same machine, and the channel bridged a process boundary, it wasn't a big leap of intuition to think of moving the server to a different machine, and have the channel bridge a machine boundary instead. Thus:

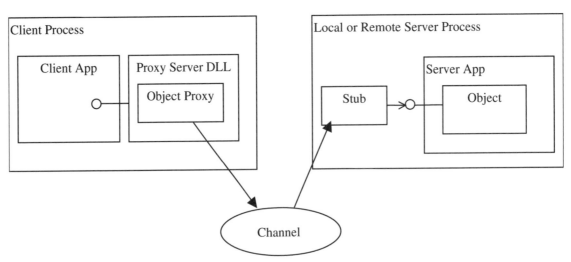

3. While DCOM can give the illusion of a client and server not knowing or caring about the other's location, sometimes the real world of programming makes it impossible to maintain this illusion. The abstraction presented by the channel is imperfect, because the underlying operating system on which it runs is also imperfect. Running COM across a network incurs costs that keeping it on a single desktop does not.

One part of that cost is slower performance. A network line isn't and cannot be made to be anywhere near as fast as a computer bus, so remote object method calls will always be slower than if the server was running the same machine as the client. DCOM's performance compares favorably with other strategies for network programming, but stuffing data through a network pipe will always be slower than thinking about it on the same machine.

Another part of that cost is increased administrative burden. The proxies and stubs for marshaling interfaces, or the type libraries used in their place, must be present and registered on both the client and the server machines. The server must have its security properly configured so that only authorized users are allowed to create and use its objects.

A third part of that cost is the necessity of rethinking your programming architecture. For example, some types of data, say, window handles, can be shared between different processes on the same machine. This is how in-place activation works. However, window handles cannot be shared from one machine to another. Any architecture that depends on this will have to be changed.

4. It will turn out that raw DCOM, as discussed in this chapter, is a very low level of abstraction, as assembly programming is a very low level of abstraction. And as programming in assembler takes too long for most uses, so programming raw low-level DCOM code will prove to take too long and cost too much for most major applications. For example, writing authorization code that deals with NT security descriptors is a colossal pain. The cool but cautionary example of the global running object table at the end of this chapter demonstrates some other problems posed by this low level of abstraction.

The new classes of problems, such as security, synchronization, data integrity and overlapping client and server lifetimes are too complex for you solve cost-effectively at this low level of abstraction. What you really need to write distributed applications in reasonable amount of time and for a reasonable cost is a higher level of abstraction that provides prefabricated solutions to these common problems. That's what COM+ provides, a much higher level of abstraction, a toolkit of prefabricated solutions to the common problems of distributed applications. That's where you really need to go if you want to write distributed applications. I highly recommend (and so do my creditors) that you read about COM+ in my book *Understanding COM+* (Microsoft Press, ISBN 0-7356-0666-8). I also publish a free quarterly e-mail newsletter on current COM+ development topics, which you can read and subscribe to on my Web site, www.rollthunder.com.

B. CREATING REMOTE OBJECTS

1. A client application may create an object on a remote system via the API function **CoCreateInstanceEx( )**, an example of which is shown on the facing page. The flag **CLSCTX_REMOTE_SERVER** specifies that the object is to be created on a remote machine which may be anywhere on the network that is visible to the calling app. The server name is specified in a structure of type **COSERVERINFO**.

COM object method calls over a network are slow compared to calls made on the same machine. To improve performance, CoCreateInstanceEx( ) allows you to query for more than one interface when the object is created. In this way, you incur the network overhead of only a single function call when obtaining all the interface pointers you want to use. You pass a pointer to an array of structures of type **MULTI_QI** as the last parameter to CoCreateInstanceEx( ). Each structure contains a pointer to the ID of the requested interface, which you must set before making the call. Each structure contains an HRESULT and an interface pointer which are filled on output. When the function returns, these will be filled with the result of the request for the specified interface and a pointer to that interface. A return code of S_OK means that all of your requested interfaces were successfully retrieved. A return code of CO_S_NOTALLINTERFACES means that at least one but not all of the requested interface was successfully retrieved.

Because DCOM is not supported in the base release of Windows 95, the function declarations which require it have been conditionally compiled out of the header files. To have the compiler be able to see them, you must define the constant **_WIN32_DCOM** ahead of <windows.h> as shown, or define the value **_WIN32_WINNT** to 0x400 or higher. To make sure it appears everywhere, the sample code for this chapter defines the former constant in its project settings.

A sample app containing the code fragment on the facing page may be found in the directory \chap07\data4\client. It contains an upgraded version of the client app from the data3 example in Chapter 2. I have added menu choices to the app which allow you to specify a remote server for an object and create an object from the remote server. The performance test menu items and advise loop functionality have been left in, allowing you to compare local versus remote operation.

```
#define _WIN32_DCOM
#include <windows.h>

extern WCHAR wServerName ; extern CLSID GUID_TimeData ;
extern LPDATAOBJECT lpd ;

case ID_DATAOBJECT_CREATEFROMREMOTESERVER:
{
/*
Set up COSERVERINFO structure specifying name of remote server.
*/
    COSERVERINFO si ;

    si.pwszName = wServerName ;
    si.dwReserved1 = 0 ;
    si.pAuthInfo = NULL ;
    si.dwReserved2 = 0;

/*
Set up array of MULTI_QI structures to specify requested interfaces and
hold returned pointers. Here we only have one.
*/

    MULTI_QI mqi [1] ;

    mqi [0].pIID = &IID_IDataObject ;
    mqi [0].pItf = NULL ;
    mqi [0].hr = 0 ;
/*
Create instance of object on remote machine.
*/
    HRESULT hr = CoCreateInstanceEx (
      GUID_TimeData,                // class ID of requested object
      NULL,                         // no aggregation
      CLSCTX_REMOTE_SERVER,         // remote server required
      &si,                          // name of remote server
      1,                            // # of interfaces to query for
      mqi) ;                        // array of MULTI_QI for each
                                    //   requested interface
/*
If call succeeded, use returned interface pointer.  Otherwise signal
error.
*/
    if (hr == S_OK)
    {
      lpd = (LPDATAOBJECT) mqi [0].pItf ;
    }
    else
    {
      MessageBox (hWnd, "Couldn't create object", "Error",MB_ICONSTOP);
    }
    return 0 ;
}
```

2. The function **CoGetClassObject( )**, which gets the class factory that manufactures a specified class of object, has been upgraded to support DCOM. The third parameter to this function, which previously was reserved, now may contain a pointer to a **COSERVERINFO** structure which specifies the remote machine from which the class factory is to be obtained. Thus:

```
LPCLASSFACTORY lpcf ;
extern WCHAR wServerName ;
extern CLSID GUID_TimeData ;

case ID_DATAOBJECT_GETREMOTECLASSFACTORY:
{
    HRESULT hr ;

/*
Set up COSERVERINFO structure specifying name of remote server.
*/
    COSERVERINFO si ;
    si.pwszName = wServerName ;
    si.dwReserved1 = 0 ;
    si.pAuthInfo = NULL ;
    si.dwReserved2 = 0;
/*
Get class factory that manufactures objects of class GUID_TimeData. We
might use it later to create an instance of the object.
*/

    hr = CoGetClassObject (
       GUID_TimeData,           // class ID made by requested factory
       CLSCTX_REMOTE_SERVER,    // remote server required
       &si,                     // server on which to get class factory
       IID_IClassFactory,       // interface ID wanted on class factory
       (LPVOID *) &lpcf) ;      // output variable

    if (!SUCCEEDED(hr))
    {
       MessageBox (NULL, "Couldn't get remote cf", "", 0) ;
    }

    return 0 ;
}
```

NOTE: The preceding code fragment does not appear in the data4cl sample program. Implementing it is left as an exercise to the student.

3. If you do not want to write code for the client application to specify the name of the remote server on which to create an object, you can arrange for that information to be stored administratively in the registry instead. Remember that when a client app calls CoCreateInstance( ), COM reads the registry looking for the InProcServer32 or LocalServer32 entries to find the server for the specified class ID. If this search fails, then COM will look for the registry key HKEY_CLASSES_ROOT\APPID\{object's app ID, usually the same as the class ID}, and find the named value "**RemoteServerName**". This contains a string value specifying the name of the remote system on which the requested object's server may be found. In the following example, the data3 sample from Chapter 2 will look for its server on the remote machine named REDTAILALE.

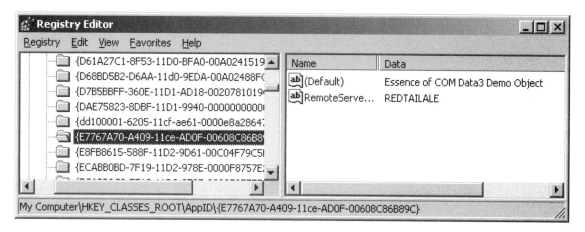

The AppID that corresponds to the specified CLSID is placed as a named value in the class's CLSID entry. For convenience, you usually choose the AppID to be the same as the class ID.

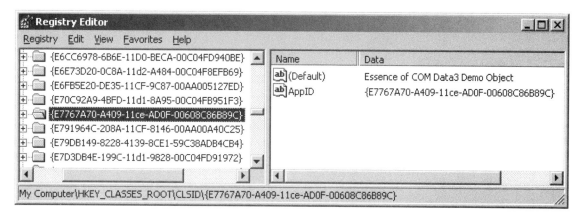

For this operation to succeed, a local server .EXE for the specified class ID must be registered on the named remote system, DCOM must be enabled on the remote machine and the client must have permission from the server machine's security system to launch that app. There is not currently a lookup service whereby a server may advertise its availability for a client to examine at runtime. The client must explicitly specify a server machine.

4. It is easy to make these registry settings with the use of *dcomcnfg.exe*, the DCOM configuration utility app. Since it changes registry settings, this app may only be run from an administrator account. When you run it, you will see a list of all the objects with local servers registered on the system. If you select an object and click the "Properties" button, you will see the following view, which will allow you to make and change the registry settings described on the previous page.

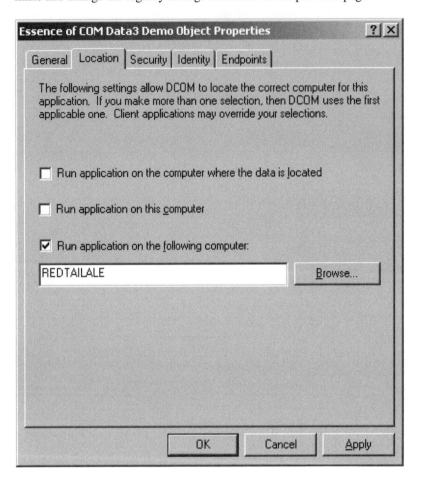

NOTE: Dcomcnfg only shows you objects that are registered with local servers. However, it is perfectly possible to have an EXE server on a remote machine take the place of an in-proc server on your local machine, although the call overhead will go up by about a factor of 1000. To do this, simply make the required registry settings via the registry editor.

5. When a client creates an object on a remote machine, the remote machine's SCM looks in the registry for the server registered as handling the requested clsid, exactly as it does for a request originating on its own machine. The base release of NT 4.0 required a .EXE server to handle a remote creation request; a .DLL server wouldn't work. With the release of Service Pack 2, NT provided a *surrogate process* which the SCM will launch to allow .DLL servers to handle remote activation requests. The surrogate process acts as a shell, loading the DLL server, obtaining its class factory and registering it with COM.

To use a surrogate process for your .DLL server, you must add the named value "DllSurrogate" to the AppID registry settings for the server, as shown below. Dcomcnfg does not provide a UI for this; you must do it yourself. This works on the same machine as well as remotely. If there is a .DLL server on your machine that you like but don't trust inside your client app's address space, you can make this registry entry and create the object using the flag CLSCTX_LOCAL_SERVER.

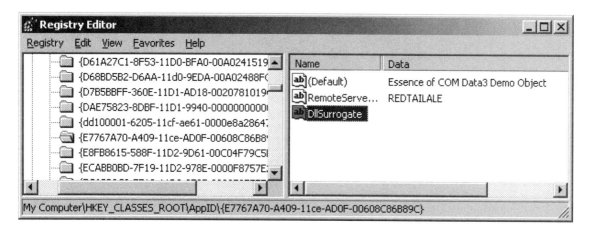

If you add the named value DllSurrogate with an empty string, as shown above, COM will launch its standard surrogate process "dllhost.exe". This suffices for the great majority of cases. However, if you ever need to write your own custom surrogate, you can find instructions in the "ActiveX/COM Q + A" in the May 1997 *Microsoft Systems Journal*.

WARNING: One of the reasons for providing an object in a DLL server is that certain types of data, such as HDC's, cannot be marshaled across process boundaries. The IViewObject interface, for example, has this problem. If your remote DLL server requires or provides data that can't be marshaled to another process, you'll be able to launch it using a surrogate, but it won't work the way you want it to.

C. LAUNCH SECURITY

1. The security features described in this section deal with allowing or forbidding users to launch an app on a remote server. This is mostly a matter of administration, not programming.

DCOM settings are maintained in the system registry to tell the SCM which users are allowed to perform which operations. Most of the default server-wide items are listed as named values under the key HKEY_LOCAL_MACHINE\SOFTWARE\Microsoft\Ole. Thus:

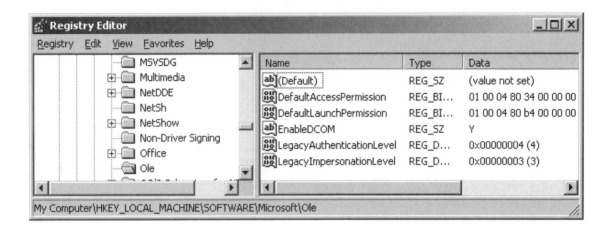

2. The first named value that we care about is "EnableDCOM". Setting it to "Y" as shown above allows remote requests to be received on the machine. Setting it to any other value, such as "N", disables incoming calls but still allows outgoing calls to proceed. Remember, however, that an object on the server machine more often than not makes callbacks to an interface provided by the client machine, such as asynchronous event notifications. With DCOM turned off on the client machine, these callbacks will fail with the error code 0x8001011C, "Remote calls are not allowed for this process."

3. These registry keys can be most conveniently set via the utility app *dcomcnfg.exe*, shown below. Since it modifies the registry, this app can only be run from an account with administrator privileges. Using it can be a little confusing, as some controls modify the server properties of the machine and some modify the client properties. The UI of the app does not always make the distinctions clear.

Checking the box shown below sets the "EnableDCOM" value to "Y", and clearing it sets the value to "N". As discussed on the previous page, this value affects the server functionality of the machine. Thus:

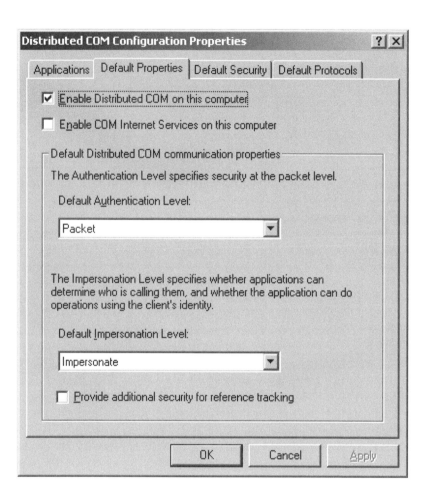

4. You may specify the users or groups that are allowed or forbidden to launch an individual app by setting the named value "LaunchPermission" in that app's AppID registry entry as shown below. This is most conveniently done via dcomcnfg as shown on the following pages.

The launch permission information is stored as an NT security descriptor in binary format. When a request for remote activation comes into a server machine from a remote client, the server's SCM looks in the registry to see if the requesting user has the authority to launch the app. If this named value is not present, then the SCM uses the value of the system's "DefaultLaunchPermission" shown on page 156. Thus:

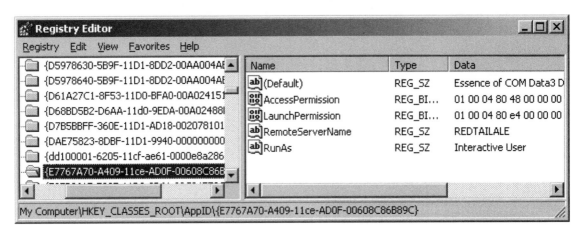

5. To configure an individual app's settings, first select the app on the "Applications" tab of dcomcnfg. Then click "Properties". Thus:

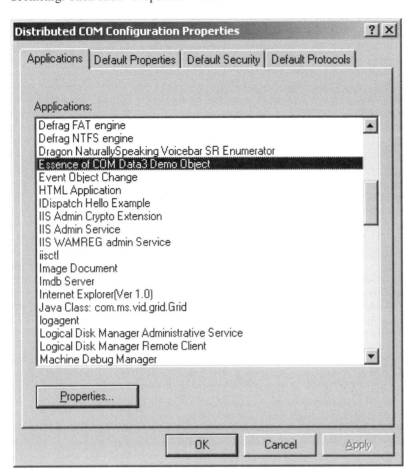

6. To configure an individual app's security settings, you use the "Security" tab of dcomcnfg. If you select the radio button for the default permission, dcomcnfg will remove "LaunchPermission" value from the app's AppID registry key. If you select the radio button for custom launch permission as shown, you will see a security administrator dialog box similar to that shown on the next page. Making selections in this dialog box will cause the editor to add the named values if necessary, and set their contents to the security descriptor containing the permissions that you have specified. Thus:

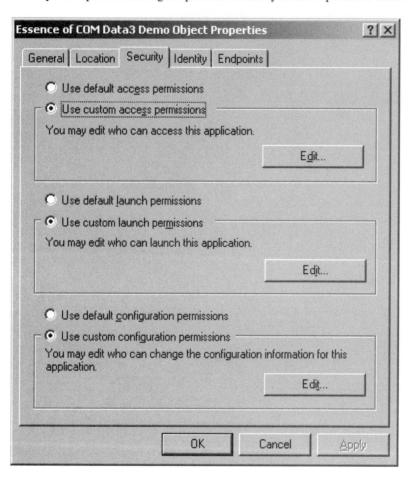

7. The dialog boxes that you use to edit security permissions are shown below. The first one shows the current settings. The default settings grant launch permission to administrators, the system user, the interactive user, and internet accounts. For development purposes, I have added launch permission for the group "Everyone".

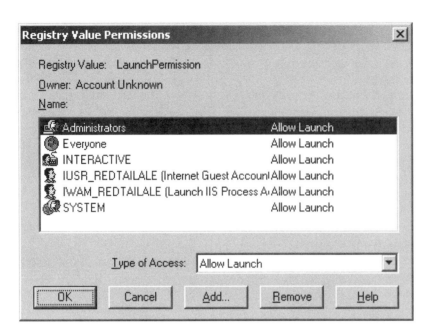

8. When you click "Add...", you will see the dialog box below. This shows you all the groups of users that your installation knows about. You select a group of users, then use the "Type of Access" control at the bottom to specify whether this group is allowed permission to launch as shown, or is denied that permission. Why would you want to explicitly deny access? The operating system checks denied accesses first, before looking for allowed access. You might set access allowed permission to Everyone, but put in an access denied permission for the group of "Disgruntled Ex-Employees". The operating system would check the latter group first, as a permission denial entry. When it did so, it would find that members of this group are denied launch permission, stop checking, and fail the call. Users who were not members of this group would be allowed access when the operating system checked far enough down the list to find that Everyone was allowed access.

You may also make entries for individual users, but this is rare. You generally grant permissions to groups and then set permissions on individual users by moving them into and out of the appropriate groups.

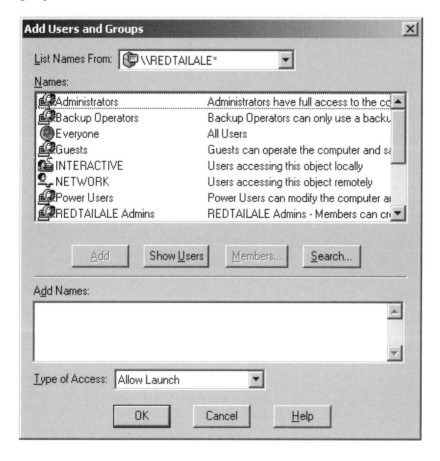

D. REMOTE CLIENT IDENTITY

1. When a client launches a server app on a remote server machine, which user ID does the server process run under? When the server process performs an action that requires the operating system to do security checking, such as opening a file, whose identity does the operating system use when checking if the operation is permitted or not?

By default, the server process runs by impersonating the launching user. Suppose an app running on George's machine calls CoCreateInstanceEx( ) to create an object on Mary's machine. Unless Mary has made registry entries directing otherwise, the server process (if it runs at all) will be launched on Mary's machine with George's identity. The server process is said to be "running as the activator." Any operations that George would have been unable to perform on Mary's machine via other channels, such as browsing her private files with Explorer, he will be unable to accomplish via DCOM either.

This makes sense from the point of not freaking out users and opening up gaping security holes when they upgrade to NT 4.0. However, it has two major drawbacks. First, it is very resource intensive. When you launch a process as the activator, the operating system creates an entirely new *window station*. A window station is a securable object that contains a desktop (where all the windows live), running object table, clipboard, and atom table. You can think of a window station as a clone machine that happens to inhabit the same physical box as all the other window stations. When a user logs on to NT, a window station called the *interactive window station* is created and given access to the keyboard, mouse, and display device. Other window stations on a machine cannot interact with the input or output devices, which is why you don't see the server's window when it runs as the activator. Window stations can only interact with each other if you specifically write code to make that happen, which hardly anyone ever does.

Window stations are expensive, costing at least 3 Megabytes of memory. Each activator gets his own window station. The interactive window station is created when Mary logs on to her machine. If George creates an object on Mary's machine, COM will create a second window station and launch an instance of the server process on it. If Lee then creates the same class of object as activator on Mary's machine, COM will create a third window station and launch a third instance of the server process in it. This brings a server machine to its knees very quickly.

The second problem of running as the activator is that a process which is impersonating a user is allowed a lower level of privilege than one that is legally logged on as the same user. On NT 4.0, an impersonating process is allowed to perform actions on its own machine, but not allowed to perform actions on other machines. If George launches a server process as activator on Mary's machine, the process will be able to do anything on Mary's machine that Mary has granted permission for George to do. However, since the server process is only impersonating George, the server process won't be able to do anything on any other machine, even George's. Any action on any other machine that requires any security checking at all will fail, even if George would normally be allowed to do it. In the data4 example, if you launch the remote server as activator and select "Data Object — DAdvise" from the main menu, you probably won't receive updates, although you will when you create the same object from a local server. The reason is that the server process is only impersonating the client, which won't allow the server to make calls to any other machine, even the original client's. The only way around this is to set the authentication level (see next section) on both machines to "none", which means that it won't even check to see if the caller is impersonating or not. Most real life administrators don't like to do this.

2. Is there a way around this? Fortunately, yes. A remote server app does not have to run as the activator. The administrator of the server machine may specify that the server process run as a specific user or as the interactive user, the one who is currently logged in via the user interface. Most real apps want one or the other. The "RunAs" named value in the AppID section of the registry, shown on the facing page, specifies the user whose identity the launched server will assume. You can set it with dcomcnfg, shown below, or via the registry editor.

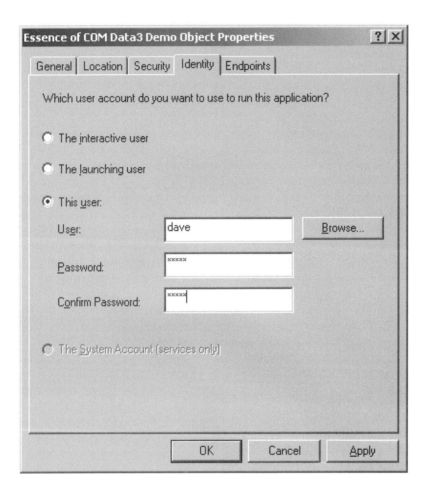

NOTE: Running as the interactive user or as a specific user does not require your app to supply a password at runtime. The identity of the remote user, as confirmed by the domain server, is all the ID required of a remote client. If there is no domain server, then the ID and password of the remote client need to match those of the specified user on the object's server.

3. If you choose "The interactive user", the RunAs registry setting will be "Interactive user". In this case, a server launched by a remote user shares the window station of the interactive user who is currently logged on. Any windows that the server shows will be visible on the desktop of the server machine. If George creates an object that launches a server and Lee comes along and creates another object of the same class, the same server app will handle both requests. The only drawback is that if no user is logged in, no app will run, and if the user logs out, any running servers will be terminated. Choose this option during development so you can see debugging information on the server app's window.

You may also elect to run a server app as a specific user. This will create one new window station, which isn't a terrible resource hit. A server here may still provide objects to multiple remote clients. The only real difference is that the interactive user won't be able to see the server's windows.

In either of these cases, the server process will not run under impersonation; it will be legally logged in as the specified user. If the server wants to make a call to another machine, it will be allowed to do so subject to the other machine's security.

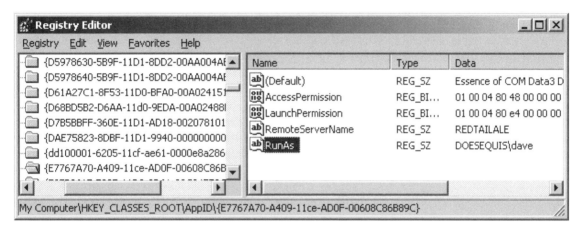

4. It is frequently useful for a server to be able to temporarily impersonate the client that is making an object method call. Server apps tend to have high levels of permissions, for example, frequently having the privilege of opening any file on their machines. The remote client generally has a much lower level of permission. When a DCOM client makes an object method call that requires secured operations, for example opening a file, you usually want the operation to succeed only if the client making the call has permission to do so. Rather than write your own security checking and administration code, it would be great if the server could take on the client's identity and security attributes and attempt to open the file in the usual way. The operating system would treat the server as if it were the client, and refuse to open the file if the client was not permitted to do so, rather than using the higher access privilege of the server.

A server impersonates a client via the API function **CoImpersonateClient( )**. The server takes back its own security identity by calling the API function **CoRevertToSelf( )**, which is called implicitly when the method returns if you haven't done it sooner. The sample app in \chap07\data4\server performs its impersonation on every call to IDataObject::GetData( ) and places the results on the main window for you to see. Thus:

```
extern HRESULT LastImpersonateResult ;
extern char LastImpersonatedName [] ;
extern HWND hMainWnd ;

STDMETHODIMP CTimeData::GetData (LPFORMATETC lpfe, LPSTGMEDIUM lpstg)
{

/*
Impersonate the calling client. Place the result code where it will be
shown on the server's main window for administrator to see.
*/

    LastImpersonateResult = CoImpersonateClient( ) ;



    < perform operations >

/*
Take back server's own identity.
*/

    CoRevertToSelf ( ) ;

    InvalidateRect (hMainWnd, NULL, TRUE) ;
    return retval ;
}
```

NOTE: This function might be slow because it may require a round trip to the domain controller to get the information of the client it needs to impersonate.

5. A client app sets an *impersonation level* that specifies which impersonation actions the client will allow the server to perform. DCOM-aware apps may provide this setting via the API function CoInitializeSecurity( ) shown in the next section. I find it more logical to think of this as the trust level – the client is saying how much it trusts the server to do while using the client's identity. Apps which do not call this function are given the value specified in the LegacyImpersonationLevel registry setting shown on page 156. The settings available to the client are:

Name	Value	Operations allowed
Anonymous	1	Server cannot find out who client is.
Identify	2	Server can read identity of client, cannot perform operations as client.
Impersonate	3	Server can perform operations as client on server's own machine but not on other machines, even the client's.
Delegate	4	Server can perform operations as client on other machines on network (not supported on NT 4.0, scheduled for Windows 2000).

A client may choose not to allow itself to be impersonated. However, a server may refuse to perform operations for a client that doesn't allow this. Good DCOM clients need to allow the server to impersonate them. If you don't trust the server, you shouldn't connect to it.

If the server calls CoImpersonateClient( ) and the client doesn't allow impersonation, the call will still return a value of S_OK. However, if the server then tries to perform any secured operations before reverting to itself, the call will fail, because the client has refused to provide the information necessary for the server machine's operating system to check if the operation should be allowed or not.

6. A server may need to find out the identity of a client that it is impersonating. The API function GetUserName( ) would seem to do the trick, but it only provides the user's name and not its domain. To get both user name and domain, it is necessary to open the thread's security token and read its actual data. A full discussion of the security mechanism is beyond the scope of this book, but the code shown on the facing page does the trick in the data4sv sample app. It can appear anywhere after the call to CoImpersonateClient( ) and before the call to CoRevertToSelf( ). It reads the domain and user information of the impersonated thread and displays it on the main window, as shown in the screen shot below.

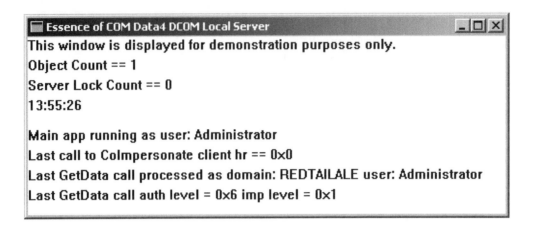

```
/*
Get user and domain name to display on screen.
*/

char LastImpersonatedName [80] = "", LastImpersonatedDomain[80] = "" ;

STDMETHODIMP CTimeData::GetData (LPFORMATETC lpfe, LPSTGMEDIUM lpstg)
{
    < code omitted >

    CoImpersonateClient ( ) ;

#define BUFSIZE 512
    HANDLE hToken ;
    char buf [BUFSIZE] ;
    DWORD bufsize = BUFSIZE ;
    SID_NAME_USE snu ;

/*
Open security token of this thread.
*/
    OpenThreadToken (GetCurrentThread(), TOKEN_QUERY,
      TRUE, &hToken) ;

/*
Get the information from the token that identifies the user thereof.
*/
    GetTokenInformation (
      hToken,
      TokenUser,    // const defined in system header file, see docs
      buf, bufsize,
      &bufsize) ;
/*
Query the operating system for the domain and user names that apply to
the user information from the token. Store in global variables that the
main window's WM_PAINT code draws on the screen.
*/

    DWORD NameSize = sizeof (LastImpersonatedName) ;
    DWORD DomainSize = sizeof (LastImpersonatedDomain) ;

    LookupAccountSid (
      NULL,
      ((PTOKEN_USER)buf)->User.Sid,
      LastImpersonatedName,
      &NameSize,
      LastImpersonatedDomain,
      &DomainSize,
      &snu) ;

    InvalidateRect (hMainWnd, NULL, FALSE) ;
    CoRevertToSelf( );
}
```

E. CALL SECURITY AND AUTHENTICATION

1. DCOM uses Microsoft's Secure RPC as its underlying communication mechanism. Secure RPC provides several *authentication levels* of security checking for a programmer to choose from. The available authentication levels are:

Name	Value	Security checking done
None	1	No checking done at all.
Connect	2	Client identity checked only on first RPC to server. Automatically upgraded to Packet in NT 4.0.
Call	3	Same as Connect, plus encrypted sequence number on each call to foil a recording attack. Automatically upgraded to Packet in NT 4.0.
Packet	4	Same as Call, except encrypted sequence number is on every packet of every call (sometimes a call's data is split into multiple packets). Packets that do not match the expected sequence number are discarded.
Packet Integrity	5	Same as Packet, plus RPC calculates and encrypts a checksum of the packet's data. Server recalculates and checks this checksum to be sure that packet wasn't tampered with.
Packet Privacy	6	Same as Packet Integrity, plus RPC encrypts all the data in the entire packet so an eavesdropper can't read any of it.

The authentication level set by a client specifies the construction of the packets it sends to the server. The authentication level set by a server indicates the minimum level at which the server will accept an incoming call from a client. During the initial connection process, RPC sets the level to the higher of the two.

The levels Packet Integrity and Packet Privacy require the secure RPC mechanism to examine all the data in the packet, first to generate the checksum (and encrypt the data for Packet Privacy) on the client side; then to regenerate the checksum (and decrypt data for Packet Privacy) on the server side. This burns microseconds, so use them only for sensitive data. If you find yourself doing that a lot, consider buying encrypted network cards to speed up the operation.

RPC performs its authentication functions at a lower level than COM. On an outgoing COM call from a client, it takes place after the call is marshaled by the interface proxy. On an incoming COM call to a server, it takes place before the call is presented to the interface stub.

The secure RPC functionality is provided by a *security service provider* (SSP), a package that lives on the operating system to provide security services. On NT 4.0, the only available security provider is the one that ships with the operating system. Windows 2000 provides support for installable SSP's, notably Kerberos.

2. A DCOM app specifies the security settings for all interfaces in its process via the API function **CoInitializeSecurity( )**. If this granularity is too high, you can change it for individual interfaces as shown on the following pages. If an app has not called this function by the time it makes the first COM call that marshals an object pointer, such as CoCreateInstance( ), COM will automatically call it for you, specifying default settings from the registry.

The first parameter allows you specify a security descriptor instructing the secure RPC mechanism as to which users are or are not allowed access to interfaces of which this app is the server. This mechanism is somewhat complicated and is explained on page 176.

The authentication level that you set in this call is the outgoing level used in calls to interfaces of which this process is the client. The same value is used for the minimum authentication level that will be accepted for incoming calls to interfaces of which this process is the server. If COM calls this function automatically, it will use the "LegacyAuthenticationLevel" registry value shown on page 156.

The impersonation level set in this call is discussed in the previous section. If COM calls this function automatically, it will use the "LegacyImpersonationLevel" registry value shown on page 156.

The code shown below comes from the DCOM sample client app data4cl. It is called when you select "Data Object — Set Process Security..." from the menu. **For this feature to work in the sample app, you must make these settings before you create the remote object.** Thus:

```
DWORD g_AuthenticationLevel, g_ImpersonationLevel ;

case ID_DATAOBJECT_SETSECURITY:
{

/*
Pop up dialog box to get security settings from user.
*/
    if (DialogBox (hInst, MAKEINTRESOURCE (IDD_DIALOG3), hWnd,
      (DLGPROC) SecurityDlgProc) == IDOK)
    {
      HRESULT hr = CoInitializeSecurity (
            NULL,                       //security descriptor, use defaults
            -1,                         //count of authorization services
            NULL,                       //authorization srvc, NULL==default
            NULL,                          // reserved
            g_AuthenticationLevel,         // authentication level
            g_ImpersonationLevel,          // impersonation level
            NULL,                          // reserved
            EOAC_NONE,                     // additional capabilities
            NULL) ;                        // reserved

      if (hr != S_OK)
      {
            MessageBox (NULL, "Couldn't initialize security", "", 0) ;
      }
    }
    return 0 ;
}
```

3. The authentication level set in CoInitializeSecurity( ) specifies the authentication level used for all outgoing calls made by the client process. This granularity may be too coarse for your purposes. Suppose you had a distributed commerce client app that had two different interface pointers to the server. Interface IMarketingInfo has methods that the client app calls frequently but which transfer only non-sensitive information, like the latest unadvertised specials. You would not want to spend the microseconds on an authentication level higher than Packet, and maybe not even that much. On the other hand, you also have the interface IPurchase, whose methods transfer sensitive information such as the customer's credit card number. You want these calls to be made at the packet privacy level so that any eavesdropper can't see its information. What you really want is to be able to specify different authentication levels for different interface proxies.

You can do this via the API function **CoSetProxyBlanket( )**. This function sets the authentication level and impersonation level used on a single proxy without affecting any other proxies in the process. The API function **CoQueryProxyBlanket( )** will read the current security settings on an individual proxy. The sample app uses the latter to get and the former to set the authentication and impersonation level on the proxy to the remote data object, as shown on the facing page. The code shown is executed when you select "Data Object — Set Proxy Security ..." from the main menu. This code will work any time you have an object proxy for it to work on.

If you like fixups for kludges, you'll love the API function **CoCopyProxy( )** (not shown). This makes a new copy of an interface proxy so you can access the same remote interface at two different levels of authentication. When a single interface contains sensitive and non-sensitive methods, you make two copies of the proxy. You set one's authentication level low and use it to call the interface's non-sensitive methods. You set the other's authentication level high and use it to call the interface's sensitive methods. It allows you to hack your way securely around a bad interface design.

```
typedef struct _MySecurityDlgParms {
    DWORD AuthenticationLevel ;
    DWORD ImpersonationLevel ;
} MYSECURITYDLGPARMS ;

case ID_DATAOBJECT_SETPROXYSECURITY:
{
    HRESULT hr ;  SECURITYDLGPARMS sdp ;
/*
Get current authentication and impersonation levels of this particular
IDataObject interface proxy. Store in a structure for passing to a
dialog box.
*/
    hr = CoQueryProxyBlanket (
      lpd,                        // proxy to obtain security settings for
      NULL, NULL, NULL,          // output we don't care about
      &sdp.AuthenticationLevel,  // output of authentication level
      &sdp.ImpersonationLevel,   // output of impersonation level
      NULL, NULL) ;              // more stuff we don't care about
/*
Pop up dialog box passing current authentication and impersonation
level for end user to modify.
*/
        if (DialogBoxParam (hInst, MAKEINTRESOURCE (IDD_DIALOG3), hWnd,
            (DLGPROC) SecurityDlgProc, (LPARAM)&sdp) == IDOK)
        {
/*
If user clicks OK, then set authentication and impersonation levels on
this one proxy to those specified by the end user. This does not affect
other proxies in the same process, if any.
*/
                hr = CoSetProxyBlanket (
                    lpd,                        // proxy to change settings on
                    RPC_C_AUTHN_WINNT,
                    RPC_C_AUTHZ_NONE,
                    NULL,
                    sdp.AuthenticationLevel, // new authentication level
                    sdp.ImpersonationLevel,  // new impersonation level
                    NULL,
                    EOAC_NONE) ;
        }
    return 0 ;
}
```

4. The authentication level set in CoInitializeSecurity( ) specifies the minimum incoming authentication level that the server will accept on any of its objects. This, too, is very coarse granularity. Consider the hypothetical distributed commerce application discussed in the previous pages. If the server set packet privacy as its minimum level, both client and server would waste a lot of microseconds encrypting and decrypting non-sensitive marketing information. On the other hand, if the server sets its minimum security level lower, it might accept sensitive data at a low authentication level, thereby exposing it to eavesdropping. What you really want is for the server to be able to accept information at two different levels for two different interfaces.

Since the client initiates all conversations, the server can't prevent the client from sending sensitive information unencrypted. The server can, however, detect this situation and refuse to use the information. The API function **CoQueryClientBlanket( )** fetches the authentication level used by the client in the incoming call. If that level is lower than the one you think the client should have used, you can reject it. The sample app simply displays the level on the screen. The code isn't executed until the client actually makes a call to IDataObject::GetData( ). Thus:

```
DWORD g_AuthenticationLevel ;

STDMETHODIMP CTimeData::GetData (LPFORMATETC lpfe, LPSTGMEDIUM lpstg)
{

/*
Get authentication levels to display on screen.
*/
        CoQueryClientBlanket (
                NULL, NULL, NULL,         // don't care
                &g_AuthenticationLevel, // output ptr
                NULL, NULL, NULL) ;      // don't  care either

    <other code omitted>
}
```

NOTE: If you run the client app and connect to the server on a local machine, you will find that the server always reports a level of 6 (packet privacy) no matter what the client sets. COM is saying that the data is as secure as it could possibly be because it hasn't been on the network at all. Furthermore, if the client app sets its authentication level to connect or call (2 or 3) and then creates an object on a remote server, you will see that NT has upgraded these levels to 4 (packet).

NOTE: This function has an output parameter that seems to want to return the impersonation level used by the client, but it doesn't currently work. You just have to try to impersonate the client, which will work or it won't.

This page intentionally contains no text other than this sentence.

5. The final piece of call security is specifying which users are or are not allowed to make calls to your app's interfaces. You can specify this in several ways, based on the first parameter you pass to called CoInitializeSecurity( ).

If you pass NULL as the first parameter, as in this example, access permission will be set based on registry entries. COM will first look at the security descriptor set in the "AccessPermission" value of your AppID section. This is set with dcomcnfg in a similar manner as the "LaunchPermission" value set on page 158. If your app doesn't have this registry setting, access permission will default to the global "DefaultAccessPermission" registry value shown on page 156. If this granularity and responsiveness is good enough for you, and it usually is, you can handle the entire access control issue administratively, without having to program anything.

Suppose that's not enough control. Maybe your system administrator is too lazy or maybe your permitted user set changes too quickly. For whatever reason, to sell your app and make money, your app needs to check when it starts up to see which clients are and are not allowed to access its objects. Your app can create an NT security descriptor at runtime based on its own private data and pass that descriptor as the first parameter of CoInitializeSecurity( ). COM will use the security descriptor to decide who is or is not allowed access. A demonstration of NT security descriptors and models is beyond the scope of this book, but they're not too terrible if you can find a prefabricated C++ class library that does it for you. This technique only works on Windows NT and 2000.

If you don't like NT security descriptors, you can pass as the first parameter to CoInitializeSecurity( ) a pointer to an interface of type *IAccessControl*, also adding the capability flag **EOAC_ACCESS_CONTROL** to the eighth parameter. This technique will work on Windows 95 as well as NT, although anyone who expects real security from Windows 95 would probably ask his barber for open heart surgery. The methods of this interface are:

GrantAccessRights	*// Add new access permissions to the existing list.*
SetAccessRights	*// Replace existing access rights list with new list.*
SetOwner	*// Set an item's owner or group.*
RevokeAccessRights	*// Remove access permissions from existing list.*
GetAllAccessRights	*// Get the entire list of access rights.*
IsAccessAllowed	*// Decide if client is allowed access to the object/property.*

DCOM provides a standard implementation of this interface, which you create by calling CoCreateInstance( ) with a clsid of **CLSID_DCOMAccessControl**. Although CoInitializeSecurity( ) is usually called implicitly with default parameters if you haven't done so before calling CoCreateInstance( ), this particular object is special cased by COM so that you can create it first and pass it as a parameter to CoInitializeSecurity( ). You use the first five methods of this interface to set up an access control list that specifies who is allowed to do what to the object. It requires using a number of complicated structures and isn't much less painful than the NT security descriptor. COM will then call the last method when it needs to know if a user is permitted access. The standard implementation of the object looks at the access control list that you have set up and says yea or nay.

6. Suppose checking at startup time isn't fine enough access control for your app. If you need to check for up-to-the-second access permission every time a client asks for access to an object, you can write your own implementation of the IAccessControl interface. You can stub out the first 5 methods. The only one that COM will ever call is the last one, **IAccessControl::IsAccessAllowed( )**. You place in this method whatever code you want to decide if the user is allowed access or not. Thus:

```
virtual HRESULT STDMETHODCALLTYPE IsAccessAllowed(PTRUSTEEW pTrustee,
    LPWSTR lpProperty, ACCESS_RIGHTS AccessRights,
    BOOL *pfAccessAllowed)
{

    if ( <whatever access checking I need to do succeeds> )
    {
      *pfAccessAllowed = TRUE ;
    }
    else
    {
      *pfAccessAllowed = FALSE ;
    }

    return S_OK ;
}
```

F. PERFORMANCE IN DCOM

1. When designing a DCOM server app, thinking about its performance in the initial design stages is vital to avoid writing and then trying to sell a pig-dog of an app. DCOM requires network traffic, and network calls are slower than local calls by at least one order of magnitude, frequently more. It's not just complex code that bogs down, either. It's anything that generates lots of network traffic. Look at the remote running object table sample in the next section for an example of very simple code that generates an awful lot of network traffic. You need to think about it at design time.

If you run the timing test on the sample app, you will find some interesting things. The table below sums up the performance data measured with the data3 legacy apps on two Pentium Pro 200 machines connected by a 10Mbit Ethernet with no other users:

bytes transferred	ms per call
100	1.2
200	1.4
10,000	11.0
20,000	21.8

As you can see, the call overhead is about 1 ms per call. Transferring data takes about 1 ms per 1000 bytes, which is just about the raw speed of a 10 MBit Ethernet. So for small amounts of data transferred, the call overhead dominates the timing. To optimize this, you need to minimize round trips. For example, if your server exposed an object representing a customer, you would make a performance profit by providing a method that returned a customer's first name, middle name, and last name in a single call, rather than exposing them as separate properties, each of which required a round trip to read.

As the amounts of data transferred get larger, then copying the data starts to dominate the overhead. The break-even point is somewhere around 1000 bytes transferred, which isn't a whole lot as data models go these days. To optimize this, you need to avoid transferring unnecessary data. For example, don't transfer the entire 1 Mbyte customer database to a client app that only cares about a single customer.

2. What else can you do? Here are a few ideas. First, make sure you are using the fastest hardware you can buy. I'm sure that 100 MBit Ethernet would make the numbers above go down considerably, probably more in the data transfer than the call overhead. But remember that your customers won't always have the latest hardware, and that future releases of software invariable get bigger and slower. It has long been a truism of the software industry that, "It doesn't matter how good the hardware boys are, the software boys will toss it away." In other words, "Andy Grove giveth, but Bill Gates taketh away." Don't add your name to the end of the sentence.

Second, make sure that you can pass as many small properties as possible in the same call. Instead of exposing each property individually, or perhaps in addition so that designers using your server can choose what they want, have a method called GetCustomerData( ) which takes output pointers to all of a customer's properties and gets it all in one trip.

3. About the neatest way I can think of optimizing the performance is with a custom marshaling proxy. Your server app has a method like ISomeApp::GetCustomer( ), which returns a pointer to an ICustomer interface, for which you provide a custom marshaling proxy, an advanced topic not dealt with in this book. When DCOM calls your server's method IMarshal::MarshalInterface( ), you write all the customer's data as a blob into the IStream used as a marshaling packet. On the client side, DCOM will create your custom marshaling proxy and call IMarshal::UnmarshalInterface( ). The proxy then unpacks the stream and uses its data, exposing methods that the client uses to access it locally. All the data is transmitted in a single call, and your client is none the wiser. If the client makes changes to the customer's properties, your proxy can cache them locally and only transmit them to the server when instructed to do so. This approach would work especially well for an object that had many small properties.

G. Cool But Cautionary Example: Global Running Object Table

1. One of the things that I get asked in every class on DCOM that I teach is if there is a global running object table. There really isn't, but I decided to sit down and write one as an exercise. Getting the running object table from a remote machine is trivial if you can place a server on that machine, which in turn is trivial using DCOM. The sample app server is found in the directory \Chap07\drotdll. The subdirectory \test contains an app for testing the sample server. While very easy to write, this app demonstrates almost every possible pitfall in DCOM. Specifically:

A. Your remote server can only get the running object table of the window station on which it runs. If the remote server is configured to run as the interactive user, as is the sample, then it accesses the same running object table as the interactive user's apps on that system. If the server is running as a specific user, it will be on a separate window station and not be able to see the interactive apps, although it will see the running object table used by all other remote servers configured to run as the same user. This may be what you want in a distributed object application.

B. Even if you get a pointer to an object container in a remote running object table, unless the server that put the pointer there has granted you permission to use it, you can't call any of its methods.

C. This conceptually simple app generates a hellacious amount of network traffic. Looking at the source code on the following pages; the call to get the remote object table is one remote call; the call to IRunningObjectTable::EnumRunning is a second. Each call to IEnumMoniker::Next( ) is another; each call to IMoniker::GetDisplayName( ) is another. Furthermore, the bind context used in the latter call is on the client machine, so any call the moniker makes to the bind context in composing its display name is another remote call. You can really bog a system down by writing distributed code with a single-desktop mindset.

D. The moniker comes from a remote system. If you try to bind to it on the local machine, it might reference data on the remote machine and thus not work.

I wrote my own custom interface called IRemoteROT. It contains the single method GetRemoteRunningObjectTable( ). Thus:

```
interface DECLSPEC_UUID("23901471-FD2A-11D0-806E-006097418C73")
    IRemoteROT : public IUnknown
    {
        public:
            virtual HRESULT STDMETHODCALLTYPE
                GetRemoteRunningObjectTable(IRunningObjectTable **ppRot)=0;
    };
```

Implementing this interface is about as trivial as it gets. Thus:

```
STDMETHODIMP CRemoteROT::GetRemoteRunningObjectTable(
    IRunningObjectTable **ppRot)
{
    return GetRunningObjectTable (0, ppRot) ;
}
```

2. The test client app does about what you think it ought to do. It creates an object of the correct clsid on the specified remote system, then calls the method IRemoteROT::GetRemoteRunningObjectTable( ). Once it had the running object table, it enumerated the monikers in it and placed their display names in a list box for the user to look at. Its appearance is shown below. Its code is shown on the two following pages. Thus:

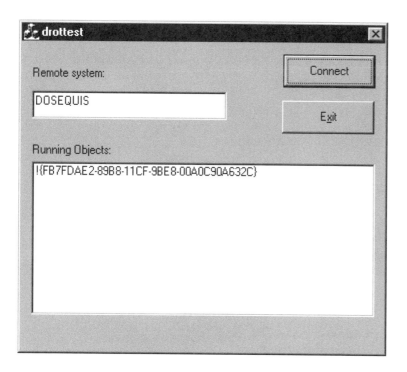

```
/*
This method called when user clicks "Connect".
*/

void CDrottestDlg::OnConnect()
{

/*
Create remote running object table server on specified machine. Query
for IRemoteROT interface.
*/

    CString RemoteSystemName ;
    GetDlgItemText (IDC_REMOTENAME, RemoteSystemName) ;

    USES_CONVERSION ;

    HRESULT hr ;
    COSERVERINFO si ;

    si.dwReserved1 = 0 ;
    si.pwszName = A2W(RemoteSystemName) ;
    si.pAuthInfo = NULL ;
    si.dwReserved2 = 0 ;

    MULTI_QI mqi [1] ;

    mqi [0].pIID = &IID_IRemoteROT ;
    mqi [0].pItf = NULL ;
    mqi [0].hr = 0 ;

    hr = CoCreateInstanceEx (
      CLSID_RemoteROT,
      NULL,
      CLSCTX_REMOTE_SERVER,
      &si,
      1,
      mqi) ;

    if (hr != S_OK)
    {
      char out [256] ;
      wsprintf (out, "Couldn't launch remote server, hr == 0x%x", hr) ;
      MessageBox (out, "RemoteROT") ;
    }

    IRemoteROT *pGet = (IRemoteROT *) mqi [0].pItf ;
```

```
/*
Now that we have the IRemoteROT interface, use it to get the running
object table from the remote machine.
*/

    hr = pGet->GetRemoteRunningObjectTable (&m_pRot) ;
    pGet->Release ( ) ;

/*
Iterate through running object table. Get each moniker's display name
and place in the list box for the user to see. First, get the
enumerator of all the objects in the running object table.
*/

    IEnumMoniker *pEnum ;
    hr = m_pRot->EnumRunning (&pEnum) ;

/*
Step through each moniker it.
*/
    IMoniker *pMoniker ;

    while ((hr = pEnum->Next (1, &pMoniker, NULL)) == S_OK)
    {
      IBindCtx *pBindCtx ;
      CreateBindCtx (0, &pBindCtx) ;

      WCHAR wout [256], *pwout ;
      pwout = wout ;
/*
Get display name from moniker. Place in list box.
*/

      pMoniker->GetDisplayName (pBindCtx, NULL, &pwout) ;
      m_List.AddString (W2A(pwout)) ;

/*
Clean up.
*/
      pBindCtx->Release ( ) ;
      pMoniker->Release ( ) ;
    }
    if (pEnum)
    {
      pEnum->Release() ;
    }
}
```

Chapter 7
Lab Exercises
Custom Moniker and Remote Running Object Table

Directory: \EssenceOfCOM\Chap07\data4
Directory: \EssenceOfCOM\Chap07\drotdll

1. Make sure the data3 server from Chapter 2 is registered according to its instructions on both client and server machine. For this quick demo, make sure that both machines are running with the same user ID and password. On both client and server machines, run dcomcnfg.exe and use it to enable DCOM. On the client machine, use dcomcnfg.exe to configure the client machine's registry as follows. From the "Applications" tab, choose "Essence of COM Data3 Demo Object" and click the "Properties ..." button. Select the "Location" tab. Clear the "Run application on this computer" checkbox. Check the "Run application on the following computer" box, then click "Browse...". Use the browser to select the client machine, click OK. Click OK again to close DCOMCFNG. Run the data3 client app from the chap02 directory. Pick "Create from .EXE server". The object will run on the remote machine. Try the "Get Data" and "Get Data Time Test..." options.

2. On the client machine, run the registry editor, go to the CLSID for the server and comment out the InProvServer32 key, as you will see that dcomcnfg.exe has already done for the LocalServer32. Run the client app again, this time choosing "Create from .DLL server". The server app will appear on the server machine. There is at the time of this writing no way to make the server machine use an in-proc server for this request.

3. Register the data4 server app on local and remote machine. Run the data4 client app. Create objects both locally and remotely. The "Create from Remote Server" menu item will not be enabled until you have set a remote server name. Perform the time test.

4. Log in as different user on the client machine. Create a remote object using the data4 server. Note that server performs impersonation on remote machine.

5. Register the server \Chap10\drotdll\drotdll.dll on a remote system. Using dcomcnfg, set the security parameters so your client machine will have access. Run an app on the remote machine that registers a moniker, such as VC++ v5.0. Now go back to your client machine, run the app "drottest.exe" from the \test subdirectory. Type in the name of the remote machine, click the connect button. You should see the moniker from the remote system.

EXTRA CREDIT: Install netmon and see how many remote COM calls are generated by the seemingly simple remote running object table. Figure out how you would design a different interface to optimize this operation. Hint: What interface does IMoniker derive from?

Chapter 8

Persistent Objects

A. Concepts and Definitions

1. A COM client will often invest a fair amount of time and effort getting an object from its default state, hot off the class factory, into a different state that the client prefers. For example, a programmer using Visual Basic will often place a control from the toolbox onto a form, then set the control's properties such as color and font. The programmer wants the properties that he has so laboriously set, not the object's original default properties, to be remembered and applied when the object next created. He could write code explicitly creating the object and then setting its properties, but it would be much easier if the object's state could somehow be transparently saved and later transparently restored, without writing all of this code. Furthermore, if the programmer was writing code to set and get individual properties, he might not know about properties that he didn't set but that were important to the object, such as version number. Since an object's client has no idea how the object is organized internally, it is unable to perform this action without the object's assistance.

This is a generic problem and has a generic solution. An object that wants to provide a client with the capability of storing and retrieving an object's state to some persistent medium implements a *persistent interface*, which is an interface that causes the object to write its state to or read its state from some type of storage medium. Some standard persistent interfaces include:

IPersistStream	*Persist object to/from a stream.*
IPersistStorage	*Persist object to/from a storage within a structured storage file.*
IPersistFile	*Persist object to/from a separate file of any type the object recognizes.*
IPersistMemory	*Persist object to/from a block of memory.*
IPersistPropertyBag	*Persist object to/from name/value pairs in a text file.*

This is such a handy concept that there are many other persistent interfaces, too many to list here. You can also write your own if you so desire. A *persistent object* is an object which supports one or more persistent interfaces. A persistent object knows how to save itself to a persistent storage device and then restore its state from that device during some later instantiation. An object written in Visual Basic (see Chapter 13) can inherit a prefabricated implementation of IPersistStream and IPersistPropertyBag from VB. An object written in the ATL can likewise inherit implementations of persistent interfaces (not dealt with in this book, but see Chapter 6 of *ATL Internals* by Rector and Sells, Addison-Wesley, ISBN 0-201-69589-9).

Note that remembering an object's state using a persistent interface is different from remembering an object's state by the use of a moniker, described in the next chapter. Persistent objects are used when the actual persistent data is held by the client, for example, in compound document embedding. Monikers are used when only a reference to the data is held by the client, for example, in compound document linking.

2. The operation of persistent interfaces is fairly simple, and doesn't change conceptually from one persistent interface to another. To save state, a client queries an object for a persistent interface. The client then creates a persistent medium of the desired type. The client calls the persistent interface's Save( ) (or similar) method. In response, the object writes its data into the storage medium provided by the client. Think of this as dehydrating the object, but hanging onto the powder in a bag. Thus:

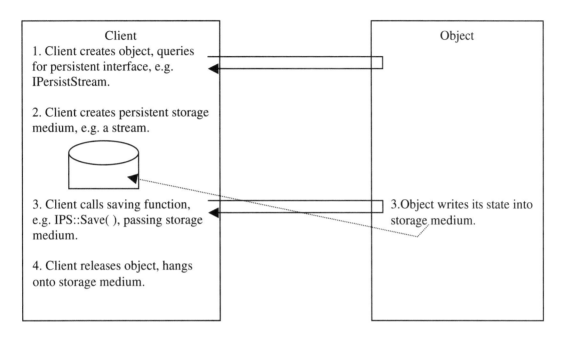

When the client creates a new object at some later time, the client restores the object's previous state by querying for the persistent interface. The client calls the persistent interface's Load( ) (or similar) method, passing the storage medium in which the object previously saved its state. The object reads and restores its previous state from the storage medium. Think of this as adding water to reconstitute the previously dehydrated object. Thus:

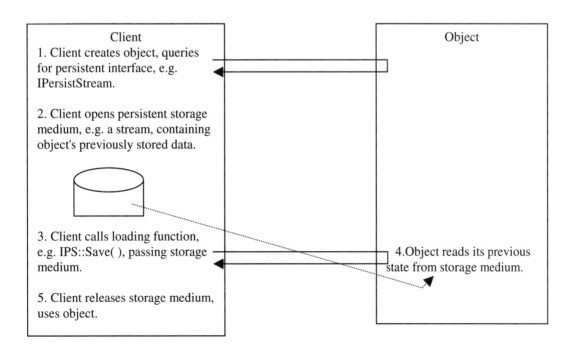

3. The use of persistent objects is not restricted to the simple case of restoring the visual properties of a control in a VB form. There are many other uses as well. For example, MSMQ, Microsoft's store-and-forward messaging system uses persistent interfaces to send objects asynchronously from a client to a server, as shown below. The sender posts a message containing a persistent object to MSMQ, specifying a recipient. MSMQ takes the message and saves the object's CLSID and state in persistent storage. The client application can then shut down. MSMQ will send the message containing the persisted object to the specified recipient at such time as the connectivity of its network routing allows. Eventually the message appears at the recipient machine, often when the sender machine isn't running. MSMQ on the recipient machine reads the object's CLSID from the message, calls CoCreateInstance to create a new object of the specified class on the recipient machine. Obviously, for this strategy to work, the recipient machine must have a server configured for the object's CLSID. MSMQ then the uses the object's persistence mechanism to load the object's original state from the message. The recipient thus transparently receives an exact copy of the object as it existed on the sender's system. This mechanism is also used in the Queued Components service of COM+. Thus:

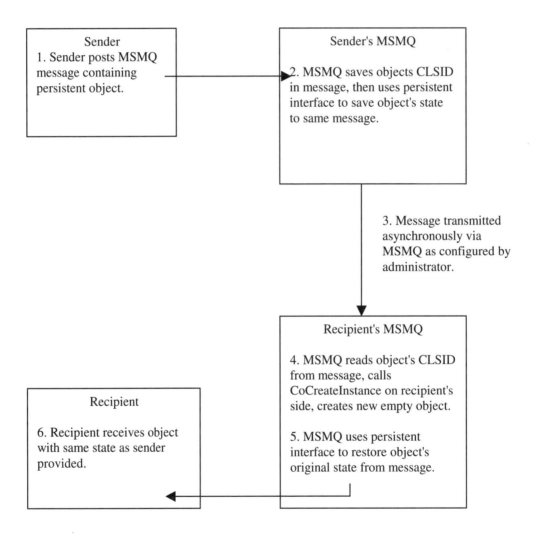

B. USING PERSISTENT OBJECTS

1. All persistent interfaces derive from the base interface IPersist. In addition to IUnknown, this interface contains only one method:

IPersist: GetClassID   *// Get CLSID of object to be loaded/stored.*

The simplest persistent object interface is *IPersistStream*. In addition to IPersist, the methods of this interface are:

IPersistStream::IsDirty   *// Ask object if it thinks it's dirty.*
IPersistStream::Load   *// Load object's data from stream.*
IPersistStream::Save   *// Store object's data to stream.*
IPersistStream::GetSizeMax   *// Ask object how big its data might get.*

A sample program that uses this interface is supplied for you in the directory \chap08\perstream. It is similar to the data3 sample provided in Chapter 2, except that in this sample, the data object representing the current time has been made persistent by having the object also support the IPersistStream interface. The menu selection "Save to Stream" uses this interface to save the object's state (the current time) into a stream provided by the client. The menu selection "Create from Stream" creates a new object and uses its IPersistStream interface to restore its previous state from the stream.

2. A stream is a logically contiguous sequence of bytes within a storage, analogous to a file within a file. The operations that are available for streams should remind you of the functions you are accustomed to using to manipulate the contents of ordinary files. A stream is manipulated via the *IStream* interface, which contains the following methods:

IStream::Read   *// Read bytes from stream to memory.*
IStream::Write   *// Write bytes from memory to stream.*
IStream::Seek   *// Set position of stream pointer.*
IStream::SetSize   *// Preallocate space for stream (streams are expandable anyway).*
IStream::CopyTo   *// Copy bytes from one stream to another.*
IStream::Commit   *// Not yet implemented.*
IStream::Revert   *// Not yet implemented.*
IStream::LockRegion   *// Not yet implemented.*
IStream::UnlockRegion   *// Not yet implemented.*
IStream::Stat   *// Get statistics about this stream.*
IStream::Clone   *// Create new stream pointer accessing same stream.*

You use the first three methods 98% of the time.

3. A client app that wants to provide a persistent stream in a document file can do so by creating a *structured storage* file. This is a file that uses an internal structure defined by Microsoft, originally for object linking and embedding, but available to any app that wants to use it. You create such a file via the API function **StgCreateDocfile( )** which returns an IStorage interface pointer. The method **IStorage::CreateStream( )** allows you to create streams inside the file. Thus:

```
/*
Create storage file, clobbering any previous version.
*/

    HRESULT hr ; IStorage *pStor ;  IStream *pStream ;

    hr = StgCreateDocfile (L"adata4.ips",
      STGM_CREATE | STGM_READWRITE | STGM_SHARE_EXCLUSIVE,
      0,  &pStor) ;

/*
Create a stream within the storage file.
*/
    hr = pStor->CreateStream (L"Data",
      STGM_CREATE | STGM_WRITE | STGM_SHARE_EXCLUSIVE,
      0, 0, &pStream) ;

    <use stream>
```

To open an existing stream, you use the function **StgOpenStorage( )**, which again returns an IStorage interface pointer. The method **IStorage::OpenStream( )** will open an existing stream in the file. Thus:

```
    HRESULT hr ; IStorage *pStor ;  IStream *pStream ;

    hr = StgOpenStorage (L"adata4.ips", NULL,
      STGM_READ | STGM_SHARE_EXCLUSIVE, NULL, 0,
      &pStor) ;

    hr = pStor->OpenStream (L"Data", 0,
      STGM_READ | STGM_SHARE_EXCLUSIVE, 0, &pStream) ;
```

If you want a non-durable stream, for example, to transfer a persistent object to another running app on the same machine, you can ignore all of the file-related nonsense and create a memory stream via the API function **CreateStreamOnHGlobal( )**. Thus:

```
    IStream *pStream ;
    CreateStreamOnHGlobal  (
      NULL,        // memory handle, NULL means system allocates one
      TRUE,        // free memory when stream released ?
      &pStream) ; // output variable
```

4. When you have an object whose state you want to save to a stream, you ask the object if it is capable of doing so by querying for the IPersistStream interface. If the object knows how to do this, it will return a pointer to this interface.

Unless your client app only deals with one class of object, you will probably want to record in the stream the class ID of the stored object so you know which class to create when reconstituting the object. You can find the class ID via the method **IPersist::GetClassID( )**, and write it to the stream via the API function **WriteClassStm( )**. The latter is a simple utility function that takes a CLSID and writes it into a stream, saving you the trouble of picking the structure apart. You then call the **IPersistStream::Save( )** method to tell the object to save its data to the stream. The layout of data in the stream looks like this:

Class ID (written by client)	Object state data written by object's IPersistStream::Save( ) method

```
0            16 17          ...        N
```

```
extern IStream *pStream ;        // IStream with stream seek ptr at start

case ID_STREAM_SAVETOSTREAM:
{
    HRESULT hr ;
/*
Query the data object for the IPersistStream interface, to see if the
object is capable of saving itself to a stream.
*/
    IPersistStream *pPerStream ;
    hr = lpd->QueryInterface (IID_IPersistStream,(LPVOID*)&pPerStream);
    if (!SUCCEEDED(hr))
    {
      MessageBox (NULL, "Data object does not support IPersistStream",
            "Error", MB_ICONSTOP) ;
      return 0 ;
    }

/*
Ask the object for its class ID.  Write it into the stream.
*/
    CLSID clsid ;
    pPerStream->GetClassID (&clsid) ;
    WriteClassStm (pStream, clsid) ;

/*
Tell the object to save its data into the stream.
*/

    pPerStream->Save (pStream, TRUE) ;

/*
Release IPersistStream interface pointer when done.
*/
    pPerStream->Release ( ) ;
    return 0 ;
}
```

5. When the client wants to reload the object from its stream, it uses the API function **ReadClassStm( )** to read the class ID that the client wrote to the stream. This retrieves the class ID that the client needs to call CoCreateInstance( ), launching the server and creating a new object in whatever default state the server provides. We then query the newly created object for the IPersistStream interface, and use the **IPersistStream::Load( )** method to make the object read from the stream the state that it saved in the previous session. Thus:

```
extern IStream *pStream ;        // IStream with stream seek ptr at start

case ID_STREAM_LOADFROMSTREAM:
{

/*
Read the class ID from the stream.  Attempt to create an object based
on it.
*/
    CLSID clsid ;
    ReadClassStm (pStream, &clsid) ;

    hr = CoCreateInstance (clsid, NULL, CLSCTX_LOCAL_SERVER,
            IID_IDataObject, (LPVOID *)&lpd) ;

    if (!SUCCEEDED(hr))
    {
      MessageBox (NULL, "Couldn't create object", "Error",MB_ICONSTOP);
      return 0 ;
    }

/*
Query the object for its IPersistStream interface.   If found, tell
object to load its data from the stream.
*/

    IPersistStream *pPerStream ;

    hr = lpd->QueryInterface (IID_IPersistStream,
      (LPVOID*)&pPerStream);

    if (!SUCCEEDED(hr))
    {
      MessageBox (NULL, "Data object does not support IPersistStream",
            "Error", MB_ICONSTOP) ;
      return 0 ;
    }

    pPerStream->Load (pStream) ;

/*
Release interface pointers when done.
*/
    pPerStream->Release ( ) ;
    return 0 ;
}
```

C. Implementing Persistent Objects

1. The objects used in this example support both the IDataObject and IPersistStream interfaces. The easiest way of writing an object that supports multiple interfaces is by multiple inheritance. You simply write a class that derives from both the desired interface definitions. Thus:

```
class CPersistTimeData : public IDataObject, public IPersistStream
{

    public:
      ULONG    m_RefCount ;
      BOOL     m_bIsDirty ;

    public:

        CPersistTimeData(void);
        ~CPersistTimeData(void);

    // IUnknown member functions

        STDMETHODIMP     QueryInterface(REFIID, LPVOID *);
        STDMETHODIMP_(ULONG)  AddRef(void);
        STDMETHODIMP_(ULONG)  Release(void);

    // IDataObject member functions

      STDMETHODIMP GetData (LPFORMATETC, LPSTGMEDIUM) ;
      STDMETHODIMP GetDataHere (LPFORMATETC, LPSTGMEDIUM) ;
      STDMETHODIMP QueryGetData (LPFORMATETC) ;
      STDMETHODIMP GetCanonicalFormatEtc (LPFORMATETC, LPFORMATETC) ;
      STDMETHODIMP SetData (LPFORMATETC, STGMEDIUM *, BOOL) ;
      STDMETHODIMP EnumFormatEtc (DWORD, LPENUMFORMATETC *) ;
      STDMETHODIMP DAdvise(FORMATETC *, DWORD, LPADVISESINK, DWORD *) ;
      STDMETHODIMP DUnadvise  (DWORD) ;
      STDMETHODIMP EnumDAdvise  (LPENUMSTATDATA *);

    // IPersistStream member functions

      STDMETHODIMP GetClassID(CLSID *) ;
      STDMETHODIMP IsDirty( void) ;
      STDMETHODIMP Load(IStream *) ;
      STDMETHODIMP Save(IStream *, BOOL) ;
      STDMETHODIMP GetSizeMax(ULARGE_INTEGER *) ;
};
```

2. The only GOTCHA! in this multiple inheritance operation is that every time you use the `this` pointer, you must cast it to specify which of the VTBLs it refers to. Don't worry, the compiler will remind you with an error if you forget. Thus:

```
HRESULT CPersistTimeData::QueryInterface(REFIID riid, LPVOID *ppv)
{

/*
Caller is asking for IUnknown or IDataObject interface.  Respond with a
pointer to our IDataObject VTBL.  IUnknown, as the root class of both
base classes, is available through either VTBL.
*/

    if (riid == IID_IUnknown || riid == IID_IDataObject)
    {
      *ppv = (IDataObject *) this ;
      AddRef();
      return S_OK ;
    }

/*
Caller is asking for the IPersistStream interface or the IPersist from
which it derives. Respond with a pointer to our IPersistStream VTBL.
*/

    else if (riid == IID_IPersist || riid == IID_IPersistStream)
    {
      *ppv = (IPersistStream *) this ;
      AddRef();
      return S_OK ;
    }

/*
Caller is asking for an interface that we don't support.
*/

    else
    {
      *ppv = NULL;
      return  E_NOINTERFACE ;
    }
}
```

3. The methods of the IPersistStream interface are fairly simple. **IPersistStream::GetClassID( )** and **IPersistStream::IsDirty( )** are trivial, thus:

```
/*
Object has been asked for its class ID.  Return in the output variable.
*/

extern GUID GUID_PersistTimeData ;

STDMETHODIMP CPersistTimeData::GetClassID(CLSID * pClsID)
{
    *pClsID = GUID_PersistTimeData ;
    return S_OK ;
}

/*
Object has been asked whether it is dirty or not.  If it is, return
the success code S_OK (which has a numerical value of 0).  Otherwise,
return the error code S_FALSE. WARNING: S_FALSE has a value of 1. The
high bit is not set, so the SUCCEEDED macro will not detect it as a
failure.
*/

STDMETHODIMP CPersistTimeData::IsDirty( void)
{
    if (m_bIsDirty)
    {
      return S_OK ;
    }
    else
    {
      return S_FALSE ;
    }

}
```

4. **IPersistStream::GetSizeMax( )** is trivial to implement, but takes a little thinking about what you ought to say. The caller is asking how big a buffer is required to save the object in its current state. The estimate that you return should be conservative, because the caller's memory might not be expandable. This example is easy because the object's data is always the same size. Thus:

```
/*
This data object saves its size in a SYSTEMTIME structure.   That's
always exactly how much space we need.
*/

STDMETHODIMP CPersistTimeData::GetSizeMax(ULARGE_INTEGER *pLint)
{
    pLint->LowPart = sizeof (SYSTEMTIME) ;
    pLint->HighPart = 0 ;
    return S_OK ;
}
```

5. The method **IPersistStream::Save( )** instructs the object to save its data in its own native data format into the provided stream. The flag bClearDirty tells the object whether or not to clear its dirty flag. The client might be making a copy of the object, in which case this will be FALSE.

The saving object cannot depend on being the only owner of data in the stream. The client might have class ID or data format information stored in the stream ahead of the object's data, and might have other objects' data stored after it. The client is responsible for having the stream's seek pointer in the proper position, pointing to the beginning of the object's saved data before calling this method. The object is responsible for somehow detecting the end of its own data (in this example, the data is always of a fixed size) and leaving the stream's seek pointer positioned there at the end of this method. An object whose data size varied might write the length of its data as the first DWORD in the stream. Thus:

```
extern SYSTEMTIME LocalTime ;

STDMETHODIMP CPersistTimeData::Save (IStream *pStream,
    BOOL bClearDirty)
{

/*
If the clear flag is set by the caller, clear this object's dirty flag.
*/

    if (bClearDirty)
    {
      m_bIsDirty = FALSE ;
    }

/*
Write our own native data to the provided stream.
*/
    return pStream->Write ((LPVOID) &LocalTime, sizeof (SYSTEMTIME),
      NULL) ;
}
```

6. The method **IPersistStream::Load( )** tells the object to read its own native data from the provided stream. The client is responsible for providing a pointer to the stream in which data has been previously saved by the method IPersistStream::Save( ) of this object, with the stream pointer at the beginning of the area in which the object's data resides. Thus:

```
/*
Load our object's data from the provided stream.  Clear the dirty flag,
as the data is now new.
*/

extern SYSTEMTIME LocalTime ;

STDMETHODIMP CPersistTimeData::Load(IStream *pStream)
{
    m_bIsDirty = FALSE ;

    return pStream->Read ((LPVOID) &LocalTime,
       sizeof(SYSTEMTIME), NULL);
}
```

Directory: \EssenceOfCOM\chap08

1.   Register   the   persistent   object   server   by   running   the   registration   script \chap08\perstream\iperstreamsv.reg.

2. Run the client app \chap08\perstream\client\iperstreamcl.exe. Pick "Data Object – Create from .EXE server" from the main menu. The server window should appear.

3. Note the time on the server window, then click "Stream – Save to Stream" from the main menu. The client will query the server for IPersistStream and save the object's state in a file called "Adata4.ips". You may hear the disk thrash. Now close down the client; the server should also close down.

4. Run the client again. Pick "Stream – Create from Stream". The client will create a new object; the server window will appear. The client will then restore the new object's previous state from the stream in the file. The time that appears on the client's main window will be the time at which the object was saved, not the time that the server is currently displaying. The object's state has been successfully saved and restored by using persistent interfaces.

5. If you want to examine the internals of a structured storage file, you can use the system utility "dfview.exe", the "DocFile Viewer", which comes with the platform SDK.

Chapter 9

Monikers

A. CONCEPTS AND DEFINITIONS

1. A moniker is a COM object that represents the intelligent name of another COM object. A moniker exposes the IMoniker interface, which a client uses to create or connect to the COM object which the moniker names. A moniker is somewhat analogous to the class factory object described in Chapter 2, in the sense that it is a COM object that exists to create other COM objects. A moniker differs from a class factory in that a class factory always creates a new object in a default state. There is no way to tell a class factory anything about the initial state of the new object that it creates. A moniker, on the other hand, can and generally does contain additional data describing the state of the new object that the client wants to create. For example, a client using a class factory can create an Excel object only in its default empty state. A client using a moniker, on the other hand, can create an Excel object that contains the contents of a specific file. Thus:

A. Creating object with a class factory.

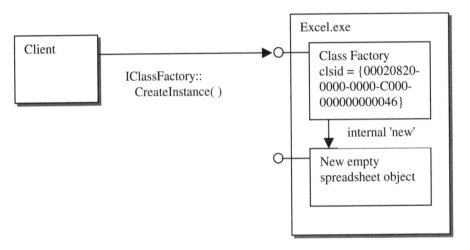

B. Creating object with moniker.

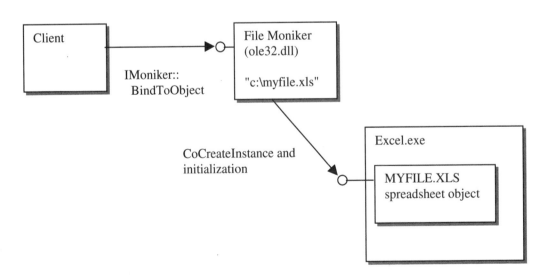

2. Why is this type of architecture useful? Monikers were originally designed for use in OLE, specifically for linking. A compound document container app wanting to display linked data needed to be able to create not just an object of a certain class (say, any old Excel spreadsheet), but rather one particular non-interchangeable object of that class (say, the Excel spreadsheet containing last month's sales figures). During the process of pasting the link into the container app, Excel would provide the container with a moniker containing the data necessary to reconstitute that particular object. The container would store the moniker in its compound document file, as shown in the diagram below (most monikers are persistent objects, as described in the previous chapter). When it came time to display the linked data, the container app would reconstitute the moniker from its file and use it to bind to the spreadsheet object that the container wanted to display (as shown on the previous page). Thus:

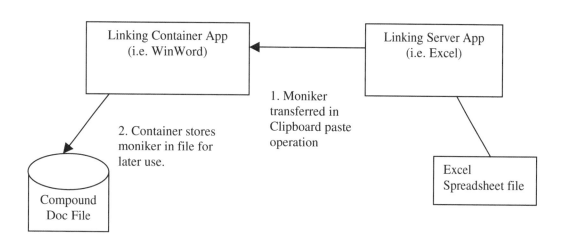

A moniker used in this manner may be seen as the object's intelligent business card. It is a COM object containing all the code and data necessary to locate the original object's server and instruct the server to recreate the original object. The moniker does not contain the Excel spreadsheet's data, but rather a reference to it, such as a file name. You can think of each individual moniker as an autodialer that contains the phone number of one particular object that the client cares about. The client doesn't have to know the format of a phone number or know how to dial phone numbers. The client only has to know how to trigger the autodialer, which is the same for all monikers: calling the method IMoniker::BindToObject( ).

3. As always happens in computing, once a particular feature gets released, programmers start using it for all sorts of things that never occurred to its original designers. Monikers have evolved from their original compound document use described on the preceding page to become a general abstraction of an object creation algorithm that allows a client to specify arbitrary initialization data.

Suppose you were writing a C++ object class that represented a patient in a hospital. It would have such methods as CPatient::ChargeLotsOfMoney( ) and CPatient::Amputate(DWORD dwWhichLimb). Obviously it is vital to know which human being each individual instance of that class represents, since removing money or limbs from the wrong patient is a bad idea. Good software engineering practice would require that none of these methods work unless the object represented a properly identified patient. The classic approach in C++ would be to require a patient identifier in the object's constructor, such as CPatient::CPatient(BSTR PatientID). In this manner, no client could ever create a patient object without first specifying an identifier.

CoCreateInstance( ) can't do that directly in COM, since you can't pass any information to the class factory. The classic approach in COM would be to have the patient interface contain a method, say IPatient::Initialize(BSTR PatientID), which the client would have to call before using any of the other methods on the IPatient interface. But now you have to write code in every other method on that interface (and any other interfaces that depend on patient ID) to check that the initialization had been done properly and to refuse to function if it hadn't. That's a lot of duplication of code, a bad idea anywhere. Plus what does your object do if a client calls Initialize( ) twice on the same instance? Keep the old patient ID? Switch to the new one? Fail quickly before it hurts someone?

What you'd really like to have is a separate "patient factory" object, a COM class separate from the patient that exists solely to create patient objects. We call this a *meta-object* in COM parlance because it exists solely to provide access to another object. It would expose one interface, say ICreatePatient, containing a method such as CreatePatient ([in] BSTR PatientID, [out, retval] IPatient *pNewPatient). The patient object itself would not be creatable through a standard COM class factory, but only through your patient factory. In this manner, you would ensure that a client could never create a new patient object without specifying a valid patient identifier. Writing this patient factory object would be pretty simple, and the architecture foolproof from a client use standpoint. That's a good combination, but it still has a number of shortcomings which the moniker architecture can remedy.

First, it takes two steps for the client to create a patient object; one to create the factory and another to use the factory to create the patient. This doesn't sound like much code to write, but if you are writing a server for sale on the open market, you want it to be as simple and transparent as possible for clients to use. You'd be surprised how attractive cutting the number of required lines of code in half is to prospective customers, even if it's only from two lines to one. That's why Microsoft wrote a new class of moniker, called the "queue moniker", for activating the call recorder used in COM+ Queued Components (see my book *Understanding COM+* from Microsoft Press, or my article in the June 1999 Microsoft Systems Journal for more information on Queued Components).

Second, the patient factory approach is not persistent. Every time a client wants to create a patient, the client app developer has to write specific code. You can't just give another application a reference to a particular patient for the other app to store and use later. The other app would have to store the patient ID and then use the patient factory as well. The creation algorithm has been imperfectly abstracted away.

Third, if you think about the previous drawback, you will realize that the client has to have intimate knowledge, not just of the data required for identifying a patient, but also of the code necessary to make use of that data. Your patient creation process will be different from that of other vendors. And unless you are very careful and ruthlessly disciplined, you will find that the steps your client apps use to create patient objects are different from the steps that they use to create objects representing other entities in the system, say, doctors and insurers. Clients don't like this complexity.

Fourth, the patient factory approach doesn't allow for easy extension. Suppose a patient is known by one ID in one medical facility but a different one in another facility (happens all the time). When you write code to identify patients in a different facility, you have to change all the client code that was ever written.

4. Monikers solve the architectural problems described on the previous page. A moniker is a COM object that abstracts the creation algorithm of another class of object. A server vendor will develop its own type of moniker, in this case, say, a patient moniker. A client that wants to create a patient moniker, which in turn will be used to create an object representing a specific patient, can easily do so via the function MkParseDisplayName( ), passing its initialization information in the form of a string, as shown beginning on page 206. The client can then store this moniker or transmit it to another program. Thus:

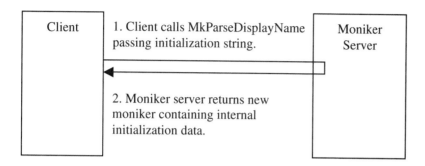

A client that already has a moniker and wants to use it to create the object which it names, in this case, one particular patient, does so via the method IMoniker::BindToObject( ), as described on page 208. A client app that wants to both create a moniker and bind to it in one single function can do so via the functions CoGetObject( ), or its VB and VB Script equivalent GetObject( ), as described beginning on page 209. The client doesn't need to know anything about how the creation is processed. The creation and initialization process, no matter how complex, is abstracted away. Thus:

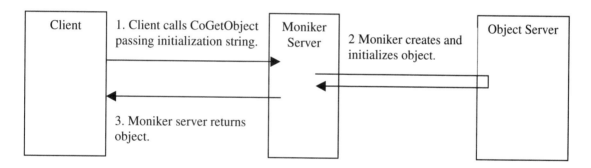

If the naming scheme gets complex, the server vendor can nest monikers together. The client can then make use of additional levels of naming hierarchy by varying only its initialization string, without changing its code. This process is described beginning on page 216.

NOTE: As always happens in evolution, a new beast contains vestigial remnants of its previous existence that don't seem to have any use in its current life, like your appendix, or the finger bones inside a whale's flipper. You will find that this applies to monikers as well. If they seem at times to be somewhat kludgey, or contain lots of methods that don't seem to be used for anything, it's because they weren't originally designed as a general purpose mechanism. They were originally designed for compound document linking.

B. TYPES OF MONIKERS

1. Monikers come in many different types, depending on the type of data that they use to create and initialize the objects that they name, and the algorithms that they use to accomplish this. The data required by a moniker, and the algorithm that it uses to create and initialize an object based on this data, are entirely up to the developer of the moniker, and will vary drastically from one moniker type to another. For an example, I will now briefly describe the file moniker, a class of object provided by the operating system that knows how to create and initialize an object based on a file name that the client specifies.

A moniker is a COM object that is creatable through a class factory. As such, it has a registered CLSID, just like any other creatable COM object. To operate properly with the moniker API functions, a moniker must also have a registered ProgID, as do most but not all creatable COM objects. The ProgID is the name of the moniker, in this case, "file", as shown in the registry screen shot below. The "DefaultIcon" and "shell" entries are there for the use of the Explorer UI and have nothing to do with monikers; it's an unfortunate overloading of the term "file". Other types of monikers will not have these. Thus:

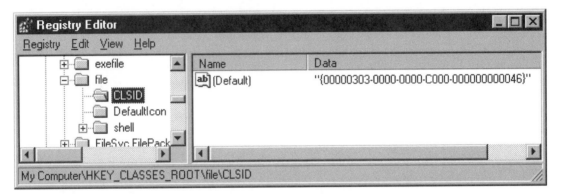

A file moniker can be created via the general API function MkParseDisplayName( ), as described on page 209. The file moniker also has its own dedicated API function, CreateFileMoniker( ). Not all system monikers have dedicated creation functions, and essentially no private monikers do, but they all work with MkParseDisplayName( ). When the client creates a file moniker through either method, it must specify the name of the file which the file moniker is to use when it creates the object.

When a client of a file moniker calls IMoniker::BindToObject( ), the file moniker first uses the API function GetClassFile( ) to find the CLSID of the server that handles that type of file. The moniker then calls CoCreateInstance( ) to create an object of the server class, querying for the IPersistFile interface. The moniker then calls IPersistFile::Load( ), passing the name of the file and telling the object's server to read the file and initialize the object's state from its contents. Finally, the moniker will query for the interface requested by the client, and return that interface pointer to the client.

The file moniker's binding algorithm is public, so that any app that uses files can benefit from it. Microsoft did this so that any app could be a linking server. Your custom monikers will probably not do this, although you certainly can write them that way if you want to. Instead they will probably use their own private initialization algorithms.

While you are thinking about the gyrations that the moniker goes through to create and initialize the object when the client calls IMoniker::BindToObject( ), it is important to remember that the client knows nothing whatsoever about it, just as the client knows nothing about the gyrations with class factories when it calls CoCreateInstance( ). It's all been abstracted away from the client's standpoint.

2. Certain types of monikers are provided by the operating system, as shown in the table below. You can see the versatility of the moniker architecture by looking at the widely varying tasks that they accomplish. It is fairly easy to write your own moniker type for extending the power of monikers to your own objects, as described on page 210. Thus:

Name	Purpose
File	Get COM object or data from a file.
Item	Get COM object or data from sub-element within a file.
Composite	Glues together two or more other monikers into atomic whole.
Anti	Undoes action of another moniker in a composite.
Pointer	Non-persistent moniker for putting transient pointers in running object table.
URL	Get COM object or data from the Internet.
Clsid	Get class factory for a specified class.
Java	Get COM object wrapping a specified Java class.
Queue	Activate client side call recorder for an object, in COM+ Queued Components.
New	Persistent name for actual server-side object created in COM+ Queued Components.

There isn't any standard way of identifying monikers in the registry. There really ought to be a category ID or dedicated registry key for this, but there isn't. The only way to find every moniker on your system would be to create an object of every registered class and query it for the IMoniker interface (not all that difficult, but very tedious).

C. CREATING A MONIKER

1. How does a client obtain a moniker that it wants to use to create an object in a specific state? There are several ways. Monikers used for linking are often transferred through the Clipboard during a paste operation, using the Clipboard format CF_LINK. The first six monikers in the system moniker table can be obtained via their own dedicated API functions, such as CreateFileMoniker( ).

The more general case of creating a moniker works through the function **MkParseDisplayName( )**. In this function, you provide a string with the moniker's ProgID as a prefix, followed by the data that you think the moniker needs, for example, "file:c:\myfile.xls". The function takes the characters preceding the first colon as a ProgID, looks in the registry and finds the CLSID for the moniker. It then calls CoGetClassObject( ), asking the moniker's server for the *IParseDisplayName* interface. It then calls the method IParseDisplayName::ParseDisplayName( ), passing the supplied string. It is up to the class object to interpret the string and return a moniker containing the initialization data specified by that string. Obviously, the client needs to know the format of the string that the moniker expects. That's the only intimate information that the client needs to have about the moniker. The client developer obtains this knowledge by sitting down for a little old-fashioned RTFM (Read The Funny Manual, more or less).

The operation of parsing a moniker's display name requires a *bind context*, essentially a scratchpad object used internally by the parsing monikers. It becomes important in complex situations such as composite monikers. All the client does is create it via the function **CreateBindCtx( )**, and pass it atomically to the function. A sample program illustrating the creation and binding of monikers is in the directory \Chap09\bindmoniker. The code is shown below, and a diagram is shown on the facing page.

```
void CChildView::OnFileBindusingmkparsedisplayname()
{
/*
Get file name from end user.
*/
    CFileDialog dlg (TRUE);
    if (dlg.DoModal( ) == IDOK)
    {
      HRESULT hr ; USES_CONVERSION ;
      CString path = dlg.GetPathName() ;
      CString DispName = "file:" ;
      DispName += dlg.GetPathName() ;


/*
Pass the file name to the IParseDisplayName interface to
obtain the moniker.
*/
      ULONG CharsEaten ; IBindCtxPtr BC ;
      CreateBindCtx (NULL, &BC) ;

      IMonikerPtr FileMoniker ;
      MkParseDisplayName (
            BC,                 // bind context, a scratchpad
            A2W(DispName),      // string to obtain moniker for
            &CharsEaten,        // number of characters used from string
            &FileMoniker);      // output moniker

      <rest of code omitted>
    }
}
```

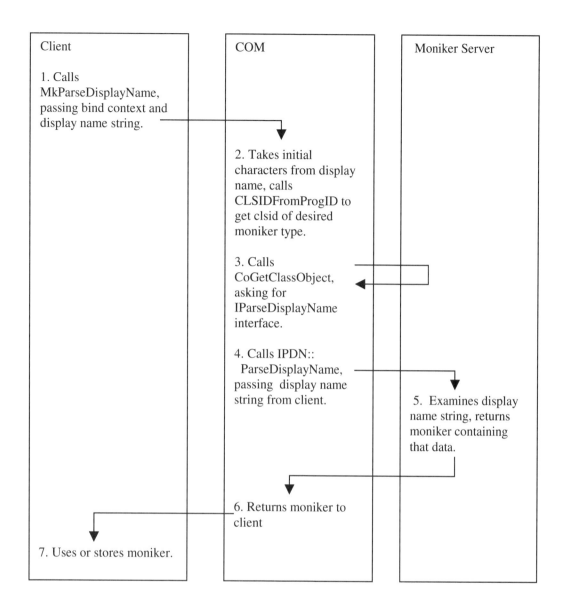

Client	COM	Moniker Server
1. Calls MkParseDisplayName, passing bind context and display name string.		
	2. Takes initial characters from display name, calls CLSIDFromProgID to get clsid of desired moniker type.	
	3. Calls CoGetClassObject, asking for IParseDisplayName interface.	
	4. Calls IPDN:: ParseDisplayName, passing display name string from client.	
		5. Examines display name string, returns moniker containing that data.
	6. Returns moniker to client	
7. Uses or stores moniker.		

D. BINDING A MONIKER

1. The process by which an object is recreated from its moniker is called *binding*, and is accomplished via the method **IMoniker::BindToObject( )**. Once the client has used the moniker to bind to the object, the client generally has no further use for the moniker and will release it. The mechanism whereby the moniker creates and initializes the object that it names is entirely up to the moniker. Thus:

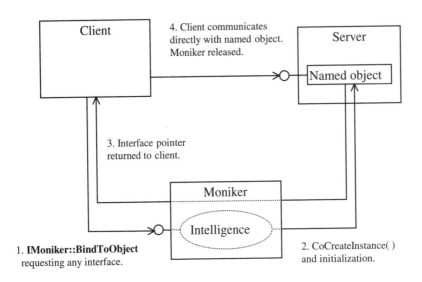

```
        IMonikerPtr FileMoniker ;

    <obtain moniker as shown previously>

/*
Tell the file moniker to bind. Ask for IDataObject interface.
*/
        IBindCtxPtr BC ;
        CreateBindCtx (NULL, &BC) ;

        IDataObjectPtr DO ;

        hr = FileMoniker->BindToObject(
            BC,                 // bind context, scratchpad
            NULL,               // used internally when binding composite
                                // monikers, client apps pass NULL
            IID_IDataObject,    // interface pointer desired on new obj
            (void**) &DO) ;     // output pointer
/*
Use interface pointer in whatever manner desired.
*/
```

NOTE: The API function **BindMoniker( )**, not shown, combines the operations of creating the bind context, binding to the moniker, and releasing the bind context.

2. The API function **CoGetObject( )**, and its VB equivalent GetObject( ), combine the operations of MkParseDisplayName and BindMoniker. This makes it possible for even the simplest of clients to access the power of monikers. The client doesn't even think about monikers in any way, it just calls the function, passing the initialization string. Think of it as CoCreateInstance( ), passing an initialization string. Thus:

```
void CChildView::OnFileBindusingownstring()
{

    CString str ;
    <assemble desired binding string>

/*
Call CoGetObject, combining MkParseDisplayName with BindMoniker.
*/
    HRESULT hr = CoGetObject (
            A2W(str),                   // name entered by user
            NULL,                       // flags
            IID_IUnknown,               // interface pointer wanted
            (void**) &pUnk) ;           // output variable

    <use object in whatever way you want>
    }
}
```

E. WRITING YOUR OWN CUSTOM MONIKER

1. If you are writing a COM server and the notion of persistent references to individual objects is attractive to you, then writing your own custom monikers to provide access to your objects in addition to or instead of a standard class factory is a useful thing. While this may seem daunting at first, it really isn't so bad. The IMoniker interface has 15 members, the IPersistStream interface from which it derives has 5, and many of them look quite bloody. However, when you start breaking them down into groups, you will find that many of them are only important in the moniker's original compound document use, particularly those in the Composition group. You can get the moniker to totter to its feet and say "Hello, World" by implementing only two of them, shown in bold below The rest are optional, and most of them outside the Composition group are trivial. The methods of the interface are:

Binding Group:
    BindToObject
    BindToStorage

Running Object Table Group:
    IsEqual
    Hash
    IsRunning
    GetTimeOfLastChange

Display Name Group:
    GetDisplayName
    ParseDisplayName

Composition Group:
    Reduce
    ComposeWith
    Enum
    Inverse
    CommonPrefixWith
    RelativePathTo
    IsSystemMoniker

2. To demonstrate writing a custom moniker, I decided to write a moniker called the "thunder" moniker. It would create new automation objects based on a supplied ProgID, and also allow their properties to be set. For example, if a client called:

```
CoGetObject("Thunder:EssenceOfCOM.HelloAutomation HelloMessage=Goodbye")
```

then the moniker would create the automation object from Chapter 4 and initialize the property whose name was HelloMessage to say "Goodbye" instead of "Hello, World".

This turned out to be relatively simple using the ATL. I first had to generate a new DLL project and a new simple object class. I added **IMoniker** to the inheritance list and to the interface map, and then added declarations and shell implementations of the methods of that interface. No problem, took about 15 minutes.

Remember that a moniker's class factory must support the IParseDisplayName interface. The prefabricated ATL class factory didn't support that, so I then had to override the default class factory via the macro **DECLARE_CLASSFACTORY_EX**. This tells the ATL not to use its own class factory, that you will provide one instead. Thus:

```
class ATL_NO_VTABLE CThunderMk :
    public CComObjectRootEx<CComSingleThreadModel>,
    public CComCoClass<CThunderMk, &CLSID_ThunderMk>,
    public IDispatchImpl<IThunderMk, &IID_IThunderMk,
      &LIBID_THUNDERMONIKERLib>,
    public IMoniker
{
public:
    CThunderMk()
    {
    }

    CComBSTR m_DisplayName ;

DECLARE_REGISTRY_RESOURCEID(IDR_THUNDERMK)

DECLARE_CLASSFACTORY_EX (CThunderMkFactory)

DECLARE_PROTECT_FINAL_CONSTRUCT()

BEGIN_COM_MAP(CThunderMk)
    COM_INTERFACE_ENTRY(IThunderMk)
    COM_INTERFACE_ENTRY(IDispatch)
    COM_INTERFACE_ENTRY(IMoniker)
END_COM_MAP()

// IMoniker methods


    public:
        virtual HRESULT STDMETHODCALLTYPE BindToObject (IBindCtx  *pbc,
          IMoniker *pmkToLeft, REFIID riidResult, void  **ppvResult) ;

< rest of IMoniker and IPersistStream methods>
}
```

3. The class factory itself is shown below. It inherits from the ATL's CComClassFactory base class, and I added my own support for the IParseDisplayName interface. It only has one method, ParseDisplayName( ), the functionality of which is duplicated in the method IMoniker::ParseDisplayName( ). So all my implementation here has to do is to strip off the leading portion of the string that contains the moniker name "thunder:", create a new empty Thunder moniker, and delegate the call to that moniker. The new moniker will return a different moniker containing the specified initialization string, as shown on the next page. Thus:

```
class ATL_NO_VTABLE CThunderMkFactory : public CComClassFactory,
    public IParseDisplayName
{
public:
    CThunderMkFactory() {}

DECLARE_PROTECT_FINAL_CONSTRUCT()

BEGIN_COM_MAP(CThunderMkFactory)
    COM_INTERFACE_ENTRY(IParseDisplayName)
END_COM_MAP()

    HRESULT STDMETHODCALLTYPE ParseDisplayName(IBindCtx *pbc,
        LPOLESTR pszDisplayName, ULONG *pchEaten, IMoniker **ppmkOut)
    {
/*
Find the colon. Point to the character after it. Figure out how many
characters we've skipped.
*/

        WCHAR *pAfterColon = wcschr (pszDisplayName, ':') + 1 ;
        ULONG nPrefixChars = pAfterColon - pszDisplayName ;


/*
Create a new, empty Thunder moniker.
*/
        IMonikerPtr pMoniker = new CComObject <CThunderMk> ( ) ;


/*
Pass the remaining display name string to the moniker. Give
the resulting new moniker back to the caller.
*/

        ULONG CharsEatenByMoniker ;
        pMoniker->ParseDisplayName(pbc, NULL, pAfterColon,
            &CharsEatenByMoniker, ppmkOut) ;

/*
Calculate the correct number of eaten characters and give that
back to the caller as well.
*/
        *pchEaten = nPrefixChars + CharsEatenByMoniker ;
        return S_OK ;
    }
};
```

4. The method IMoniker::ParseDisplayName accepts an initialization string and returns a new moniker that contains that string internally. This is somewhat non-intuitive, that one moniker creates another moniker of the same class but containing different internal data, but that's how Microsoft designed it. Thus:

```
HRESULT STDMETHODCALLTYPE CThunderMk::ParseDisplayName(IBindCtx  *pbc,
    IMoniker  *pmkToLeft, LPOLESTR pszDisplayName, ULONG  *pchEaten,
    IMoniker  **ppmkOut)
{

/*
Create a new moniker of our own class.
*/
    IThunderMk *pThunderMk = new CComObject <CThunderMk> ;

/*
Use our own internal custom interface to set its internal display name.
*/

    pThunderMk->put_DisplayName (CComBSTR(pszDisplayName)) ;

/*
Give the new moniker back to the caller. It was already AddRef'd by the
constructor.
*/

    pThunderMk->QueryInterface (IID_IMoniker, (void**)ppmkOut) ;

/*
Tell the caller that we ate the whole thing.
*/
    *pchEaten = wcslen (pszDisplayName) ;
    return S_OK ;
}
```

5. The method IMoniker::BindToObject contains whatever code the developer of the moniker decided he needed to create a new object and initialize it, based on the string with which the moniker was created. In this sample, I treat the first string as a ProgID and the second as a property name/value pair. You will write whatever code your creation and initialization algorithm requires. Thus:

```
HRESULT STDMETHODCALLTYPE CThunderMk::BindToObject(IBindCtx  *pbc,
    IMoniker  *pmkToLeft, REFIID riidResult, void  **ppvResult)
{

/*
The token following the ProgID is of the form "PropName=PropVal", no
spaces allowed. The token before the = sign is the name of the
property, that after is the string value of the property.
*/

    WCHAR *pPropName, *pPropValue, *pProgID ;

    CComBSTR StringToHack = m_DisplayName ;
    pProgID = wcstok (StringToHack, L" =") ;
    pPropName = wcstok (NULL, L" =") ;
    pPropValue = wcstok (NULL, L" =") ;

/*
The first token in the string should be the ProgID. Convert to a CLSID
and create the object, asking for the IDispatch interface.
*/
    CLSID clsid ;
    CLSIDFromProgID(pProgID, &clsid) ;

    IDispatch *pDisp ;
    HRESULT hr = CoCreateInstance (clsid, NULL, CLSCTX_SERVER,
      IID_IDispatch, (void **) &pDisp) ;

/*
Call IDispatch::GetIDsOfNames to get the dispatch ID of the property.
*/
    long dwDispatchID ;
    hr = pDisp->GetIDsOfNames (IID_NULL, &pPropName, 1,
      LOCALE_SYSTEM_DEFAULT, &dwDispatchID) ;

/*
Call IDispatch::Invoke to set the value of the property.
*/
    hr = _com_dispatch_propput (pDisp, dwDispatchID, VT_BSTR,
      CComBSTR (pPropValue)) ;

/*
Give object back to caller.
*/
    pDisp->QueryInterface (riidResult, ppvResult) ;
    return S_OK ;
}
```

6. Monikers were originally designed to be persistent by making the IMoniker interface derive from the IPersistStream interface. The standard persistence model is for every moniker to implement the methods of this interface, as described at the end of the last chapter. It isn't very hard, and I won't burden you with another implementation of it here.

Making IMoniker derive from IPersistStream is an unfortunate choice. Not all monikers are or want to be persistent. My sample Thunder moniker, for example, doesn't support persistence, but there is no way to query a moniker for its support of this interface. A client that wants to persist a moniker into a stream just has to try it and see if it works. A moniker can support any other persistence mechanisms that it cares to by supporting their interface in addition to IMoniker.

F. Complex Binding Hierarchies

1. Monikers become even more useful as the namespace within which the binding operation takes place becomes more complex. Consider the case of the object representing the medical patient discussed at the beginning of this chapter. Suppose a single ID did not suffice to identify this patient. Suppose instead that a patient can appear in the records of several different medical providers (hospitals, doctors' offices, insurers, etc.), with different ID strings used in each. (This happens all the time in real life, and is one of the major stumbling blocks to greater integration of medical data.) In order to fully identify a patient, a client app would need to provide both the patient ID string and the provider within whose database that string had the correct meaning. To obtain an object identifying a particular patient, a client app would need to know how to connect to the specified provider (and you know they'd all have different mechanisms), and then how to negotiate with that provider to resolve the patient ID into a patient object (ditto).

Monikers are great for this. The client could simply call CoGetObject( ), specifying a string containing the necessary information for the binding operation. It would be entirely up to the moniker to perform the necessary negotiations, however complex they might be. This painful logic could be written once and encapsulated, shielding the user from needing to know or care about it.

2. A moniker developer has several options in this situation. The first is to have one class of moniker that knows how to parse all the information in the binding string. For example, if the client called:

```
CoGetObject  ("patient:Provider=GeneralHospital ID=12345" ...) ;
```

the patient moniker would know how to use the provider string in conjunction with the patient ID to resolve the call into an object that represents the correct patient. This is OK if the binding algorithm is simple. It gets more cumbersome as the hierarchy gets more complex (specifying the department within the provider, for example).

3. The second option is for you to write a moniker that knew how to use other monikers. For example, you could write two separate monikers, say, the provider moniker and the patient moniker. The former would know how to use the latter. If the client called:

```
CoGetObject  ("provider:GeneralHospital patient:12345" ...) ;
```

the provider moniker would parse the string and internally create a patient moniker. The provider moniker would, perhaps, know how to connect to the provider's system, transfer the patient moniker to it, bind it there, and return the result to the client. The patient moniker would not know anything about the provider moniker. Again, this works well for relatively simple hierarchies that don't change often.

4. The final alternative would be to use a composite moniker. You saw back on page 214 that the method ParseDisplayName( ) returns the number of characters that it has used from the binding string. If the first moniker doesn't eat the whole string (don't say it), then MkParseDisplayName continues to try to create monikers with the rest of the string. For example, if the provider moniker at the bottom of the previous page returned 25 (the length to the end of "Hospital") for the number of characters eaten instead of 38 (the length of the entire string), then MkParseDisplayName would continue to try to create another moniker with the remaining substring starting at the 26th character, in this case, "patient:12345". MkParseDisplayName would then return the two monikers wrapped up inside a third moniker, known as the *composite moniker*, a system-provided class that exists for the sole purpose of containing other monikers. The first moniker found, in this case the provider, would be on the left of the second moniker inside the composite. Conceptually it would look like this:

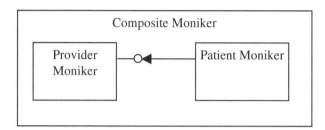

When the client calls BindToObject( ), the composite moniker would call that same method on the rightmost moniker in the composite, in this case the patient. The second parameter of this call contains the IMoniker interface of the moniker located on that moniker's left in the composite, in this case, the provider moniker. Thus:

```
HRESULT STDMETHODCALLTYPE IMoniker::BindToObject(IBindCtx  *pbc,
    IMoniker  *pmkToLeft, REFIID riidResult, void  **ppvResult)
```

In the simple cases that we have looked at so far, this has always been NULL, but now it isn't. The patient moniker knows that it can't stand on its own, that it has to look to its left for its outer context (or perhaps the patient moniker uses a default binding algorithm if there isn't a provider moniker to its left). The patient moniker would query the moniker on its left for an agreed-upon interface. *IOleItemContainer* was popular in OLE, but it carries a lot of extra baggage that you probably don't want any more. This interface can be anything that both patient and provider expect, say IResolvePatientId. The patient would then call a method on this interface, say ResolvePatientID, passing its ID; saying in effect, "Hey, go look up patient ID 12345 in whatever database you have", and the provider moniker would do whatever it needed to make that happen. The advantage of this approach is that the patient and provider monikers don't need to have intimate implementation knowledge of each other, they just need to know the interface that connects them. For example, the patient moniker wouldn't care if the moniker on its left was a department moniker, which in turn delegated to a provider moniker on *its* left, and so on to arbitrary complexity. Monikers for composition are a little harder to write, as you then have to implement the Composition group of methods, but it really isn't that bad. When you need it, it works.

Lab Exercises
Chapter 9
Monikers

Directory: \EssenceOfCOM\chap09\bindmoniker

1. The first sample program illustrates the process of creating a moniker and using it to bind to an object. Run the file "bindmoniker.exe" and select any of the first three entries on the main menu. A dialog box will appear. Select the file "gas.xls" from the same directory as the sample program. The program will create a file moniker and attempt to bind it. If you have Microsoft Excel on your system, you will see the picture of a spreadsheet appear in the window. If you don't have Excel, try selecting any file for which you have a registered OLE server type. The binding operation will work; it's just the display portion that depends on Excel.

2. To experiment with other moniker types, select "Bind using own string" from the main menu. Enter a moniker string in the resulting dialog box. The program will attempt to create a moniker with that string and bind to it. It will report whether or not the operation was successful, but will not display a spreadsheet.

Directory: \EssenceOfCOM\chap09\thundermoniker

3. This sample program demonstrates the functionality of our custom moniker. Register the file "thundermoniker.dll" using the utility program regsvr32.exe. Also register the automation server from Chapter 4. Run the sample client app "Project1.exe" from the \vbtest directory. You will see message boxes appear showing the progress of the binding operation, and then the automation server's window will appear on the screen. Click the "Say Hello" button on the client app. You will see that the server's message has been changed to "Good bye". NOTE: This sample only works on Unicode systems (NT and W2K).

Chapter 10

Asynchronous COM

A. CONCEPTS AND DEFINITIONS

1. When a COM server takes a long time to complete a method call, say, a minute or two for searching a large database and returning a record set, the client doesn't want its calling thread to have to block for the entire duration of the call. Instead, the client would rather call one method to start the process and return immediately; then obtain the results at some convenient later time. In the meantime, the client can perform other useful tasks that don't depend on the result of the call. That's what you do when you drop off your dry cleaning, go grocery shopping, and pick up your clean clothes afterwards. It doesn't necessarily solve every throughput problem, as some operations can't be started until others are completed, but proper interleaving of tasks can greatly increase a client apps productivity by reducing idle time.

COM programmers have traditionally accomplished this task by exposing a method for starting the process, say, StartSearch( ). The client calls it, passing the input parameters (drops off the laundry, specifies no starch) and returns (leaves the store to go about its other errands). At some later time, the client calls another method, say GetResultSet( ) to harvest the results (go back to the dry cleaner and pick up the clean clothes), which returns an error code if the task is not yet complete (the counter guy says, "They're not done yet.") Alternatively, the client can provide a callback interface (give the dry cleaner your cell phone number). When the server completes the task, it calls a method on the callback interface to notify the client of the completed task and pass the results to the client.

The main advantage of this approach was that it didn't require any operating system support, and thus was feasible from the very first release of COM. It does, however, contain a number of disadvantages. First, it requires some tricky multithreaded programming work on the server side. In the StartSearch( ) method, the server has to store the client's input parameters, then switch the job to a worker thread for execution. This worker thread has to be managed and scheduled and pooled and synchronized, and the correct result gotten back to the correct client. It's harder than it sounds. Inter-thread object marshaling considerations come into play, which aren't any fun either. Second, there's no good way for the client to cancel the operation of the long call if he changes his mind (going back to the dry cleaner and saying you need your pants back right away even if they're still dirty). Finally, it isn't really standardized, every server runs in a different way.

Using COM+ Queued Components (QC) is another alternative for asynchronous operation. This is a part of Windows 2000 that uses MSMQ instead of RPC for communication between client and server. You can find more information in my book *Understanding COM+* (Microsoft Press, ISBN 0-7536-0666-8), or in my article in the June 1999 issue of *Microsoft Systems Journal*. QC was designed for completely portable operation, where the client is not connected to the server when it makes its calls, so its architecture is completely decoupled and it's harder for the client to get output from the server. It's designed for the large class of environments where the presence or absence of connections is not deterministic. It's not a great match for the situation above, where the client is running in an environment where the server is available but you just don't want to wait for it. Additionally, using QC requires you to install MSMQ, which not everyone wants to do.

2. In Windows 2000, Microsoft introduced *non-blocking* COM calls, or *asynchronous* COM, as shown in the diagram below. In this architecture, a client creates an object and calls a method that the server has marked for asynchronous completion. The client thread returns immediately, while COM transmits the call to the server and makes the method call on the server side. Since the client has already returned, the server can simply execute the method call on its incoming thread without having to reschedule, and returns the output data to COM. COM buffers the output data until the client makes another call to harvest it. Thus:

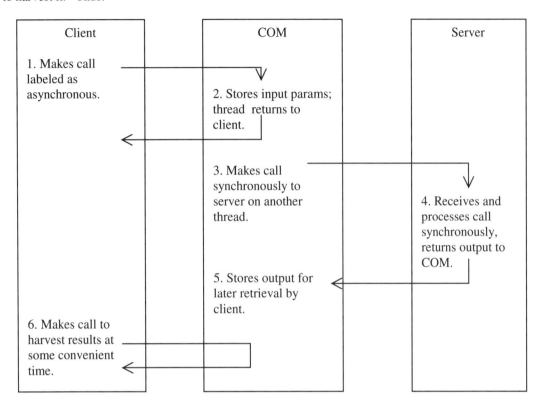

3. Windows 2000 is the first release of non-blocking COM calls. It shouldn't surprise you that the current implementation has some fairly serious rough edges, including these three major drawbacks: First, as you will see, the client side of disconnected operation is somewhat tedious to code, although significantly less so than writing your own multithreaded code instead. I'd hope to see a proxy generator appear in Visual Studio sometime in the future, that will generate the repetitive code for non-blocking calls, much as the #import directive generates the repetitive code for IDispatch calls today. I sent this request in to comwish@microsoft.com. If all of you readers do also, then maybe they'll do it.

Second, non-blocking calls don't work for COM+ configured components, which are COM object classes that have been installed in COM+ applications using the COM+ Explorer. That means that non-blocking calls currently can't work with COM+, only with classic COM and DCOM. Finally, non-blocking calls don't work with the IDispatch interface, or any interface derived from it, which rules out all dual interfaces. Since IDispatch is required for scripting, and essentially no object vendor is willing to give up scripting compatibility, this will severely restrict the utility of the Windows 2000 non-blocking COM call mechanism. I hope Microsoft fixes all of these problems soon, but nothing has been announced at the time of this writing (Jan 2000).

B. DECLARING ASYNCHRONOUS INTERFACES

1. The programmer of a server that wants its client to be able to make non-blocking calls to it uses the .IDL tag **async_uuid** to signify this to the MIDL compiler. Thus:

```
[
  object,
  uuid(1E007E4C-A2C0-46B3-94D6-5346969F9183),
  async_uuid(1E007E4D-A2C0-46B3-94D6-5346969F9183),
  pointer_default(unique)
]
interface IChap10Demo : IUnknown
{
  HRESULT DoSomething([in] long InputParm,
        [out, retval] long *pOutputParm);
};
```

When MIDL compiles the above fragment, you will find that it generates two interface definitions. The first is the standard definition that you would expect to see, thus:

```
MIDL_INTERFACE("1E007E4C-A2C0-46B3-94D6-5346969F9183")
IChap10Demo : public IUnknown
{
    public:
        virtual HRESULT STDMETHODCALLTYPE DoSomething(
            /* [in] */ long InputParm,
            /* [retval][out] */ long __RPC_FAR *pOutputParm) = 0;

};
```

The second is an asynchronous version of that interface. The name of the interface is the name of the original interface with the characters "**Async**" prepended to it. Each method in the original interface has been replaced with two methods; one for starting the operation asynchronously and one for harvesting the results. The former contains the input parameters from the original interface and has the name "**Begin_**" prepended to it. The latter contains the output parameters from the original interface and has the name "**Finish_**" prepended to it. Thus:

```
MIDL_INTERFACE("1E007E4D-A2C0-46B3-94D6-5346969F9183")
AsyncIChap10Demo : public IUnknown
{
    public:
        virtual HRESULT STDMETHODCALLTYPE Begin_DoSomething(
            /* [in] */ long InputParm) = 0;

        virtual HRESULT STDMETHODCALLTYPE Finish_DoSomething(
            /* [out][retval] */ long __RPC_FAR *pOutputParm) = 0;

};
```

2. The two interfaces are registered in the normal way, in the HKEY_CLASSES_ROOT\Interface section of the registry. However, there are two new entries signifying that each is the other-time version of the other. The standard interface's registry entries contains the key "AsynchronousInterface", shown in the screen shot below, telling the operating system which asynchronous interface contains the Begin_ and Finish_ methods that map to its standard methods. The asynchronous interface's registry entries contain the key "SynchronousInterface", which tells the operating system which synchronous interface its Begin_ and Finish_ methods map to. The use that the operating system makes of these entries will become clear when you see the process used for building and making an asynchronous call, as shown on the next few pages.

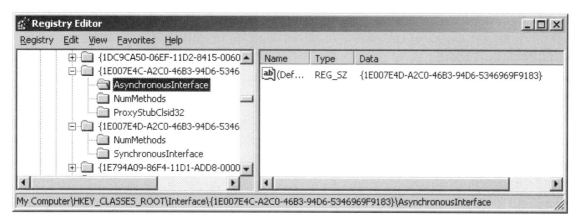

C. SIMPLEST ASYNCHRONOUS EXAMPLE

1. Making an asynchronous call from the client side is a little bit tedious. You don't just query for an interface and make the call the way you are used to doing with a synchronous call. Instead, you must create a separate *call object* for each asynchronous call you want to make. This call object exposes the asynchronous interface, and also the ISynchronize and ICancelMethodCalls interfaces that you use to control that particular asynchronous call. This call object is manufactured by a *call factory object*, accessed via the **ICallFactory** interface, which is provided by the operating system exposed on the standard COM proxy manager. The process is diagrammed below.

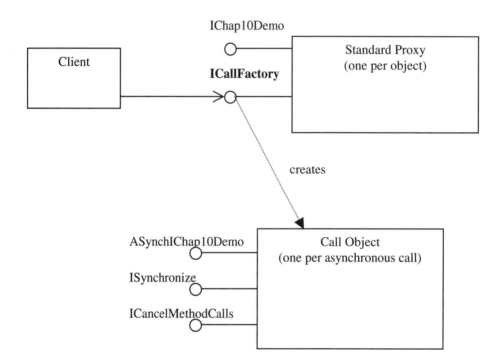

The code required to do this is shown on the facing page. The client creates the object as usual (not shown), then queries the object for the ICallFactory interface. The client then manufactures the call object via the method **ICallFactory::CreateCall( )**, asking for the asynchronous version of the interface. Finally, the client calls the Begin_ method on the asynchronous interface, which starts the asynchronous call process.

NOTE: The HRESULT value returned from the Begin_ method indicates only the result of the call being accepted by COM. It does not indicate success or failure of the actual method call on the server, because it hasn't been done at the time the Begin_ call returns to the client.

```
/*
User clicked the Begin button. Create a call object, get the
asynchronous version of the desired interface, then call the "Begin_"
version of the desired method.
*/


IUnknownPtr g_pObject ;
AsyncIChap10DemoPtr g_pAsyncIChap10Demo ;

void CClientDlg::OnButton2()
{

/*
Query the proxy manager for the ICallFactory interface. This is
provided by COM's standard proxy manager. The server does not have to
implement it.
*/

    ICallFactoryPtr pCallFactory ;

    g_pObject->QueryInterface (IID_ICallFactory,
      (void **) &pCallFactory) ;

/*
Call the method ICallFactory::CreateCall to create the call
object, requesting the asynchronous version of the desired
interface.
*/

    pCallFactory->CreateCall (
      __uuidof (AsyncIChap10Demo),   // ID of asynchronous interface
      NULL,                          // aggregation, here none
      __uuidof (AsyncIChap10Demo),   // interface wanted on call object
      (IUnknown **) &g_pAsyncIChap10Demo) ; // output pointer


/*
Call the "Begin_" version of the desired method on the
asynchronous interface.
*/

    g_pAsyncIChap10Demo->Begin_DoSomething (GetDlgItemInt (IDC_EDIT1));

}
```

2. After accepting the call from the client, COM transmits the parameters to the server side. The server only needs to provide an implementation of the synchronous version of the interface, as shown in the class below. The server does not need to implement the Begin_ and Finish_ methods of the asynchronous interface. They are solely synthesized by COM on the client side. The server's implementation of QueryInterface does not even have to indicate support for the asynchronous interface. Thus:

```
/*
This class need only implement the synchronous version of the
interface. COM, specifically the call object, will worry about the
Begin_ and End_ methods.
*/

class ATL_NO_VTABLE CChap10Demo :
    public CComObjectRootEx<CComSingleThreadModel>,
    public CComCoClass<CChap10Demo, &CLSID_Chap10Demo>,
    public IChap10Demo
{

/*
The server-side class doesn't even have to place the asynchronous
interface ID into its QueryInterface map. Again, that is handled on the
client side.
*/

BEGIN_COM_MAP(CChap10Demo)
    COM_INTERFACE_ENTRY(IChap10Demo)
END_COM_MAP()

// IChap10Demo
public:
    STDMETHOD(DoSomething)(/*[in]*/ long InputParm,
        /*[out, retval]*/ long *pOutputParm);

};
```

3. The server simply implements the synchronous interface as if it was being called synchronously. When the client calls Begin_, COM will allow the call to return to the client, then turn around and call the synchronous method on the server on another thread. From the server's point of view, the operation appears to be synchronous. The server doesn't know that the client isn't waiting around. In this example, the server waits for a number of seconds specified by the client. Thus:

```
STDMETHODIMP CChap10Demo::DoSomething(long InputParm,
    long *pOutputParm)
{

/*
Sleep for the number of seconds specified in the input parameter.
*/
    int i ;
    for (i = 0 ; i < InputParm ; i ++)
    {
      Sleep (1000) ;
    }

/*
Return the input parameter incremented by one, so the caller knows
that we have successfully done what he asked for.
*/

    *pOutputParm = InputParm + 1 ;
    return S_OK;
}
```

4. When the client needs the results from the server, it harvests them by calling the Finish_ method on the asynchronous interface that it got from the call object. This will return to the client the results generated by the server. The call object is useless after harvesting the results. Any subsequent calls to the Finish_ method will fail, so you might as well release it now.

If the client calls Finish_ before the server has returned its results, the call will block until the server does return the results. So the client will call the Finish_ method when it has reached the point where it can no longer proceed without them (you've finished all your other errands in the shopping center, but you can't drive home until your dry cleaning is done). Thus:

```
/*
User clicked the "Finish" button.
*/

void CClientDlg::OnButton4()
{

/*
Attempt to harvest the result of the method call by calling the
"Finish_" version of the desired method of the asynchronous interface.
This call will block until the results are ready.
*/


    long l = g_pAsyncIChap10Demo->Finish_DoSomething ( ) ;
    SetDlgItemInt (IDC_EDIT2, l) ;

/*
Release the call object.
*/

    g_pAsyncIChap10Demo = NULL ;
}
```

5. The client can, without blocking, check whether or not the server has returned the results of the asynchronous call. The client will do this if it still has other things that it can do while waiting for the results of the asynchronous call (other errands in the shopping center while waiting for your dry cleaning). When the server returns, the operating system will signal a synchronization event contained within the call object. The client accesses this event via the **ISynchronize** interface. The sample code queries for this interface and calls its **Wait( )** method. A return value of S_OK indicates that the server has finished the operation, the results are waiting inside the call object, and a call to the Finish_ method will return immediately. A return value of RPC_S_CALLPENDING means that the server has not yet finished its work, that the call object does not yet contain the results, and that a call to the Finish_ method will block until the server actually is finished. Thus:

```
/*
User clicked the "Poll" button. Check to see whether the server has
completed the call or not.
*/

void CClientDlg::OnButton6()
{
    HRESULT hr ;

/*
Query the call object for the ISynchronize interface.
*/
    ISynchronizePtr pSynch ;
    g_pAsyncIChap10Demo->QueryInterface (IID_ISynchronize,
      (void **)&pSynch) ;

/*
Call ISynchronize::Wait with immediate return.
*/

    hr = pSynch->Wait (
      COWAIT_WAITALL,            // events to wait for, here all of them
      0) ;                       // timeout interval in milliseconds

/*
If return code is S_OK, it means that the wait has cleared. If it's
RPC_S_CALLPENDING, then the call hasn't completed yet.
*/

    if (hr == S_OK)
    {
      AfxMessageBox ("Call finished") ;
    }
    else if (hr == RPC_S_CALLPENDING)
    {
      AfxMessageBox ("Call still pending") ;
    }
    else
    {
      AfxMessageBox ("Wait error") ;
    }
}
```

6. The longer the time the asynchronous method takes to complete, the more likely it is that the client will change its mind and decide it would rather cancel the call. (How long do you wait on hold for an airline reservation clerk?) Canceling calls is supported by the operating system. The client signals the server that it wants to cancel the call via the method **ICancelMethodCalls::Cancel( )**, as shown below.

It is important to note that this is merely a signal to the server. As shown on the next page, it sets a flag in the server's context, which the server can examine when and if it feels like it, and then take whatever action it feels like whenever it feels like it, or completely ignore the client if it wants to. It is still up to the client to check when the call completes. Thus:

```
void CClientDlg::OnButton3()
{

/*
Query the call object for the ICancelMethodCalls interface.
*/

    ICancelMethodCallsPtr pCancel ;
    g_pAsyncIChap10Demo->QueryInterface (IID_ICancelMethodCalls,
      (void **)&pCancel) ;

/*
Call the ICancelMethodCalls::Cancel method to send the cancellation
request to the server. Pray that the server is watching for it and will
obey.
*/

    pCancel->Cancel (0) ;

}
```

7. On the server side, the server's call context, available via the function **CoGetCallContext( )**, supports the ICancelMethodCalls interface. The method **TestCancel( )** will tell the server whether or not the client has requested a cancellation. The server can return the error code RPC_E_CALL_CANCELED, which the client will receive in its Finish_ method. The client will thus know that its cancellation request has been received and honored, and that it shouldn't rely on any of the output. Thus:

```
STDMETHODIMP CChap10Demo::DoSomething(long InputParm,
    long *pOutputParm)
{

/*
Get our call context for checking whether or not there has been a
cancel request.
*/

    ICancelMethodCallsPtr pCancel ;
    HRESULT hr = CoGetCallContext (IID_ICancelMethodCalls,
      (void **) &pCancel) ;

/*
Sleep for the number of seconds specified in the input parameter,
pausing every second to see if we are supposed to cancel.
*/
    int i ;
    for (i = 0 ; i < InputParm ; i ++)
    {
      Sleep (1000) ;

      if (pCancel->TestCancel ( ) == RPC_E_CALL_CANCELED)
      {
            MessageBox (NULL, "Cancel detected by server", "", 0) ;
            return RPC_E_CALL_CANCELED ;
      }
    }

/*
Return the input parameter incremented by one, so the caller knows
that we have successfully done what he asked for.
*/

    *pOutputParm = InputParm + 1 ;
    return S_OK;
}
```

D. CALLBACKS FOR COMPLETION

1. The previous example shows polling for completion. Polling is often a bad idea because the client wastes a lot of time saying "Are you done yet?", and the server wastes a lot of time saying "No, I'm not". Even though these are handled at the call object level, it's still a waste of time. Sometimes we'd rather be notified, essentially have the dry cleaner beep us when the clothes are finished (you see this more with perishable items such as restaurant tables than with non-perishable items such as dry cleaning). We would really like asynchronous COM to support some sort of callback notification, and it does.

In the previous example, the client polled for completion by using the ISynchronize interface provided by the standard proxy. If we want to be notified of completion by means of a callback, we have to provide our own implementation of the ISynchronize interface. We then have to aggregate that in with the call object in place of the COM-provided ISynchronize interface. The code to do it is shown on the facing page.

The ISynchronize interface only has three methods, and they are relatively simple. I've just put in message boxes so you can see when they get hit. You will find that the operating system will call Reset( ) immediately when you create the call, and Signal( ) method when the server finishes its work and returns the results. It's really not hard to set up at all. Thus:

```
class ATL_NO_VTABLE CSynchronizeDemo :
    public CComObjectRootEx<CComSingleThreadModel>,
    public CComCoClass<CSynchronizeDemo, &CLSID_SynchronizeDemo>,
    public ISynchronize
{
    <omitted>

    virtual HRESULT STDMETHODCALLTYPE Wait (DWORD dwFlags,
      DWORD dwMilliseconds) ;
    virtual HRESULT STDMETHODCALLTYPE Signal (void) ;
    virtual HRESULT STDMETHODCALLTYPE Reset (void) ;

} ;

HRESULT STDMETHODCALLTYPE CSynchronizeDemo::Wait (DWORD dwFlags,
    DWORD dwMilliseconds)
{
    MessageBox (NULL, "Wait Hit", "", 0) ;
    return S_OK ;
}

HRESULT STDMETHODCALLTYPE CSynchronizeDemo::Signal (void)
{
    MessageBox (NULL, "Signal Hit", "", 0) ;
    return S_OK ;
}

HRESULT STDMETHODCALLTYPE CSynchronizeDemo::Reset (void)
{
    MessageBox (NULL, "Reset Hit", "", 0) ;
    return S_OK ;
}
```

```
void CClientDlg::OnButton7()
{

/*
Query the proxy for the ICallFactory interface.
*/

    ICallFactoryPtr pCallFactory ;
    g_pObject->QueryInterface (IID_ICallFactory,
      (void **) &pCallFactory) ;

/*
Instantiate  an   object   of   our   own   design   that   implements   the
ISynchronize interface.
*/

    IUnknownPtr pSynch = new CComObject <CSynchronizeDemo> ( )   ;

/*
Call  the  method  ICallFactory::CreateCall  to  create  the  call  object,
requesting  the  asynchronous  version  of  the  desired   interface. Supply
our  own  implementation  of  the  ISynchronize  interface  to  be  aggregated
in.
*/

    IUnknownPtr * pUnk ;

    pCallFactory->CreateCall (
      __uuidof (AsyncIChap10Demo),   // ID of asynchronous interface
      pSynch,                        // outer aggregate
      IID_IUnknown,                  // interface wanted on call object
      (IUnknown **) &pUnk) ;         // output pointer

/*
Query  the  call  object  for  the  asynchronous  interface. We couldn't ask
for  it  directly  in  the  previous  call  because  creating  an  object  with
aggregation  requires  us  to  ask  for  the  IUnknown  interface.
*/

    pUnk->QueryInterface (__uuidof (AsyncIChap10Demo),
      (void**) &g_pAsyncIChap10Demo) ;

/*
Call the "Begin_" version of the desired method on the
asynchronous interface.
*/

    g_pAsyncIChap10Demo->Begin_DoSomething (GetDlgItemInt (IDC_EDIT1));
}
```

Lab Exercises
Chapter 10
Asynchronous COM

Directory: \EssenceOfCOM\chap10\data1\templ

1. Register the DLL "AsyncDemoDll.Dll" using RegSvr32.

2. Run the client program \client\client.exe. The sample app will appear. Click "Create Object" to create an object supporting a sample asynchronous interface. The buttons will then offer the choices of operations to exercise the functions discussed in the chapter.

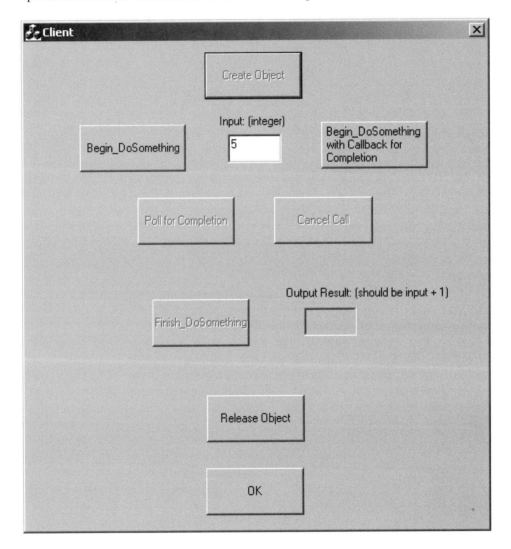

Chapter 11

COM Support in Visual C++

A. SMART POINTERS

1. One of the biggest problems in COM is getting the reference count right. You spend an awful lot of your debugging time tracking down nasty and hard-to-reproduce bugs that invariably turn out to be caused by an extra or missing call to AddRef( ) or Release( ). With the release of VC++ 5, Microsoft added a new C++ wrapper class to automate reference counting or at least make it consistent. The class is called **_com_ptr_t**. It contains a member variable called `m_pInterface`, which represents a raw interface pointer (the type used throughout this book). The idea is that you will no longer call AddRef( ) or Release( ) directly. Instead, the class contains overloaded methods and operators which call AddRef( ) and Release( ) on the internal pointer in a consistent and (relatively) logical manner, thereby preventing you from forgetting. For example, the destructor of this class automatically calls Release( ) on the internal interface pointer if it is non-NULL when the outer wrapper is destructed.

The facing page shows the Clipboard sample program from Chapter 1 rewritten to use smart pointers. The sample code may be found in the directory \Chap11\SmartPtrData1. First, you must include the system header file **<comdef.h>,** which defines smart pointer classes for all standard interfaces, and also provides the templates used for defining your smart pointer classes for your own interfaces. The name of the smart pointer class is the name of the interface with the characters "Ptr" added to the end. You generally use these classes instead of using _com_ptr_t directly. Remember, IDataObject is a binary, language-independent interface specification. IDataObjectPtr is a convenient, Microsoft C++ specific utility wrapper class. In this case, instead of a dumb pointer LPDATAOBJECT or IDataObject*, we instantiate on the stack a smart pointer of the class **IDataObjectPtr**, which wraps an internal pointer to an IDataObject interface.

WARNING: Nothing will screw your project up faster or worse than using dumb pointers in some places and smart ones in others. Pick ONE model and follow it throughout your entire app, better yet, your entire company, no matter what.

When we call OleGetClipboard( ), we use the & operator to pass the address of the IDataObjectPtr. The _com_ptr_t base class overloads this operator to return the address of the internal interface pointer m_pInterface. In this way, OLE returns the clipboard data object pointer straight into the wrapper. The wrapper does not AddRef( ) the pointer in this case because it knows that, since this operator is used for obtaining interface pointers returned from functions, the AddRef( ) should have already been done before the function returns.

When we compare the IDataObjectPtr to NULL, we use the == operator. This, too, has been overloaded to operate on the inner interface pointer. We then call QueryGetData( ) using the arrow operator, which has also been overloaded to operate on the inner interface pointer.

Finally, the IDataObjectPtr goes out of scope and its destructor is called. When using dumb pointers, we had to remember to release it ourselves, first checking for NULL. The smart pointer contains this functionality prefabricated inside its destructor, so we don't call Release( ). If you forget and in fact do call Release( ) on the smart pointer, you will have one too many calls to Release( ) and the destructor will crash.

NOTE: The ATL has its own version of smart pointers, based on a class called CComPtr. They are conceptually very similar, and differ from the native VC smart pointers only on fine points of syntax. I won't bother describing them separately; they work in pretty much the same way.

```c
#include <comdef.h>

case WM_INITMENU:
{

/*
Get a data object pointer to the current Clipboard contents. Assign it
into a smart pointer. The & operator is overloaded so as to assign the
raw pointer returned by the function directly into the smart pointer's
m_pInterface variable. Smart pointer does not AddRef( ) it because it
knows that as the return value from a function, it already has been.
*/
    IDataObjectPtr lpd ;
    HRESULT hr ;

    hr = OleGetClipboard (&lpd) ;

/*
Fill out a FORMATETC structure.
*/

    FORMATETC fe ;

    fe.cfFormat = CF_TEXT ;
    fe.ptd = NULL ;
    fe.tymed = TYMED_HGLOBAL ;
    fe.dwAspect = DVASPECT_CONTENT ;
    fe.lindex = -1 ;

/*
Smart pointer overloads the == operator to compare directly to its
internal interface pointer m_pInterface, so the test for NULL works
correctly. It also overloads the -> operator so the call to
QueryGetData is made correctly from the internal interface pointer.
*/
    if (lpd == NULL ||  lpd->QueryGetData (&fe) != S_OK)
    {
      EnableMenuItem ((HMENU)wParam, ID_DEMO_PASTETEXT, MF_GRAYED) ;
    }
    else
    {
      EnableMenuItem ((HMENU)wParam, ID_DEMO_PASTETEXT, MF_ENABLED) ;
    }

/*
Smart pointer releases Clipboard data object in its destructor when it
goes out of scope. Don't you do it, or you'll have one too many and
crash.
*/

    return 0 ;
}
```

2. What happens with smart pointers that don't live on the stack? Suppose in the same example we rewrote our drop target class to use a smart pointer. Thus:

```
class CDropTarget : public IDropTarget
{

    protected:
      ULONG             m_RefCount ;
      IDataObjectPtr    m_pIDataSource ;

    <rest of class definition>
};
```

3. Our DragEnter( ) method would be similar, except that we would not call AddRef( ) on the source IDataObject pointer when we saved a copy of it. The smart pointer class overloads the = operator to do that for us automatically if the pointer is not NULL. It will also automatically release any previous pointer it might have held. Thus:

```
 STDMETHODIMP CDropTarget::DragEnter(LPDATAOBJECT pIDataSource,
    DWORD grfKeyState, POINTL pt, LPDWORD pdwEffect)
{
/*
Check to see if the data is in a format we can handle (in this case,
only text).  If so, keep a copy of the data object pointer and add to
its reference count.
*/
    FORMATETC fe ;
    < fill out FORMATETC>

    if (pIDataSource->QueryGetData (&fe) == S_OK)
    {
/*
Smart pointer automatically does an AddRef( ) in its assignment. It
also releases any previous object that might have been held (in this
case, there shouldn't be one).
*/
      m_pIDataSource = pIDataSource ;
    }
    else
    {
/*
This sets the internal interface pointer to NULL, which is the result
that we want.
*/
      m_pIDataSource = NULL ;
    }
/*
Call our own DragOver( ) method to set the effect code.
*/
    DragOver(grfKeyState, pt, pdwEffect) ;
    return S_OK ;
}
```

4. When we are finished with the data object pointer, we cause the smart pointer to release it by assigning the smart pointer the value of NULL. Thus:

```
STDMETHODIMP CDropTarget::Drop(LPDATAOBJECT pIDataSource,
    DWORD grfKeyState, POINTL pt, LPDWORD pdwEffect)
{
    if (m_pIDataSource != NULL) // != operator overloaded by smart ptr
    {
/*
Get point on screen where data was dropped.  Convert to client
coordinates, store in global variables xText and yText, which will
cause main window to display the text where it was dropped.
*/

        <code omitted>
/*
Fetch text from data object and display it.
*/

        STGMEDIUM stg ; FORMATETC fe ;
        <code omitted>

        m_pIDataSource->GetData (&fe, &stg) ;


/*
Copy data into string for display in main window and Invalidate to
cause a repaint.
*/
        <code omitted>

/*
Release storage medium. This isn't a smart pointer, in fact it isn't
any type of COM object, so we have to do it ourselves.
*/

        ReleaseStgMedium (&stg) ;

/*
Smart pointer releases internal pointer when its value is set to NULL.
*/
        m_pIDataSource = NULL ;

    }

/*
Call our own DragOver( ) method to set the effect code.
*/

    DragOver(grfKeyState, pt, pdwEffect) ;
    return S_OK;
}
```

5. Smart pointers are especially useful when your app uses exception handling. When a function throws an exception which is caught higher up the stack, any pointers on the stack are discarded when the stack is unwound, possibly leaking away objects. With smart pointers, the objects are released when their pointers are discarded. Thus:

```
/*
This top-level function calls a middle function from within a try-catch
block.
*/

TopFunc ( )
{
    try
    {
      MiddleFunc ( ) ;
    }
    catch (CSomeException)
    {
      HandleException ( ) ;
    }
}

/*
The middle function gets a data object from the Clipboard and stores it
in a dumb pointer. It then calls the deepest function.
*/

void MiddleFunc ( )
{
    IDataObject lpd ;
    OleGetClipboard (&lpd) ;
    DeepestFunc ( ) ;
    if (lpd) lpd->Release ( ) ;
}

/*
The deepest function does some work and throws an exception to be
caught by the top function, causing the stack to be unwound. If
MiddleFunc( ) above uses a dumb pointer as shown, the object to which
it points will be leaked away as the stack is unwound, because the dumb
pointer doesn't know to call Release( ). If MiddleFunc( ) had used a
smart pointer instead, the smart pointer's destructor would have
released the Clipboard data object when the smart pointer got discarded
during the stack unwinding.
*/

DeepestFunc ( )
{
    if (DoSomeWork())
    {
      throw new CSomeException ;
    }
}
```

6. As always, there's one place where the magic bullet doesn't work. When you write a function or method that returns a pointer to an object, such as OleGetClipboard( ) or QueryInterface( ), the rules require you to AddRef( ) the pointer before the function returns. The smart pointer class is not smart enough to detect this situation and automatically AddRef( ) the pointer being returned. You must call it manually.

You'd like smart pointers to free you from ever having to think about reference counts, but they don't, so now you have to think about when you need to think about them and when you don't. Thus:

```
IDataObjectPtr pMyDataObject ;

HRESULT CSomeObject::QueryInterface(REFIID riid, LPVOID *ppv)
{

/*
Caller  is  asking  for  the  IDataObject  interface,  which  I  keep  in  a
separate pointer for this example.
*/

    if (riid == IID_IDataObject)
    {

/*
Give  caller  a  pointer  to  the  IDataObject  interface.  The  smart  pointer
knows that the = operator means to give back the raw internal pointer.
*/
        *ppv = pMyDataObject ;

/*
Since  this  pointer  is  being  returned  from  an  interface  method,  the
rules  require  that  its  AddRef( )  be  called.  The  smart  pointer  is  not
smart  enough  to  differentiate  the  situation  where  its  value  is  being
returned,  as  here,  which  requires  an  AddRef( ),  from  that  where  it  is
simply  being  examined,  which  wouldn't.  Therefore  we  must  manually  call
AddRef( ) on the smart pointer.
*/

        pMyDataObject->AddRef( ) ;

        return S_OK ;
    }

    <rest of QueryInterface( )>
}
```

7. Writing a smart pointer class for your own interfaces is trivially easy. You simply use the macro **_COM_SMARTPTR_TYPEDEF**, plugging in your interface name and IID. Thus:

```
_COM_SMARTPTR_TYPEDEF(IFoo, IID_IFoo);
```

When all the substitutions and expansions take place, this comes out to be:

```
typedef _com_ptr_t <com_IIID <Interface, &IID>> Interface IFooPtr
```

And you simply use it, thus:

```
IFooPtr pFoo ;
```

This page intentionally contains no text other than this sentence.

B. WRAPPER CLASSES USING TYPE LIBRARIES FOR C++ CLIENTS

1. One of the cooler features added to VC++ in version 5 was its ability to automatically generate C++ wrapper classes for a dispinterface based on the dispinterface's description in a type library. The preprocessor now automatically translates the language-independent object and interface definitions in a type library into C++ classes that you can use directly. As always, you need to have an accurate type library at compile time. The example shown in this section uses this feature to generate a class that replaces the CHelloDriver wrapper class that we wrote manually in the previous chapter. The source code may be found in the directory "\EssenceOfCom\chap11\typelibhellodrv".

To import a type library, you use the new Microsoft-specific preprocessor directive **#import**, specifying the type library file that you want to import. This causes the compiler to read the specified type library, generate C++ language header files based on its contents, and include those header files in the C++ source file. The new header files are stored in the project's output file directory (such as \Debug or \Release), and regenerated whenever the type library changes.

The wrapper class generated by this directive is based on the new standard C++ class **_com_ptr_t**, also known as a "smart com pointer," described in the previous section of this chapter. Looking back at the sample IDispatch shown in the previous chapter, you will see that it contains a dispinterface named "IDHello". When you import the type library, the preprocessor will use the _com_ptr_t class to create a wrapper class based on this dispinterface. The name of this class is always the name of the dispinterface with the characters "Ptr" appended to it, in this case "**IDHelloPtr**".

The imported class is by default placed into its own C++ namespace, which has the name specified in the "library" attribute of the type library. This was done to avoid possible name conflicts with your existing C++ code, but I find it more confusing than helpful. To turn this feature off, add the keyword **no_namespace** to the #import directive as shown on the facing page. If I had not done this, I would have to refer to my IDHello pointer by its full namespace name, "hello32::IDHelloPtr".

As in the original example, simply instantiating the pointer does not create the server object to which it refers. This requires a separate method, **CreateInstance( )**, which belongs to the class _com_ptr_t. Internally this calls CoCreateInstance( ) and assigns the resulting pointer to the smart pointer. The directive **__uuidof( )** returns the class ID of the HelloApplication object, which you will also see in the generated wrapper class. Thus:

```
/*
Tell the preprocessor to read in this type library and generate a
wrapper class based on it.
*/

#import "hello32.tlb" no_namespace

/*
This is the smart pointer class, based on com_ptr_t that wraps the
IDHello dispinterface specified in the type library.
*/

IDHelloPtr pHello ;

extern BOOL CALLBACK HelloDlgProc (HWND, UINT, WPARAM, LPARAM) ;


int WINAPI WinMain(HINSTANCE hInst, HINSTANCE hPrevInstance,
    LPSTR lpCmdLine, int nCmdShow)
{
    MSG msg ;
    OleInitialize (NULL) ;

/*
Create the driver object based on COM's smart pointer classes generated
by the #import directive.
*/


    HRESULT hr = pHello.CreateInstance (__uuidof(HelloApplication)) ;

    if (hr != S_OK)
    {
      char out [256] ;
      wsprintf (out, "Couldn't create object, hr == 0x%x", hr) ;
      MessageBox (NULL, out, "", 0) ;
    }

/*
Pop up dialog box giving user interface to automation object. This
function returns when the user clicks "Exit".
*/

    DialogBox (hInst, MAKEINTRESOURCE(IDD_DIALOG1), NULL, (FARPROC)
      HelloDlgProc) ;

    OleUninitialize ( ) ;

    return msg.wParam;
}
```

2. The file "hello32.tlh" is the main type library header generated by the preprocessor in response to the #import directive. It contains C++ specific classes based on the language-independent information provided by the type library. Here you will find the C++ declaration of the wrapper class for the dispinterface IDHello. The new C++ keyword **__declspec(uuid)** attaches a uuid to a structure which you can read later with the __uuidof() directive as shown on the previous page. Simplified and commented for clarity, the C++ files look like this:

```
// C++ source equivalent of Win32 type library hello32.tlb
// compiler-generated file created 06/21/97 at 10:06:17 - DO NOT EDIT!

#include <comdef.h>

// Forward references and typedefs

struct __declspec(uuid("6ced2902-a1dd-11cf-8a33-00aa00a58097"))
    IDHello;

// Smart pointer typedef declarations. This line actually generates the
// IDHelloPtr class from com_ptr_t

_COM_SMARTPTR_TYPEDEF(IDHello, __uuidof(IDispatch));

// Type library items

struct __declspec(uuid("6ced2902-a1dd-11cf-8a33-00aa00a58097"))
IDHello : IDispatch
{
    // Properties

    __declspec(property(get=GetHelloMessage,put=PutHelloMessage))
    _bstr_t HelloMessage;

    // Methods:

    HRESULT SayHello ( );

    // Property accessor functions

    _bstr_t GetHelloMessage ( );
    void PutHelloMessage ( _bstr_t _val );
};

struct __declspec(uuid("6ced2900-a1dd-11cf-8a33-00aa00a58097"))
    HelloApplication;

// Wrapper method implementations

#include "Debug/hello32.tli"
```

3. The file "hello32.tli" contains the type library implementations for the wrapper class's methods and properties. It uses the new library functions **_com_dispatch_method( )**, **_com_dispatch_propget( )**, and **_com_dispatch_propput( )** to handle the standard cases of accessing properties and methods through an IDispatch interface. Thus:

```
//
// Wrapper implementations for Win32 type library hello32.tlb
// compiler-generated file created 06/21/97 at 10:06:17 - DO NOT EDIT!

//
// dispinterface IDHello wrapper method implementations
//

inline HRESULT IDHello::SayHello ( )
{
    return _com_dispatch_method(this, 0x2, DISPATCH_METHOD, VT_EMPTY,
      NULL, NULL);
}

inline _bstr_t IDHello::GetHelloMessage ( )
{
    BSTR _result;
    _com_dispatch_propget(this, 0x1, VT_BSTR, (void*)&_result);
    return _bstr_t(_result, false);
}

inline void IDHello::PutHelloMessage ( _bstr_t _val )
{
    _com_dispatch_propput(this, 0x1, VT_BSTR, (BSTR)_val);
}
```

4. The dialog box response function shown below has been modified to use the smart pointer wrapper class. Remember that the _com_ptr_t object is itself a C++ object that contains a pointer to the COM interface as a member variable. To access this COM interface pointer, you must use the overloaded arrow operator as shown; not the dot operator used in the CreateInstance( ) method a few pages ago. Thus:

```
#import "hello32.tlb" no_namespace
extern IDHelloPtr pHello ;

BOOL WINAPI HelloDlgProc (HWND hDlg, UINT msg, WPARAM wParam,
    LPARAM lParam)
{

    switch (msg)
    {
      case WM_COMMAND:
      {
            switch (LOWORD(wParam))
            {
/*
User clicked "Say Hello" button.   Call driver object's SayHello( )
method,  which uses the IDispatch interface to control the server's
automation object and invoke its "SayHello( )" method.
*/
                case ID_SAYHELLO:
                {
                        pHello->SayHello( ) ;
                        return TRUE ;
                }
```

5. The native compiler support also extends to VTBL interfaces. VC++ will generate a wrapper class that provides data passing and error handling that makes a COM object look and feel more like a native C++ object. Suppose I have a raw interface method defined thus:

```
HRESULT ICatalogCollection::get_Item(long lIndex, IDispatch** pDisp);
```

When I #import it in VC++, the wrapper class will pass the necessary output pointer to the function and return the output data as the return value of the function call. It will also check the result code and throw a C++ exception if it fails. Thus:

```
inline IDispatchPtr ICatalogCollection::GetItem ( long lIndex )
{

/*
Make call to raw interface, passing output variable.
*/

    IDispatch * _result;
    HRESULT _hr = get_Item(lIndex, &_result);

/*
Check for error. If found, throw C++ exception.
*/

    if (FAILED(_hr)) _com_issue_errorex(_hr, this, __uuidof(this));

/*
Return output data as return value of this function.
*/
    return IDispatchPtr(_result, false);
}
```

The client uses it as shown below. The **_com_error** object is another native VC class, containing any error information that might have been made available by the object. It encapsulates checking for the ISupportErrorInfo interface. Thus:

```
COMAdmin::ICatalogObjectPtr NewApp ;

try
{
    NewApp = Apps->GetItem (i) ;
}
catch ( _com_error &e)
{
    <handle error>
}
```

C. BSTR Support

1. All automation-compatible COM interfaces must use the data type BSTR to handle strings. That's over ¾ of all COM interfaces, and many of the others do it anyway for consistency. A BSTR is a string data type that is length prefixed, NULL terminated, and contains Unicode characters. You create a BSTR using the API function SysAllocString( ), and delete them using the API function SysFreeString( ).

Using these functions is a pain. We'd really like a C++ class wrapper class that made them easier to use and harder to get wrong. Microsoft provided that with the native VC++ class **_bstr_t**, which encapsulates the functionality of a BSTR into an intelligent class. For example, the =, +, and cast operators have been overloaded so as to work smoothly and logically. Thus:

```
/*
User    clicked    "Get    String"    button.      Call    wrapper    object's
GetHelloMessage() method, which uses the IDispatch interface to read
the value of the server object's "HelloMessage" property.
*/
                case ID_GETSTRING:
                {
                        _bstr_t bstrHello = pHello->GetHelloMessage ();
/*
The (char *) cast operator of the _bstr_t class automatically performs
conversion from the BSTR's native Unicode to ANSI.
*/
                        SetDlgItemText (hDlg, IDC_EDIT1,
                            (char *) bstrHello);
/*
BSTR's memory freed when it goes out of scope.
*/
                        return TRUE;
                }
/*
User clicked "Set String" button. Fetch the desired string from the
edit control where the user has typed it. Assigning it to the _bstr_t
object automatically converts it to BSTR. Call driver object's
SetHelloMessage( ) method.
*/
                case ID_SETSTRING:
                {
                    char out [128] ;
                    GetDlgItemText(hDlg,IDC_EDIT2, out,sizeof(out));
/*
Assigning ANSI string to the _bstr_t class invokes the overloaded =
operator that automatically converts it into Unicode.
*/
                        _bstr_t bstrHello  = out ;
                        pHello->PutHelloMessage (bstrHello) ;
                        return TRUE ;
                }
            }
            return FALSE ;
}       }
```

2. Another wrapper class for BSTRs is provided by the public class **CComBSTR**. Although packaged with the ATL, this class is available to any program written in VC++. The usual assignment operators have been overridden, making it very easy to use. I find it more convenient than _bstr_t when dealing with API functions that produce BSTRs as output by means of parameter list pointers. You can pass a pointer to a CComBSTR, which you can't do with a _bstr_t. The only drawback to this class is that the cast operator is not overridden as it is with a _bstr_t; instead you have to use the W2A macro to convert it to ANSI as described in the next section of this chapter. Thus:

```
/*
Get name of coclass, make it the title of the dialog box. This method
returns a raw BSTR by means of the parameter list. Assign it into a
CComBSTR.
*/

    CComBSTR CoclassName ;
    m_pTypeInfo->GetDocumentation (-1, &CoclassName, NULL, NULL, NULL);

/*
Create a new CComBSTR with our title prefix in it.
*/

    CComBSTR DlgTitle ("CoClass: ") ;

/*
Use the CComBSTR's intelligent += operator to concatenate another
string onto the end of ours.
*/

    DlgTitle += CoclassName ;

/*
Set the string into the UI. We need to use the W2A macro (see next
section of this chapter) to convert its Unicode into the ANSI required
by our UI.
*/

    SetWindowText (W2A(DlgTitle)) ;
```

D. ANSI – Unicode Conversion

1. You will by now have noticed that every string parameter to every COM API function or interface method that isn't a BSTR is defined as the type LPOLESTR, or pointer to OLECHAR. For example:

```
CLSIDFromProgID (LPCOLESTR pStr, LPCLSID pClsid);
```

Or

```
IDispatch::GetIDsOfNames( REFIID riid, OLECHAR** pNames, ...
```

Back in the 16-bit world (remember that?), this data type resolved to a string of 8-bit ANSI characters, of type char in C++, so you could ignore the entire issue. But in the 32-bit world, an OLECHAR is a 16-bit character, of C++ type WCHAR, using the Unicode character set, and an OLESTR is a null-terminated string of such 16-bit characters. For anyone who has to provide Far Eastern character sets and doesn't mind restricting himself to Windows NT, Unicode is a fantastic advantage. For anyone who doesn't care about non-Western character sets or who needs to support Windows 95 or 98, it's nothing but trouble. For a complete discussion of exactly what Unicode is and how it works, see *Advanced Windows NT* by Jeffrey Richter (Microsoft Press).

Regardless of your philosophy, COM demands to be fed Unicode, so if we want to make a COM app run, that's what we have to feed it. The easiest solution is to build your app to be Unicode-only. It's quite simple to do, you just #define the constant **UNICODE** in your system header files. This was done on some of the more involved sample apps, such as the Eliza local server in Chapter 3. Windows NT uses Unicode internally, and your app will actually run slightly faster if you do this. But Windows 95 and 98 do not speak Unicode other than in the COM API, so your Unicode app will not run on it at all. Very few markets, and no large ones, are willing to restrict themselves to NT at the time of this writing. Too bad.

The one exception to this, emerging at the time of this writing, is COM components used as middleware in three-tier systems running under Microsoft Transaction Server or COM+. Since these runtime environments run only on NT 4.0 and Windows 2000 respectively, writing Unicode-only components for them is probably the best approach.

2. In the absence of a Unicode app, you have to handle all strings on a case-by-case basis. In places where strings are hardwired into code, prepending the capital letter 'L' (as in Long) onto a string causes the compiler to make it Unicode, even if the app around it isn't. Thus:

```
case ID_DATAOBJECT_CREATEDLL:
{
    HRESULT hr ;

/*
Read class ID from registry key. Must pass a Unicode string to this
function, so prepend 'L' to the string.
*/

    CLSID clsid ;
    hr = CLSIDFromProgID (L"EssenceofOLE.Data3", &clsid) ;

/*
Create object based on class ID read from registry.
*/

    hr = CoCreateInstance (clsid, ...) ;

    <rest of creation case>
}
```

3. The operating system provides functions for run-time conversion of strings to and from Unicode. The API function **MultiByteToWideChar( )** takes an ANSI string and produces Unicode output. You'll need to do something like this when you get an ANSI string from a user and need to pass it to COM. Thus:

```
char out [256] ; WCHAR wout [80] ;

MultiByteToWideChar (CP_ACP,    // code page
        0,                      // flags
        out,                    // ANSI string to convert
        -1,                     // string is null-terminated
        wout,                   // output buffer for Unicode string
        sizeof(wout)) ;         // max # of characters to convert

<rest of code omitted>
```

When a string comes in to one of your object's methods, it is always in Unicode. To use it in a non-Unicode app, you will have to convert it to ANSI via the API function **WideCharToMultiByte( )**. Thus:

```
STDMETHODIMP CFileTextData::GetObject(LPOLESTR pWideItemName,
    DWORD dwSpeed, LPBINDCTX pbc, REFIID riid, VOID **ppv)
{

    HRESULT hr ;
    char ItemName [256] ;

/*
Convert item name from wide to the ANSI that we use internally.
*/

    WideCharToMultiByte (CP_ACP,    // code page
            0,                      // flags
            pWideItemName,          // Unicode char string to convert
            -1,                     // string is null-terminated
            ItemName,               // output buffer for ANSI string
            sizeof(ItemName),       // size of buffer
            NULL, NULL) ;           // not used

    <rest of function>
```

4. You look at this and say, "What a pain. Do I really have to write that entire function call every time I want to convert a string? It's enough to drive a geek to – gulp – VB!" Fortunately not. VC++ provides several macros that can perform the conversion inline. In the following example we need to pass a Unicode string to the COM API function CreateURLMoniker( ). The macro **A2W( )** performs this conversion in place for us. The macro **W2A( )** performs the opposite conversion (not shown). Both macros require that you include the macro **USES_CONVERSION** within the scope of their functions. All of these macros are defined in the header file "**afxpriv.h**", which must be included as well. Thus:

```
#include <afxpriv.h>

void CUrlmonikerDlg::OnBind()
{
    char name [256] ;
    HRESULT hr ;

/*
Get name from combo box control. It is in ANSI characters.
*/

    m_URLCombo.GetWindowText (name, sizeof(name)) ;


/*
Use name to create an URL moniker. Store moniker in a member variable.
This function, as do all OLE functions, requires a wide character
string.  The macro A2W( ) is an MFC macro that performs this
conversion.  The macro USES_CONVERSION must be inserted prior to it as
shown.
*/

    USES_CONVERSION ;
    hr = CreateURLMoniker (NULL, A2W(name), &m_pUrlMoniker) ;

    <remainder of code omitted>
```

Lab Exercises
Chapter 11
COM Support in VC++

Directory: \EssenceOfCOM\chap11\smartptrdata1\done

1. Run the sample program smartptrdata1.exe. It handles the Clipboard and drag-and-drop operations in the same manner as the data1.exe sample in Chapter 1. The source code demonstrates the ease of programming with smart pointers.

Directory: \EssenceOfCOM\chap11\typelibhellodrv\done

2. Register the automation sample program from Chapter 4. Run the sample client program typelibhellodrv.exe. The sample automation server will appear. The client program provides access to the single method and single property supported by the server. The source code demonstrates the ease of programming automation wrapper classes with type libraries.

Chapter 12

Active Template Library (ATL)

This page intentionally contains no text other than this sentence.

A. Concepts and Definitions

1. The *Active Template Library* (ATL) is a set of C++ code, written by Microsoft and shipped with Visual C++, that provides prefabricated implementations of the basic COM infrastructure that most COM object servers require. These features include an implementation of IUnknown and IDispatch interfaces, class factories, self-registration, and lifetime management. Using the ATL allows you to spend much less time writing COM packaging, and correspondingly more time on your business logic.

The ATL started gaining popularity when its version 2.1 shipped with Visual C++ version 5.0 in the spring of 1997. The only prefabricated COM functionality available until then resided in the MFC, into which it had been painfully shoehorned to support user interface features such as object linking and embedding. The architectural compromises necessary to cram an implementation of COM into the convoluted, user-interface-centered MFC framework made it difficult to use this implementation for standalone COM servers. For example, the MFC's implementation of IUnknown was built into its large CCmdTarget base class, which had been originally designed for handling window menu selections from human end users. Every MFC COM object had to carry around all of this base class's infrastructure in order to use the small piece of it that the object really cared about. In addition, major pieces of functionality required by many standalone COM servers didn't appear in the MFC at all. For example, object linking and embedding uses only standard interfaces, those for which the operating system contains a proxy-stub marshaler, so the MFC's implementation of COM did not include support for building IDL files that compiled into the proxy-stub marshaling DLLs required by new custom interfaces. The MFC's implementation of COM was fine for what the MFC needed it to do, but it didn't fit well outside that framework. It could be forced to serve, with effort, and many programmers did just that because no alternative then existed.

The ATL solved these problems by starting from a clean slate. Its designers thought only about providing COM-based functionality, not how to make a class factory and a toolbar live together in peace. They were also able to make use of certain features of the C++ language that Microsoft's C++ implementation did not support when the MFC was first emerging, such as templates and multiple inheritance. The result is the next step in the evolution of prefabricated COM code.

Which architecture do you choose for writing your COM servers? Basically, I've abandoned the MFC for COM. I would only recommend it when you need to add COM to an existing MFC app. I'd use the ATL everywhere else. It's simpler, it's cleaner, it's a more highly evolved organism. It's the primary reason that I removed any explanation of how to use the MFC from this edition of my book.

B. ATL OBJECT SERVERS

1. This section of the chapter demonstrates how to use the ATL to build the simplest server that I can think of, the same "Hello, World" server as we built in Chapter 4. The sample code can be found in the directory \EssenceOfCOM\Chap12\AtlHelloDll.

We first need to create an ATL server project. A server is an .EXE or a .DLL, and can contain more than one class of object. You create a project by selecting "File — New" from the main menu, selecting the "Projects" tab, and picking "ATL COM AppWizard". Thus:

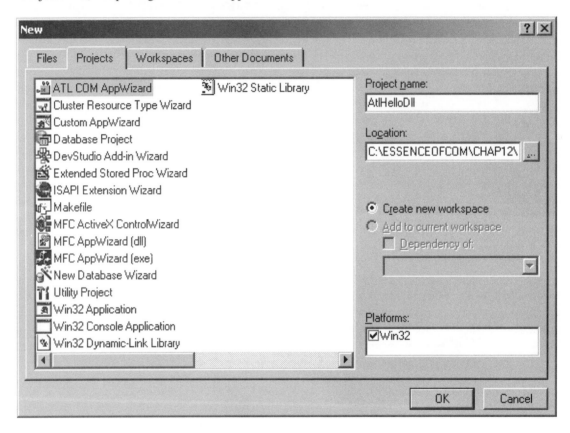

2. The ATL Wizard has only a single pane of questions, as shown below. About the only thing that it really needs to know is what type of project you want to build, a DLL, an .EXE, or a service (an .EXE automatically launched by the service control manager). The Wizard will generate code based on your choices as shown on the following pages. Thus:

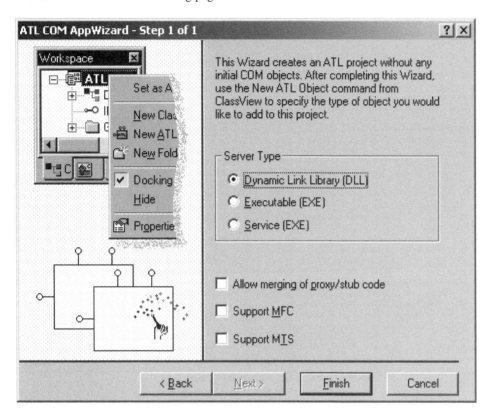

The "Allow merging of proxy/stub code" option appears when you select DLL. If your objects require marshalers, that is, if they do not use type library marshaling, you can choose either to have the marshaler live in the same DLL as the object itself (check the box) or a separate DLL (clear the box, as shown). The former is somewhat more convenient; there is only one file you need to remember to deploy to make your objects work. The latter is useful in distributed situations, where the marshaler needs to live on both client and server machines, but the actual object needs to live only on the server machine.

The "Support MFC" box exists to support whining crybabies who can't let go of their MFC CString class. Don't use it; it leads to logistical nightmares. Use the C++ STL library instead.

The "Support MTS" box is required if you are writing components that will use Microsoft Transaction Server functions, such as GetObjectContext( ), or interfaces, such as IObjectContext. It includes the necessary header files and link libraries to access these features. It only satisfies the requirements for MTS 2.0 and earlier. Anyone wanting to write code for COM+ will need to set up the relevant header files and link libraries himself.

3. The ATL COM Wizard creates a new VC++ project and the shell of a server without any COM objects inside it. The shell is represented by the ATL class **CComModule**, which is roughly analogous to the MFC class CWinApp. The server contains a single object of this class which is instantiated in the server's main file as shown below. Its name is always **_Module**. It contains methods to perform such .DLL-level or .EXE-level operations as incrementing or decrementing the global object count for locking or unlocking the server, registering or revoking class factories, and making or removing registry entries.

The Wizard also generates the four named functions that a COM server needs to expose to COM. These functions, and the use of the CComModule methods, are shown on the facing page. Thus:

```
#include "stdafx.h"
#include "resource.h"
#include <initguid.h>
#include "AtlHelloDll.h"

#include "AtlHelloDll_i.c"

/*
Instantiate the one and only _Module for this .EXE.
*/

CComModule _Module;

BEGIN_OBJECT_MAP(ObjectMap)
END_OBJECT_MAP()

//////////////////////////////////////////////////////////////////////
//////
// DLL Entry Point

extern "C"
BOOL   WINAPI   DllMain(HINSTANCE   hInstance,   DWORD   dwReason,   LPVOID
/*lpReserved*/)
{
    if (dwReason == DLL_PROCESS_ATTACH)
    {
        _Module.Init(ObjectMap, hInstance, &LIBID_ATLHELLODLLLib);
        DisableThreadLibraryCalls(hInstance);
    }
    else if (dwReason == DLL_PROCESS_DETACH)
        _Module.Term();
    return TRUE;     // ok
}
```

```
///////////////////////////////////////////////////////////////////////
//////
// Used to determine whether the DLL can be unloaded by OLE [sic, even
//     Microsoft can't make up their minds what to call it]

STDAPI DllCanUnloadNow(void)
{
    return (_Module.GetLockCount()==0) ? S_OK : S_FALSE;
}


///////////////////////////////////////////////////////////////////////
//////
// Returns a class factory to create an object of the requested type

STDAPI DllGetClassObject(REFCLSID rclsid, REFIID riid, LPVOID* ppv)
{
    return _Module.GetClassObject(rclsid, riid, ppv);
}


///////////////////////////////////////////////////////////////////////
//////
// DllRegisterServer - Adds entries to the system registry

STDAPI DllRegisterServer(void)
{
    // registers object, typelib and all interfaces in typelib
    return _Module.RegisterServer(TRUE);
}


///////////////////////////////////////////////////////////////////////
//////
// DllUnregisterServer - Removes entries from the system registry

STDAPI DllUnregisterServer(void)
{
    return _Module.UnregisterServer(TRUE);
}
```

C. ATL OBJECTS

1. Having generated an ATL project, you next add objects to the project by selecting "Insert — New ATL Object..." from the main menu. This causes the ATL Object Wizard to appear, offering the selection of all the prefabricated object types that it knows about. For the Hello sample, we use the simplest case, a "Simple Object". This is an object that can provide prefabricated support for IUnknown and IDispatch. Thus:

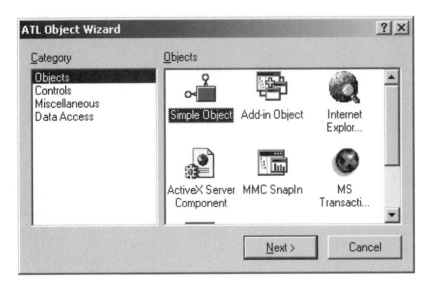

The type of objects available from the ATL Wizard are listed in the following table:

Name	Description
Simple Object	This is a bare-bones COM object containing an IUnknown and (optionally) IDispatch interface. It may be aggregatable or not, and it may use any threading model. I find myself using this one most of the time.
Add-In Object	This poorly-named object provides prefabricated functionality used to extend the Microsoft Developer Studio user interface. It would make more sense to call this one "DevStudioAdd-In", as does the attributes tab that you see after you insert this type of object. It provides support for an interface called *IDSAddIn*, with additional extensions for things like toolbars. Developer tools such as Bounds Checker, that add their own menus to Developer Studio, could use this type of object to simplify their user interface programming.
ActiveX Server Component	This type of object knows how to run within the Active Server Pages environment in Microsoft Internet Information Server. The Wizard generates an object containing the named methods OnStartPage( ) and OnEndPage( ). IIS looks for these methods by name and calls them at the appropriate time in the ASP compilation process. In the former method, the Wizard-generated code obtains the ASP intrinsic objects of its environment, such as the Request and Response objects. In the latter, it releases them.

(continued on facing page)

MMC SnapIn	Selecting this type of object causes the Wizard to generate no fewer than 4 different object classes. These classes contain all the functionality necessary to implement a snap-in panel that is compatible with the Microsoft Management Console administrative utility application, a requirement of Back Office logo compliance and a darn good idea for administrative tools anyway. It implements too many interfaces to list here. Writing this type of object will remind you of writing an in-place activation OLE server in the MFC.
Internet Explorer Object	This type of object knows how to run in the Microsoft Internet Explorer environment, but does not contain the user interface of a full control (which you will find under the "Controls" selection in the dialog box, not discussed in this book). The Wizard-generated code will provide a prefabricated implementation of the *IObjectWithSite* interface, which IE uses to talk to its objects.
MS Transaction Server Component	This type of object complies with the requirements for a component to run inside the Microsoft Transaction Server environment. The resulting component will be non-aggregatable and set its threading model registry entry to "Apartment". This is required for MTS 2.0 and earlier, but are not required for COM+. This object also has the option of supporting the *IObjectControl* interface, used for tighter integration with the MTS/COM+ runtime environment.
Component Registrar Object	This object is seldom used. It provides a prefabricated implementation of the *IComponentRegistrar* interface, which allows a knowing client to register components individually instead of all at once. I told you it was seldom used.

2. The Wizard will then show you a property page asking you to specify the names of your classes and files. As you fill in the "Short Name" box, the Wizard will fill in the others based on your entry. You can then change any of them individually if you want, but I usually don't find it worth the trouble. By accepting the defaults, I always know the transformation of, for example, C++ class name to interface name. Thus:

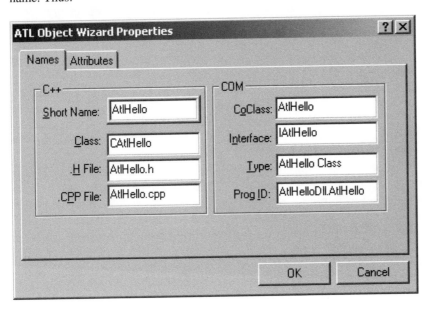

WARNING: Like most Microsoft Wizards, this one is impossible to reverse. If you click OK after entering the class name as shown above, but without examining the choices on the "Attributes" tab, you will have selected the default object attributes as discussed on the facing page, which may not be what you want. Since the Wizard is irreversible, you'll have to remove the entire object class from the project, including deleting all of your new class-level files and also editing some project-level files, and enter the object again. Don't just click OK on autopilot, STOP! And make sure you've set the right attributes before proceeding.

3. In order to properly generate code that produces the desired object behavior, the Wizard also needs to know several attributes of your new object, such as the desired threading model. A simple object will have a single property sheet labeled "Attributes". Other types of ATL objects will have other attribute choices. Your selections here will determine the ATL base classes, macro settings, and prefabricated code used for your new class. The selections for the current example are shown below.

The ATL's internal code supports all threading models. The ATL won't step on its own toes no matter which one you choose. However, it is up to you to make sure that your own code follows the rules of whatever model you select, for example, serializing access to your own global variables if you select "Apartment", as in this example.

Selecting the "Dual" radio button will cause the Wizard to generate a dual interface, exposing your object's properties and methods through both a custom interface and an IDispatch as discussed in Chapter 4. Since you'll be getting it for free, you might as well take it. If you don't want IDispatch, perhaps because you want to pass parameters of types not supported by automation, then selecting the "Custom" button will generate a custom VTBL interface without an IDispatch. The ATL does not support an IDispatch without a dual interface.

Selecting "Yes" for aggregation will select an ATL base class that allows itself to be created either as a standalone object or as part of an aggregate. Selecting "No", as in this example, allows creation as a standalone object only. Selecting "Only" specifies an object that cannot be created as a standalone object, but only as part of an aggregate.

Selecting "Support ISupportErrorInfo" will include a prefabricated implementation of the ISupportErrorInfo interface, as discussed previously in Chapter 3. Selecting "Support Connection Points" will include a prefabricated implementation of the IConnectionPointContainer and IConnectionPoint interfaces, which comprise a vastly overrated mechanism for setting up callback circuits, not discussed in this book.

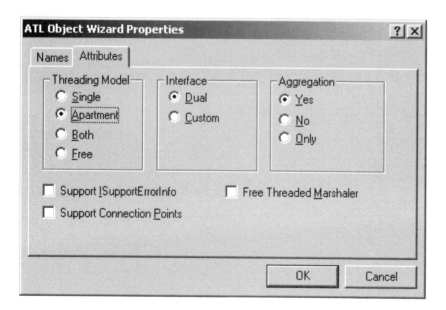

WARNING: This dialog box practically invites you to include the free threaded marshaler. You should only do this if you are writing an in-proc server that supports both threading models, and usually not even then, unless you want to write a whole lot of extra code to gain a few extra microseconds in obscure, seldom-encountered cases with clients that have already told you they don't care about performance (as discussed at the end of Chapter 6). Including it when you shouldn't will occasionally appear to give you extra speed, but I guarantee that it opens you up to the possibility of random crashes. Even if you don't see them in your development testing, your customers will. Just don't check this box. Ever.

4. Adding an object via the Wizard generates both an interface and the C++ class that implements it. When it first generated your project, the ATL App Wizard created an .IDL file. Since your project didn't then contain any COM objects, this file hasn't contained anything interesting until now. Your new object's interface is defined in the project's .IDL file, as is the CLSID of the COM class that implements it. Commented for description, the file now looks like this:

```
import "oaidl.idl";
import "ocidl.idl";

/*
Description of IAtlHello, the dual interface supported by this object.
It contains no methods or properties yet.
*/
    [
       object,
       uuid(DBA21E81-5B4C-474B-9D71-16AE917D64BA),
       dual,
       helpstring("IAtlHello Interface"),
       pointer_default(unique)
    ]
    interface IAtlHello : IDispatch
    {
    };

/*
Description of type library itself.
*/

  [
     uuid(20F0EB88-76FC-41CD-88DE-4DE29FA15493),
     version(1.0),
     helpstring("AtlHelloDll 1.0 Type Library")
  ]
  library ATLHELLODLLLib
  {
     importlib("stdole32.tlb");
     importlib("stdole2.tlb");

/*
Description of class that implements the IAtlHello interface.
*/
    [
      uuid(5BA36C8F-FF92-4710-A71C-4C89843D5199),
      helpstring("AtlHello Class")
    ]
    coclass AtlHello
    {
      [default] interface IAtlHello;
    };
  };
```

5. Based on the selections that you made on the previous pages, the Wizard will generate a new C++ class that implements your interface. Naturally, it starts without any methods or properties; these will be added as shown on subsequent pages. The class declaration uses multiple inheritance to access the ATL's prefabricated functionality. It uses C++'s template mechanism to tell the ATL which custom classes to create. Commented for explanation, the class declaration of our simple example looks like this:

```
class ATL_NO_VTABLE CAtlHello :
/*
ATL's implementation of IUnknown, using the single-threaded apartment
model.
*/
    public CComObjectRootEx<CComSingleThreadModel>,
/*
ATL's implementation of a class factory, passing the name of the C++
class that the factory creates and the class ID to which it answers.
*/
    public CComCoClass<CAtlHello, &CLSID_AtlHello>,
/*
ATL's implementation of IDispatch, telling it the custom interface it
supports and the ID of the type library which contains the description
of that interface.
*/
    public IDispatchImpl<IAtlHello, &IID_IAtlHello,
      &LIBID_ATLHELLODLLLib>
{
public:
    CAtlHello()
    {
    }

/*
Tell the component registrar which resource contains strings for this
class.
*/

DECLARE_REGISTRY_RESOURCEID(IDR_ATLHELLO)

DECLARE_PROTECT_FINAL_CONSTRUCT()

/*
Data map telling IUnknown::QueryInterface( )   which interfaces this
object supports.
*/

BEGIN_COM_MAP(CAtlHello)
    COM_INTERFACE_ENTRY(IAtlHello)
    COM_INTERFACE_ENTRY(IDispatch)
END_COM_MAP()

// IAtlHello
public:
};
```

6. ATL object servers perform their own registration. The ATL COM Wizard generates a *registrar script* for your app, which it adds to your project in a file with the extension .RGS. This contains the various keys and values that need to be added to the registry in an almost-readable format called "Backus - Nauer". When you build your app, the contents of this file are included in your server . DLL or . EXE as a resource.

The code that actually reads the Backus Nauer resource and makes or removes registry entries based on it is a COM object called the *ATL component registrar*. The method CComModule::UpdateRegistryFromResource( ) creates the component registrar object and feeds it the relevant scripts.

You may choose either to bind the component registrar statically into your server or to rely on the copy in the system .DLL "atl.dll", which is about 18 Kbytes in size. The former option makes your app about 5 Kbytes larger but removes this external dependency. Defining the compile-time constant _ATL_STATIC_REGISTRY, done automatically when you build the "Release MinDependency" project configuration, selects this option. The latter option will reduce the size of your app by about 5k, but leave you with an external dependency, albeit a small one.

The registry file containing the Backus-Nauer description of our sample ATL object server is shown below. Thus:

```
<file AtlHello.rgs>

HKCR
{
    AtlHelloDll.AtlHello.1 = s 'AtlHello Class'
    {
      CLSID = s '{5BA36C8F-FF92-4710-A71C-4C89843D5199}'
    }
    AtlHelloDll.AtlHello = s 'AtlHello Class'
    {
      CLSID = s '{5BA36C8F-FF92-4710-A71C-4C89843D5199}'
      CurVer = s 'AtlHelloDll.AtlHello.1'
    }
    NoRemove CLSID
    {
     ForceRemove{5BA36C8F-FF92-4710-A71C-4C89843D5199}=s'AtlHelloClass'
     {
      ProgID = s 'AtlHelloDll.AtlHello.1'
      VersionIndependentProgID = s 'AtlHelloDll.AtlHello'
      ForceRemove 'Programmable'
      InprocServer32 = s '%MODULE%'
      {
            val ThreadingModel = s 'Apartment'
      }
      'TypeLib' = s '{20F0EB88-76FC-41CD-88DE-4DE29FA15493}'
     }
    }
}
```

NOTE: If you need to add registry entries besides those made by the Wizard, you can simply edit the registry script file by hand.

The registry script on the previous page produces these registry entries. First, the ProgID section:

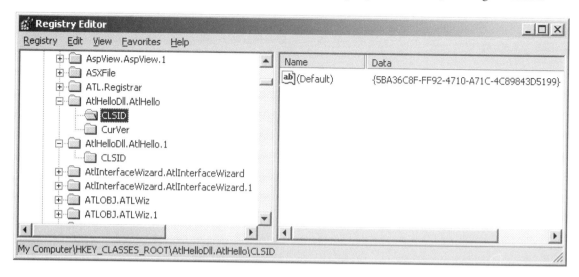

Next, the CLSID section:

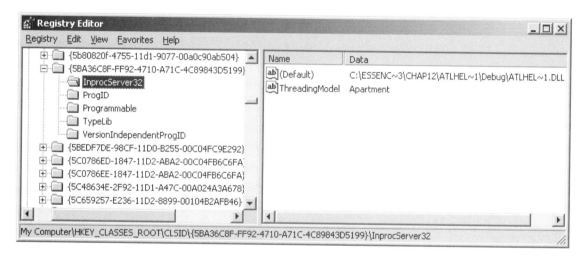

Finally, the type library section:

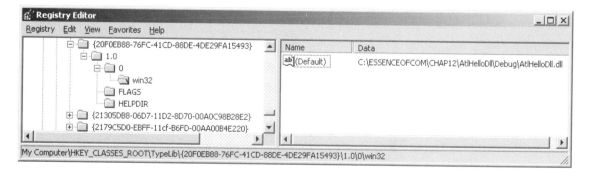

D. ATL OBJECT METHODS AND PROPERTIES

    1. You will see that the sample object supports a dual interface named IAtlHello, as shown in the Workspace window below. I've skipped a step to show you that interface containing one method and one property. Thus:

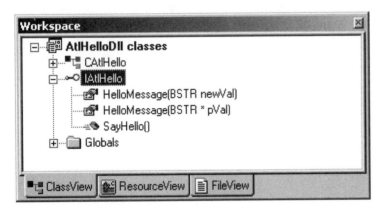

    To add properties and methods to your interface, right-click on the interface. The resulting context menu will contain the items "Add Property" and "Add Method". When you pick "Add Property", you will get the dialog box shown below. There's nothing magic about this, nothing you couldn't do yourself by going to four or five different files and making entries yourself, but it's much more convenient this way. Thus:

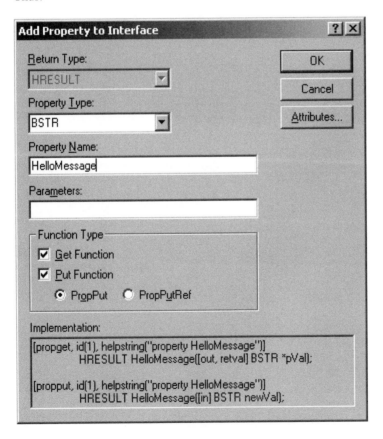

2. Adding a method is likewise simple. Thus:

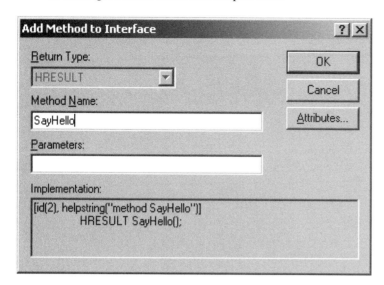

If you want to edit the attributes of a method or a property, such as hardwiring in a fixed dispatch ID, the "Attributes" button will bring up a dialog box allowing you to do this. Thus:

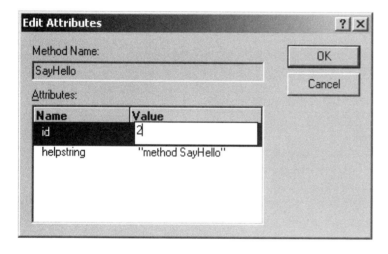

3. When you add a method or a property, the Wizard makes entries in your class's header file declaring handler functions for the method or property. In the example shown below, these handler functions appear at the bottom of the page.

You will probably need to add member variables to your class, such as m_bstrHelloMsg below. This variable is of class **_bstr_t**, which is a Microsoft-specific class that encapsulates a BSTR, released as part of the smart pointer package that came with VC++ 5.0. Its function is discussed in more detail in Chapter 11. To use this class, you must include the header file "**comdef.h**". Thus:

```
#include "resource.h"        // main symbols
#include <comdef.h>


/////////////////////////////////////////////////////////////////////
//////
// CAtlHello
class ATL_NO_VTABLE CAtlHello :
    public CComObjectRootEx<CComSingleThreadModel>,
    public CComCoClass<CAtlHello, &CLSID_AtlHello>,
    public              IDispatchImpl<IAtlHello,              &IID_IAtlHello,
&LIBID_ATLHELLODLLLib>
{
public:
    CAtlHello()
    {
    }

    _bstr_t m_bstrHelloMessage ;

DECLARE_REGISTRY_RESOURCEID(IDR_ATLHELLO)

DECLARE_PROTECT_FINAL_CONSTRUCT()

BEGIN_COM_MAP(CAtlHello)
    COM_INTERFACE_ENTRY(IAtlHello)
    COM_INTERFACE_ENTRY(IDispatch)
END_COM_MAP()

// IAtlHello
public:
    STDMETHOD(SayHello)();
    STDMETHOD(get_HelloMessage)(/*[out, retval]*/ BSTR *pVal);
    STDMETHOD(put_HelloMessage)(/*[in]*/ BSTR newVal);
};
```

4. The Wizard adds shell functions to your object's implementation file, as shown in bold below. You fill in whatever code you need to make your object do what you want it to do. Thus:

```
<file AtlHello.cpp>

/*
Value of HelloMessage property being requested. Provide its current
value from our member variable.
*/

STDMETHODIMP CAtlHello::get_HelloMessage(BSTR *pVal)
{
    *pVal = SysAllocString (m_bstrHelloMessage) ;
    return S_OK;
}


/*
New value of HelloMessage property being set. Remember the BSTR in our
member variable.
*/

STDMETHODIMP CAtlHello::put_HelloMessage(BSTR newVal)
{
    m_bstrHelloMessage = newVal ;
    SysFreeString (newVal) ;
    return S_OK;
}


/*
Controller wants us to show the value of our string in our window.
Output the current value of the HelloMessage property. The _bstr_t does
automatic conversion between its internal Unicode and the ANSI required
by the window.
*/

STDMETHODIMP CAtlHello::SayHello()
{
    MessageBox (NULL, (char *) m_bstrHelloMessage, "Essence Of COM",0);
    return S_OK;
}
```

5. The Wizard also makes the necessary entries in your .IDL file to describe the new interface's properties and methods. Thus:

```
import "oaidl.idl";
import "ocidl.idl";
    [
      object,
      uuid(DBA21E81-5B4C-474B-9D71-16AE917D64BA),
      dual,
      helpstring("IAtlHello Interface"),
      pointer_default(unique)
    ]
    interface IAtlHello : IDispatch
    {
      [propget, id(1), helpstring("property HelloMessage")]
            HRESULT HelloMessage([out, retval] BSTR *pVal);
      [propput, id(1), helpstring("property HelloMessage")]
            HRESULT HelloMessage([in] BSTR newVal);
      [id(2), helpstring("method SayHello")] HRESULT SayHello();
    };


[
    uuid(20F0EB88-76FC-41CD-88DE-4DE29FA15493),
    version(1.0),
    helpstring("AtlHelloDll 1.0 Type Library")
]
library ATLHELLODLLLib
{
    importlib("stdole32.tlb");
    importlib("stdole2.tlb");

    [
      uuid(5BA36C8F-FF92-4710-A71C-4C89843D5199),
      helpstring("AtlHello Class")
    ]
    coclass AtlHello
    {
      [default] interface IAtlHello;
    };
};
```

6. Finally, the object map in your project's main file is updated to tell the module which classes are manufactured by this app. The _Module uses this map when registering class factories. Thus:

```
CComModule _Module;

/*
Map that tells which classes this app supports.
*/


BEGIN_OBJECT_MAP(ObjectMap)
    OBJECT_ENTRY(CLSID_AtlHello, CAtlHello)
END_OBJECT_MAP()
```

E. INTERNALS OF ATL OBJECTS

1. If all you want to do is get your [expletive deleted] ATL object server out the door, you can stop reading now. This section goes under the hood to examine how ATL objects are connected to COM. Look at the declaration of your new dual interface class, excerpted below:

```
class ATL_NO_VTABLE CAtlHello :
    public CComObjectRootEx<CComSingleThreadModel>,
    public CComCoClass<CAtlHello, &CLSID_AtlHello>,
    public IDispatchImpl<IAtlHello,&IID_IAtlHello,&LIBID_ATLHELLODLLLib>
{

    <omitted for clarity>


// IAtlHello
public:
    STDMETHOD(SayHello)();
    STDMETHOD(get_HelloMessage)(/*[out, retval]*/ BSTR *pVal);
    STDMETHOD(put_HelloMessage)(/*[in]*/ BSTR newVal);
};
```

The first two classes in the derivation list, CComObjectRootEx and CComCoClass, contain no virtual functions; therefore they make no entries in the VTBL of the derived class CAtlHelloDisp. (Ignore the ATL_NO_VTABLE declaration for now, it is explained on page 282).

The ATL has also generated a C and C++ header file definition of your custom interface. In this example, you will find it in the file "AtlHelloDll.h". Excerpted for clarity, your new interface's definition looks like this:

```
<file AtlHelloDll.h>

    MIDL_INTERFACE("DBA21E81-5B4C-474B-9D71-16AE917D64BA")
    IAtlHello : public IDispatch
    {
    public:
        virtual HRESULT STDMETHODCALLTYPE get_HelloMessage(
            BSTR __RPC_FAR *pVal) = 0;

        virtual HRESULT STDMETHODCALLTYPE put_HelloMessage(
            BSTR newVal) = 0;

        virtual HRESULT STDMETHODCALLTYPE SayHello( void) = 0;

    };
```

2. The third ATL base class in your object's derivation list is **IDispatchImpl**. Simplified for clarity, its definition reads:

```
template <class T, const IID* piid, const GUID* plibid >

class ATL_NO_VTABLE IDispatchImpl : public T
{
// IDispatch methods
public:
    STDMETHOD(GetTypeInfoCount)(UINT* pctinfo)
    STDMETHOD(GetTypeInfo)(UINT itinfo, LCID lcid, ITypeInfo** pptinfo)
    STDMETHOD(GetIDsOfNames)(REFIID riid, LPOLESTR* rgszNames,
      UINT cNames, LCID lcid, DISPID* rgdispid)
    STDMETHOD(Invoke)(DISPID dispidMember, REFIID riid,
      LCID lcid, WORD wFlags, DISPPARAMS* pdispparams,
      VARIANT* pvarResult, EXCEPINFO* pexcepinfo, UINT* puArgErr)
    <etc.>
}
```

The first parameter passed in the declaration template to this class is IAtlHello. So in your class, the IDispatchImpl expands to be:

```
class ATL_NO_VTABLE IDispatchImpl : public IAtlHello
{
    <etc.>
}
```

You can see here that the ATL's implementation of IDispatch is actually implementing the four IDispatch methods required for the dual interface. Looking at the previous page, you can see that the additional methods of the interface, SayHello( ), get_HelloMessage( ) and put_HelloMessage( ), are implemented in the class CAtlHello.

We can see where all the methods are implemented except for those of the IUnknown interface. Where are they ?

3. Surprise! The ATL implements objects in a manner that at first glance appears to be completely backwards. As you study it and let it percolate, however, it will start to make a certain amount of twisted sense. Your class CAtlHello is not in fact the most derived class in the hierarchy. In reality, the ATL provides a class called *CComObject* that implements the outer IUnknown.

The class that you have taken such trouble to write is in fact an abstract base class. Since it does not provide VTBL entries for the IUnknown methods, you cannot create an object of your new class by saying "new CAtlHello( )". Instead, you must use your class as a base for one of the ATL classes, such as CComObject. You would say:

```
IAtlHello *pHello = new CComObject <CAtlHelloDisp> ( ) ;
```

Alternatively, you can use the ATL's class creator, which will invoke the FinalConstruct method described in a few pages:

```
CComObject <CAtlHello> *pHello ;
CComObject <CAtlHello>::CreateInstance (&pHello) ;
```

The derivation is actually done this way:

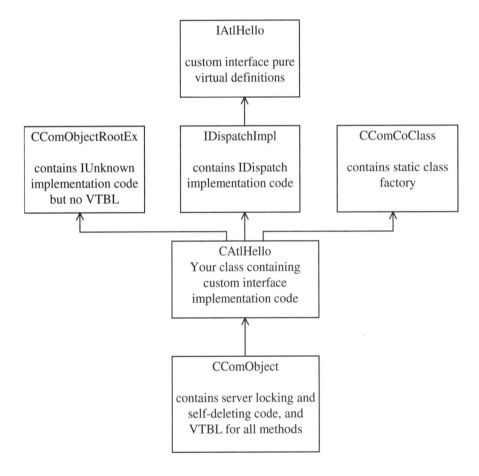

4. Why do they do such a seemingly crazy thing? It actually makes sense for flexibility reasons. COM objects differ from each other in important ways. The ATL designers wanted to provide prefabricated functionality for all the eventualities they could think of. They did that by providing 10 different classes that can be used as the most-derived class, CComObject and its siblings listed in the table below. This means no cutting or pasting, or setting obscure member variables and flags. Just choose the ATL class that has the behavior you want.

For example, most COM objects, such as your CAtlHelloDisp in this example, lock the server when they are created and unlock it when they are destroyed. The ATL base class CComObject provides this behavior by looking for the global variable named "_Module", which belongs to class CComModule, and calling its Lock( ) and Unlock( ) methods. You could use CComObject as the most-derived class for an ATL object which you want to behave in this manner.

Other objects, such as the class factory in a local server, do not lock their servers. If you were writing an object that you didn't want to lock its server, such as a new kind of class factory, you might use an ATL class called CComObjectNoLock as the most-derived class for your object. This class provides the same functionality as CComObject except that it does not lock and unlock the server. By choosing the right ATL base class as your most derived class, you can get the functionality you need without having to cut and paste.

These normal objects lock the server on creation, unlock server on destruction, and destroy themselves on final release.

CComObject	Normal case, does not support aggregation.
CComPolyObject	Same as CComObject but supports aggregation on request.
CComAggObject	Same as CComObject but requires aggregation.

These slightly strange objects do not lock the server. It is up to your server code to make sure that they are only used in cases where this behavior is appropriate:

CComObjectNoLock	No aggregation, deletes itself on final release. Used for local server class factories.
CComObjectStack	No aggregation, does not delete itself on final release. Used for stack objects that are automatically destroyed. I'd be careful with this one.
CComContainedObject	Supports aggregation, does not delete itself on final release. Used where object is contained inside another and needs to stay alive as long as its owner, such as nested classes in the MFC.

These objects have strange lifetime management for the case where an object is both used internally and exposed to outsiders. Neither supports aggregation.

CComObjectGlobal	Locks server on second and subsequent AddRef( ) calls. Does not delete itself on final release. Useful for objects which are global variables in an app, and need to stay alive as long as the app does.
CComObjectCached	Locks server on third and subsequent AddRef( ) calls. Deletes itself on final release. Useful for objects that are used internally by server and held by using pointers.

Tear-off object classes. Both support aggregation and delete themselves on final release, neither locks the server.

CComTearOffObject	Tear-offs that are created at each request.
CComCachedTearOffObject	Tear-offs that are created at first request and then cached.

5. Now you should be able to see what the ATL_NO_VTABLE macro is about. It means that your new class and its ATL base classes don't have their own VTBLs, that the most derived class, the CComObject class, will have a VTBL on their behalf. This saves a few bytes in object size and a few microseconds when constructing and destructing, as the intermediate classes won't need to have their VTBLs constructed and constantly patched up. The drawback is that you can't call any virtual functions in your class's constructor because the VTBL doesn't exist yet, or in the destructor because the VTBL has already been destroyed.

Suppose there is some functionality that you would normally place in your object's constructor, but can't because of this VTBL timing problem. The workaround is to use the method **FinalConstruct( )**, a member function of the base classes CComObjectRoot and CComObjectRootEx. The most-derived class, your CComObject relative, calls this method when its own construction process is complete and the VTBL set up. You override this method in your class and use it for your initialization that requires the VTBL. This only works if you are using the ATL creator for creating your object, the second example shown two pages ago, instead of the 'new' operator. Thus:

```
class CAtlHello: public CComObjectRootEx< ... >
{

/*
Method called after most-derived class's construction is complete.
*/

    HRESULT FinalConstruct( )
    {
      < do initialization that requires the VTBL here >
    }


    <rest of class declaration omitted>
};
```

NOTE: If you can't live with or don't trust this feature, you can always remove the ATL_NO_VTABLE macro. Everything will continue to work correctly. It'll just run a little slower and take a little more memory.

F. DEBUGGING ATL OBJECTS

1. When developing COM components, you'd often like to see which interfaces your clients are querying for, and the exact moments at which AddRef( ) and Release( ) calls take place. The IUnknown interfaces provided by the ATL contain the ability to report this information to a debugger. To see the calls to QueryInterface, simply compile your code with the line:

```
#define _ATL_DEBUG_QI
```

The resulting output will go to your debugger's output window. When the VB test client accessed the sample component built for this chapter, the output looked like this:

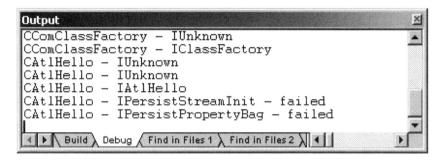

You can also see the calls to AddRef( ) and Release( ) by compiling with the line:

```
#define _ATL_DEBUG_INTERFACES
```

When the VB test client accessed the sample component built for this chapter, the output looked like this:

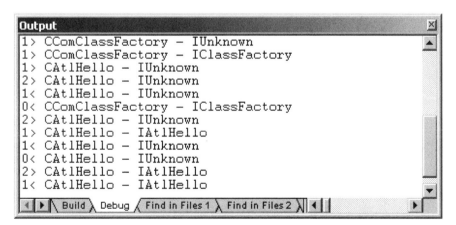

The two constants can be combined if you want to see both at once.

Directory: \EssenceofCOM\chap12\AtlHelloDll

1. The sample directory contains a DLL called "AtlHelloDll.dll". Register this component using regsvr32.exe. Then run the sample client application in the \vbclient subdirectory.

Chapter 13

COM Support in Visual Basic

A. Concepts and Definitions

1. Microsoft Visual Basic provides a prefabricated implementation of COM support that is fantastically easy and powerful, and also maddeningly difficult and crippled, both at the same time. To paraphrase Dickens, it is the best of tools and the worst of tools. How can such dichotomy exist?

As long as you are doing exactly what VB thinks you ought to be doing, in exactly the way that VB thinks you ought to be doing it, you are golden. You can crank out powerful code with almost no COM-related programming. But try just one tiny little bit to step outside the constraints that VB puts up to keep you from hurting yourself, and WHAM! Your app dies completely and it's impossible to figure out why. The quick rule of thumb in VB is that if you can't do it in about 10 minutes, you can't do it. Some programmers would argue for 5 minutes, or maybe 15, but no one who has used VB for more than a day disputes the basic premise.

VB was originally designed for corporate developers quickly cranking out relatively small applications for in-house use. The unit volume was intended to be low and the skill set easy to acquire. The designers of VB thought that their customers would buy controls, then called VBXs, and write a relatively small amount of custom code to glue them together. VB's first introduction to COM came when Microsoft Office was looking for a development environment for its macro programming capabilities. VB was the natural choice for its ease of use, but it still had large deficiencies in dealing with raw COM. The IDispatch automation scheme described in Chapter 4 was designed solely because that's what VB was capable of doing at the time (late 92 – early 93).

The philosophy that permeates VB is that the programmer should not need to know anything about COM. The programmer should write simple VB code as if he were using native VB. It is up to VB to abstract away the differences between internal VB and external COM. For throwing together a quick client app to test a COM object you just wrote, you can't beat it with a stick, not even two or three sticks. When writing a COM server, you don't have to worry about class factories or registry entries or type libraries. However, this high level of abstraction is simultaneously its greatest blessing and also its greatest curse. For a simple example, you can't easily add more registry entries than VB thinks you ought to need, say, a RunAs value for a DCOM object. For a more complex example, VB objects all have thread affinity that you just can't get rid of, which causes problems in middleware applications. There's no way to fix these today; you have to use it as is or wait until Microsoft brings out the next version.

Not only is VB's abstraction of COM imperfect, but it is also incomplete. VB does not allow you to call COM API functions directly, for example, GetRunningObjectTable( ). The designers of VB probably figured that not enough users cared about this feature to make it profitable to include in the tool, certainly not at the cost of complicating the lives of the vast majority who didn't. Most VB project teams carry at least one C++ geek, who can write an external COM object in C++ to do these things that VB can't, which VB can then use.

Alan Cooper wrote in his classic *About Face* (IDG Books, 1995, and anyone who designs human interfaces without reading this book is committing malpractice) that an interface should make simple things simple and complex things possible. It is extremely important not to sacrifice the former in order to obtain the latter. VB does the former pretty well, but doesn't do the latter at all. Microsoft Visual Java (see Chapter 14) provides a better combination, and I expect to see more users moving to it, if the lawsuit ever gets settled so Microsoft fixes its rough edges.

Despite the marketing claims, VB's abstraction of COM does not, repeat NOT, relieve you from the necessity of knowing what it's doing under the hood. You MUST understand that the VB code 'new <some object>' actually calls CoCreateInstance, which requires a registered COM server on the system. You MUST understand that assigning an object reference to a variable implies a call to QueryInterface, asking for an interface that the object might or might not support. VB makes it easy to crank out code, as a calculator makes it easy to crank out arithmetic. But without knowing the underlying COM, you're scrod. Pay me now, or pay me later.

B. COM Client Support in VB

1. Writing COM clients in VB is very easy. Even hard-core C++ geeks like me keep a copy of VB around for throwing together quick clients for testing components that they write in C++. VB clients can access automation, VTBL, or dual interfaces. Some users still think that VB is restricted to automation objects. That has never been true of 32-bit VB. A sample client program is shown in the directory \chap15\dualelizacl. It drives the IEliza dual interface sample application from Chapter 3, through both the IDispatch entry point and the VTBL entry point. It looks like this:

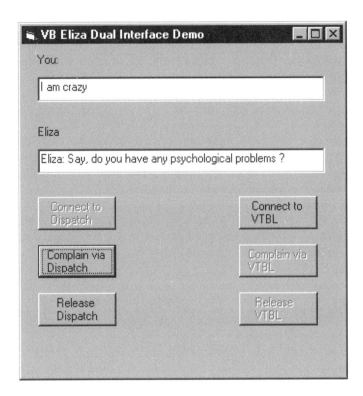

2. A VB client can create COM objects through two different mechanisms, both of which map to the API function CoCreateInstance( ). The first is the VB function CreateObject( ), to which you pass the ProgID of the class of object that you want to create, and optionally, the machine on which you want to create it. Calling CreateObject( ) internally calls CLSIDFromProgID( ) to get the object's CLSID, then calls CoCreateInstance( ) internally, always querying for the IUnknown interface.

You can see right here how VB sacrifices power for ease of use. This is the application for which ProgIDs were first created. The designers of VB knew that their programmers didn't think in terms of CLSIDs, but rather in terms of human-readable names. They decided that even though a CLSID was statistically unique in a small and fixed amount of space (16 bytes), that the computer should be made to think more like a human instead of the other way around. Furthermore, VB does not allow a creator to specify the class context for the new object; it simply uses CLSCTX_SERVER, which means any available class context. Nor does VB support creating aggregated objects, the designers figured that anyone who wanted to create an aggregated object would be programming in C++.

VB accesses all of its objects through smart pointers. Dimensioning a variable as an **Object**, as shown on the facing page, specifies the IDispatch interface for automation. Assigning an object reference into the pointer tells it to perform a QueryInterface for IDispatch, throwing a VB error if unsuccessful. You don't need to call AddRef( ) or Release( ) on your VB objects, the smart pointers take care of that internally. Objects are released when their references go out of scope, or when you set them to NOTHING, which is the VB equivalent of NULL. You can also compare an object reference to NOTHING.

When making calls to an automation object, VB automatically converts from its easy syntax to the complex packaging required by IDispatch::Invoke( ), as shown in Chapter 4. Sure makes your life easier, doesn't it?

```vb
' This declares the variable ElizaDispatch as an IDispatch
' interface pointer

Dim ElizaDispatch As Object

' Create a new object of the type specified by the ProgID.
' Assign its value to ElizaDispatch, which implies a query
' for the IDispatch interface

Private Sub btn_ConnectDispatch_Click()
    Set ElizaDispatch = _CreateObject("EssenceOfCOM.DualEliza")

    < UI handling omitted >
End Sub

' Call the method IDispatch::Invoke

Private Sub btn_ComplainDispatch_Click()
    Dim Complaint As String
    Dim Response As String

    Complaint = Text1.Text
    Call ElizaDispatch.Complain(Complaint, Response)
    Text2.Text = Response
End Sub

' Release the IEliza interface pointer

Private Sub btn_ReleaseDispatch_Click()
    Set ElizaDispatch = Nothing

    < UI handling omitted >
End Sub
```

3. The second mechanism whereby a client can create an object is to use the **new** operator, just as if the COM object that you are creating were an internal VB object. To do this, you need to include in the VB project the type library that describes the object that you want to create, which you do by selecting "Project — References" from the main menu. VB will show you the following dialog box containing all the type libraries currently registered on your system. You check the one that describes the object server that you want to use, or you can use the "Browse" button to select an unregistered type library file. Thus:

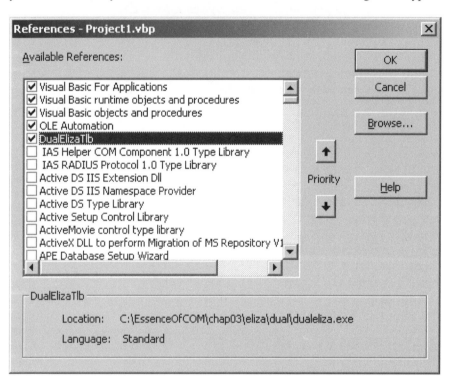

4. When you start typing "Dim <something> as", VB will look in all of its currently loaded type libraries and offer you the choices of all the different objects that it knows about from its collection of type libraries. You select the one you want. Thus:

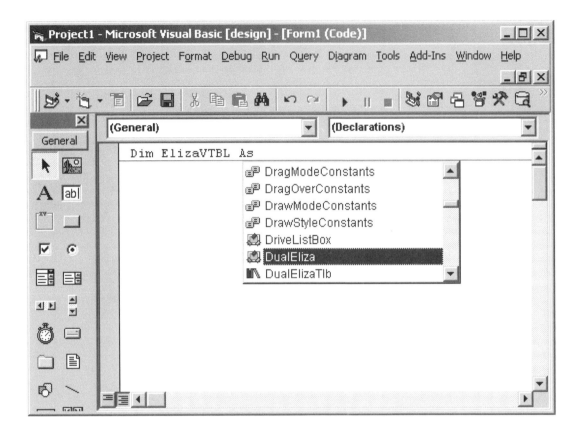

5. Once you've told it that ElizaVTBL is a DualEliza object, VB knows which type library to look in for its methods and properties. When you type the name of an object and then type a dot for accessing a property or method, VB will look in the type library and provide you with a list of the properties and methods that this object supports. Thus:

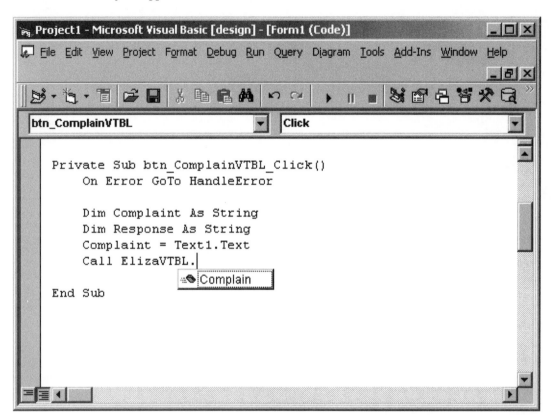

6. In the object browser view, VB shows the objects that it knows about. When you select HelloApplication in the left pane, its methods and properties appear on the right pane. When you select a method or property, VB displays the help string from its type library in the bottom pane. If you press F1, VB will read the help file name and help context from the type library and launch WinHelp, opening it to the specific topic describing the selected property or method.

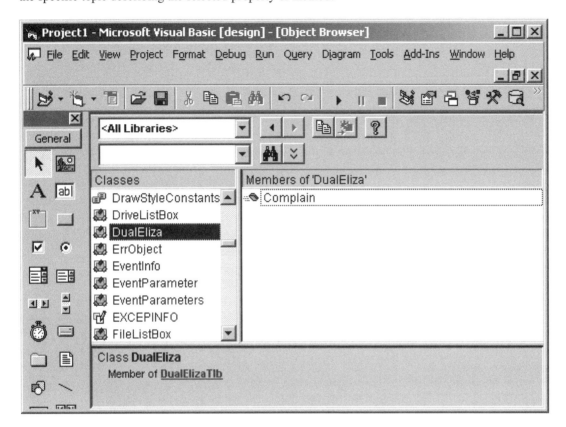

7. The sample client code for accessing an object through its VTBL interface is shown below. When you say 'New <some type>', VB knows the CLSID from the type library and calls CoCreateInstance( ), querying for the IUnknown interface. When you assign the resulting object reference into an interface pointer, VB queries for the specified interface. When you make a call to a VTBL interface pointer, VB generates the proper syntax based on the interface's description in the type library. Thus:

```vb
' Tell VB that the ElizaVTBL object is the type that it finds described
' in the type library.

Dim ElizaVTBL As DualEliza

' User clicked the "Connect VTBL" button. Create the object and connect
' to its VTBL. Assigning into the DualEliza pointer implies a
' QueryInterface for that interface.

Private Sub btn_ConnectVTBL_Click()
    If ElizaVTBL Is Nothing Then
        Set ElizaVTBL = New DualEliza

        <UI handling omitted>
    End If
End Sub

' User clicked "Complain" button. Call the complain( ) method. Because
' this object is described in a type library, VB will use the VTBL
' entry and not the dispatch entry. Since the server is in a .EXE in
' another process, it won't be faster enough to notice.

Private Sub btn_ComplainVTBL_Click()
    Dim Complaint As String
    Dim Response As String

    Complaint = Text1.Text
    Call ElizaVTBL.Complain(Complaint, Response)
    Text2.Text = Response

End Sub
```

This page intentionally contains no text other than this sentence.

C. COM SERVER SUPPORT IN VB

1. Writing a standard, vanilla COM server in VB is extremely easy. The VB philosophy, present throughout the entire development system, is that COM is transparent. You simply write VB code, either client side or server side, and VB magically makes COM out of it. VB will provide all of the infrastructure that a COM server needs – class factory, registry entries, type library, etc. And like clients, it's great as long as you want standard, ordinary, vanilla stuff. It's so easy it isn't even funny. But when you want something that's a little different, that wouldn't be too hard in C++, say, aggregation or a singleton object, VB won't do it at all and you can't make it.

To create a COM server in VB, you have to create a new "ActiveX" project. VB uses the term "ActiveX" as a synonym for COM. I call this a MINFU, which stands for MIcrosoft Nomenclature Foul-Up. See my newsletter on www.rollthunder.com for the description of this term, and my April 1999 column on www.byte.com, entitled "What the Heck is ActiveX, Anyway?" for an explanation of the mix-ups caused by this term.

When you start a new project, VB will offer you the choice of project types. This chapter will deal primarily with ActiveX DLLs, which are plain vanilla in-proc COM servers. Thus:

2. When you generate a new project, VB will generate a *class module*, which represents VB's primary abstraction of a COM class. You can also add classes yourself via the "Project – Add Class Module" menu item. Each class exposes a single dual interface. You do not have control over the CLSID of the class or the IID of its interface; these are handled internally by VB. The ProgID is always the name of the project, then a dot, then the name of the class. In the example shown, the ProgID is "EssenceOfComVbObject.MyVbClass". Its interface contains a single method called "SayHello" and a single string property called "HelloMessage". It's essentially the same functionality as the automation server shown in Chapter 4. The code is located in the directory \chap13\vbcomserver.

A VB class module contains a property known as "Instancing", which specifies the creatability of the class. The useful settings are "MultiUse", which means a standard COM object creatable through a class factory, and "PublicNotCreatable", which means a COM object that doesn't have a class factory. Only other classes in the same DLL can create the PublicNotCreatable class.

Once you have a class, you have to add properties and methods to it. Any public function that you put in the class will be automatically exposed as a COM method. Any public variable that you put in the class will be exposed as a COM property. You can also expose properties by using Property Get or Property Let functions (not shown here, but look them up, they're easy). The class module shown below contains a single method called SayHello, and a string property called HelloMessage. Thus:

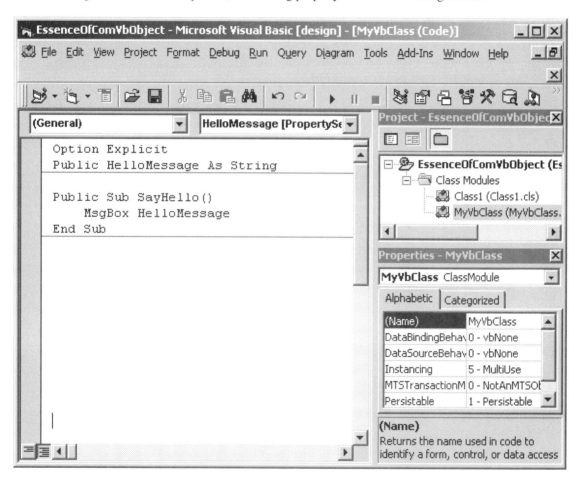

3. When you build your project into a DLL, VB creates a type library and binds it into the DLL. VB does not produce an IDL file; instead it bypasses this step by directly producing a type library via the function CreateTypeLib( ) as discussed in Chapter 5. Inspecting the type library from the sample DLL in a type library browser tool produces the following output.

```
// Generated .IDL file (by the OLE/COM Object Viewer)
//
// typelib filename: EssenceOfComVbObject.dll

[
  uuid(B494CF4F-4DD0-446F-8EB8-2E9EB0CA0806),
  version(1.0)
]
library EssenceOfComVbObject
{
    importlib("StdOle2.Tlb");

    // Forward declare all types defined in this typelib
    interface _MyVbClass;

    [
      odl, uuid(9713B644-D4BA-4F9A-889F-E6B1834D8E1D),
      version(1.0), hidden,
      dual, nonextensible, oleautomation,
      custom({50867B00-BB69-11D0-A8FF-00A0C9110059}, "4")
    ]
    interface _MyVbClass : IDispatch {
        [id(0x40030000), propget]
        HRESULT HelloMessage([out, retval] BSTR* HelloMessage);
        [id(0x40030000), propput]
        HRESULT HelloMessage([in] BSTR HelloMessage);
        [id(0x60030000)]
        HRESULT SayHello();
    };

    [
      uuid(31BF03C7-94C6-43CE-85A3-8BABEC7C68C2),
      version(1.0)
    ]
    coclass MyVbClass {
        [default] interface _MyVbClass;
    };
```

4. VB makes all the registry entries the component needs: CLSID, ProgID, type library, and IID. Thus:

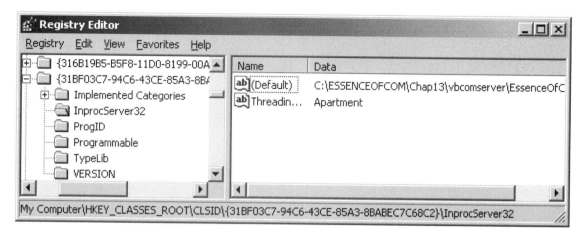

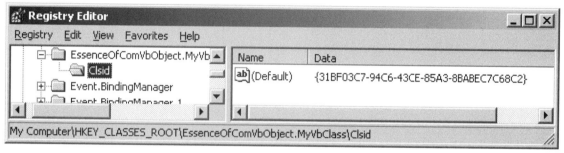

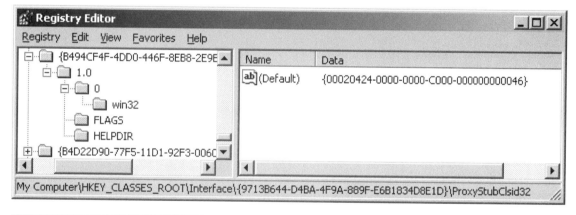

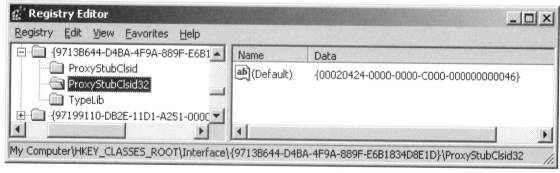

5. VB can also be used for implementing interfaces defined by other tools. To do this, you include the type library describing the interface you want to implement. You then mark your class as implementing that interface via the keyword **Implements**. VB will automatically generate a shell interface for all the methods described in the type library; you simply add your business logic. I added a class to my demo server that implemented the type library marshaled Eliza interface from Chapter 4. The code looks like this:

```
Option Explicit
Implements TypeLibMarshaledEliza

Private Function TypeLibMarshaledEliza_Complain (ByVal bstrIn _
  AsString) _As String

    < your Eliza logic goes here >

End Function
```

VB imposes some restrictions as to the interfaces that can be implemented in this manner. They can only use automation-compatible parameters, which means no structures. That's not usually a big problem. More subtle is the fact that they can't use any parameters marked only with the [out] attribute. All parameters for which output is desired have to be marked as [in, out], or the last parameter in a function can be marked as [out, retval]. I used the latter approach in this example, which required me to change the type library marshaled Eliza interface that I had originally written. There's no COM reason why this is forbidden, VB just doesn't like to do it. You get the informative error message:

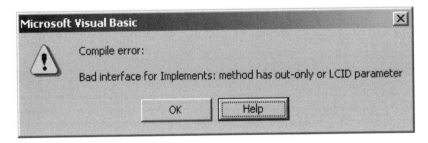

VB is terrible about this type of error message. It seems to figure that you wouldn't do this if you didn't know what you were doing, so it doesn't have to explain. VB doesn't like you coloring outside the lines, and it often seems to me that it goes out of its way to prevent you from doing so.

6. A VB component can implement as many interfaces as it wants. The type library output from the sample code is shown below. I haven't put any methods on the VB object's native interface, and there isn't any good way to get rid of it. The coclass section shows that the object supports the ITypeLibMarshaledEliza interface.

```
// Generated .IDL file (by the OLE/COM Object Viewer)
//
// typelib filename: EssenceOfComVbObject.dll

[
  uuid(B494CF4F-4DD0-446F-8EB8-2E9EB0CA0806),
  version(1.0)
]
library EssenceOfComVbObject
{

    importlib("StdOle2.Tlb");
     importlib("typelibmarshaled.exe");

    // Forward declare all types defined in this typelib

    interface _Class1;

    [
      odl, uuid(6E2D399A-571E-4001-8853-AF37CC041BDF),
      version(1.0), hidden,
      dual, nonextensible, oleautomation
    ]
    interface _Class1 : IDispatch {
    };

    [
      uuid(AD9A90C6-E507-45F5-BAFE-793AE5346CB9),
      version(1.0)
    ]
    coclass Class1 {
        [default] interface _Class1;
        interface ITypeLibMarshaledEliza;
    };
};
```

7. As previously stated, you don't have control over your CLSIDs or IIDs of the native interface provided to an object by VB, this is entirely up to VB (although VB will not change the IIDs of any interfaces that you specify with the Implements keyword). This can cause trouble when VB changes them behind the scenes and your clients aren't expecting it. The changes that VB will make are controlled by the settings in the Component tab of the Project Properties dialog box. Remember, they only apply to the one native interface on a VB class, not to any interfaces that you specify with the Implements keyword. Thus:

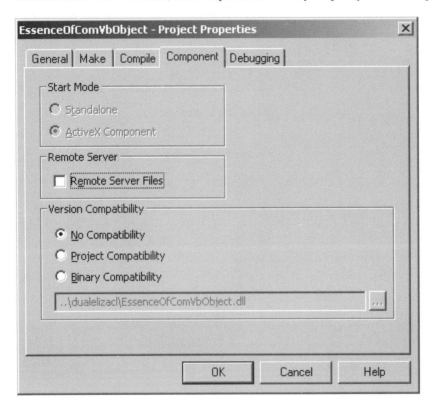

Choosing No Compatibility means that every time you rebuild the project, VB generates a new IID, CLSID, and type library ID. A client app that looks for the COM server in any other way than the ProgID, and accesses it through any other way than IDispatch, is out of luck. You choose this to avoid any possibility of entangling alliances. Hardly anyone ever does it.

Choosing Project Compatibility means that every time you rebuild your project, VB generates a new IID, but leaves the CLSID and type library ID unchanged. Client apps that you compile against the new VB component will find the new information in the same type library, import it, and recompile correctly to access the new object.

Binary Compatibility is somewhat of a misnomer. It means that the VB does not change the IIDs, so it is up to you, the programmer, to make sure that it actually does stay binary compatible. Existing binary clients will create the object and query for the expected interface, so you had better make sure it's OK. You use this when you need to make a bug fix to an existing module without changing any of the existing function signatures.

8. You can make a VB object persistent by selecting the "Persistable" property from the VB UI. Remember that we saw in Chapter 8 how persistent objects work, by implementing an interface of the IPersist family. VB provides a prefabricated implementation of the IPersistStream and IPersistPropertyBag interfaces, which it automatically includes in your project when you set this property. VB will add code to your class module that provides the VB object type PropertyBag that mediates the storing of an object's properties in, or the loading of an object's properties from, persistent storage. You simply use the methods **WriteProperty( )** and **ReadProperty( )** to save or restore your object's properties. Thus:

```
Private Sub Class_InitProperties()
    HelloMessage = "Hello, World from VB"
End Sub

Private Sub Class_ReadProperties(PropBag As PropertyBag)
    HelloMessage = PropBag.ReadProperty("HelloMessage")
End Sub

Private Sub Class_WriteProperties(PropBag As PropertyBag)
    PropBag.WriteProperty "HelloMessage", HelloMessage
End Sub
```

D. COM ERROR HANDLING IN VB

1. VB has seamlessly tied COM error handling into its own native error handling scheme. When a COM object reports a COM error via an HRESULT, VB automatically obtains whatever error information the object supports, both querying for the ISupportErrorInfo interface and also checking the EXCEPINFO structure on the IDispatch interface, and wraps it up in the intrinsic VB error object named **Err**. VB then raises an error, which causes the program to jump to the statement identified in the On Error directive. Thus:

```
Private Sub btn_ComplainVTBL_Click()

' Set error handler. If a COM method returns an error HRESULT, the
' program will automatically branch to the named label.

    On Error GoTo HandleError

    Dim Complaint As String
    Dim Response As String
    Complaint = Text1.Text

' Make a COM call. If it causes an error, we'll automatically
' branch to the error handler below.

    Call ElizaVTBL.Complain(Complaint, Response)
    Text2.Text = Response

    Exit Sub

' Error detected. Report the number and description to the user.

HandleError:

    MsgBox "COM Error:" +Err.Description+" Number: "+ Str(Err.Number)

End Sub
```

2. A VB COM server that wants to report an error to the client does so by calling the intrinsic VB method **Err.Raise**. You are required to pass an error number, and may optionally pass an error source, a description string, help file and help index. VB in turn takes this information, causes the COM method to return an HRESULT other than S_OK, and makes the additional information available via the ISupportErrorInfo interface. Thus:

```
Public Sub RaiseAnError(newStr As String)

' Caller said something we object to

    If (newStr = "US Department of Justice") Then

' Raise an error informing the caller just what the problem is.

        Err.Raise 666, "EssenceOfCom.MyVbClass", _
            "You said the name of the Beast"
    End If

End Sub
```

E. COM THREADING IN VB

1. This is the place where VB's philosophy of abstracting away the details of COM crash into the real world. The designers of VB opted for ease of use, and paid the price of non-intuitive behavior and the inability to do even moderately sophisticated things. The abstraction layer creaks when it meets threads.

When you add a class module to VB, the Project – Properties dialog box offers the choice of the Single Threaded (all objects from this server must live in the same single-threaded apartment, the legacy apartment, see Chapter 6) or Apartment Threaded (objects from this server can live in any single-threaded apartment, ditto). Thus:

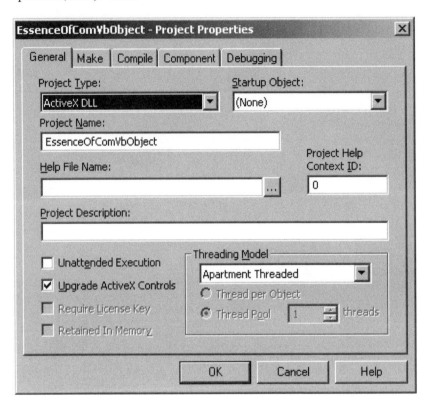

VB requires all of its objects to live in STAs because its objects have *thread affinity*. This means that a VB object depends on receiving all of its calls on the same thread. It works this way because the internal VB mechanisms use thread local storage. If you call object A from thread 1 and then call the same object from thread 2, VB will lose its mind, even if the two calls don't happen at the same time. Requiring thread affinity was a reasonable way to write single-desktop code four or five years ago, particularly code that deals with user interfaces, but it causes bottlenecks when you use it to write middleware components for distributed environments, such as COM+ or Microsoft Transaction Server.

2. As discussed in Chapter 6, selecting Single Threaded forces all objects into a single STA, which can lead to inter-thread marshaling in objects used by multithreaded clients, knocking the stuffing out of performance. It really only exists to support legacy code written for NT version 3.5, before COM worked on multiple threads. On the other hand, selecting Apartment Threaded, allowing VB objects to live in any STA, means that serialization is required to protect global variables against concurrent access by objects in different STAs. Does this mean the VB programmers now need to know and understand synchronization primitives such as critical sections, and worry about such conditions as the deadly embrace?

Fortunately, or unfortunately, not. That would be entirely out of keeping with VB's ease of use philosophy. The designers of VB decided that whatever they did had to be completely transparent to the programmer. This left them the choices of either putting automatic synchronization locks around every global variable, or making a separate copy of every global per thread so objects wouldn't fight over them. They decided that the former approach would incur unacceptable performance penalties, and therefore chose the latter approach. You don't have to think about it, it just works. At least, sort of.

Unfortunately, this means that there is no such thing any more as a true global variable in a VB apartment threaded COM server. If you are accustomed to using them in other places, all of a sudden they won't work any more and you won't know why. The technique that you've been using since Computer Science 101 (generally with the disapproval of your professor who considered it sinful) disappears for no immediately apparent reason, and without a whole lot of warning. You can live with it once you know what's happening, but it underscores my point that **THERE IS NO SUBSTITUTE, NOT IN VB, NOT IN ANY OTHER LANGUAGE, NOT NOW, NOT EVER, FOR KNOWING WHAT COM IS DOING UNDER THE HOOD.**

What do you do when you need a true global? You have several choices, none of them great. You could simply make all of your objects single threaded, forcing them all into the same apartment. Performance will stink. If you are running in a COM+ or Microsoft Transaction Server environment you can use the Shared Property Manager, which exists for this purpose. If you aren't running in that type of environment, the C++ geek on your team can write a singleton object server that will synchronize access to the items that need it. Or you can pray that Microsoft removes the thread affinity from VB, which they'll have to do if the want to keep marketing it as a middleware component development system.

Directory: \EssenceOfCOM\chap13\vbdualelizacl

1. Register the type library marshaled Eliza server from Chapter 3 by running the registration script \Chap03\Eliza\typelibmarshaled.reg. Run the client app \Chap13\vbdualelizacl\project1.exe. Click either of the "Connect" buttons; you should see the server window appear. Click the "Complain" button under your connect button; you should see Eliza's response to your complaint. Click the "Release" button under your connect button; you should see the server disappear. To see a demonstration of VB client error handling, click the "Complain via VTBL" button before the "Connect to VTBL" button. It has been left enabled for this purpose.

Directory: \EssenceOfCOM\chap13\vbdualelizacl

2. Register the DLL \Chap13\vbcomserver\EssenceOfComVbObject.dll by using regsvr32. We will use the automation client app from Chapter 4 to drive it. Register the automation server by running the registration script \Chap04\Helloau\Hello32.reg. Now open the registry editor regedit.exe. Look under the ProgID HKEY_CLASSES_ROOT\EssenceOfComVbObject.MyVbClass. Copy its CLSID to the clipboard. Now go up a few lines to the ProgID EssenceOfCOM.HelloAutomation. This is the ProgID that the Chapter 4 automation looks for. Paste the CLSID from the VB server over the CLSID on this server. Run the client application \Chap04\Helloau\Hlodrv32\Done\Hellodrv.exe; the client app will appear. Click "Say Hello"; you will see a message box containing an empty string. Type some characters into the "String to Send" box, click "Set String", then click "Say Hello". You will see a message box containing your text. Click "Get String". You will see your string appear in the "Server String" text box.

Chapter 14

COM Support in Visual Java

A. CONCEPTS AND DEFINITIONS

1. *Java* is a computer language developed by Sun Microsystems, originally for controlling intelligent household appliances such as toasters. It made a big splash around 1996 with its promise of platform independence.

When you build a Java app, the Java compiler converts your Java language source code not into native machine language instructions, as is the case in C++. Instead, it produces files with the extension *.class*, which contain *Java byte codes*. These are instructions written for the *Java Virtual Machine (JVM)*, a piece of software written for your specific operating system and processor. When your Java app runs on a machine, it is up to that machine's JVM to read the Java byte codes and interpret them into native instructions for the processor and operating system on which it runs. Thus:

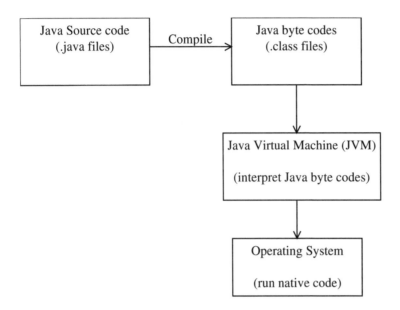

The idea is that Java byte codes are supposed to be universal. If you write an app once in Java, the JVM on any system should be able to interpret and run it, transparently handling all processor-specific questions such as little-endian versus big-endian storage. Sun's slogan is "Write once, run everywhere." For front-end programming, that's not even close to true and never has been. It's more like "Write once, test, debug, and special-case everywhere." One of my clients reported that it took him several months to tweak a Java app to run on both the Netscape 3 and Netscape 4 JVMs on Windows, never mind Windows and the Macintosh.

Furthermore, such platform independence as does exist is accomplished by reducing your Java applet to the lowest common denominator of all platforms. For example, since Windows supports object linking and embedding and other operating systems don't, your Java app will have to choose between skipping this feature (very bad if native apps provide it) or losing its platform independence. If you write anything larger than, say, Notepad, Java's architecture will be more of a hindrance than a help and a native app will clean your clock. Corel gave up trying to rewrite their entire business application suite in Java so as to cover the entire market with a single binary. It just doesn't work on a user's front end, although some of my customers are starting to report that for back end server programming, with the same version of the JVM from the same vendor, they can occasionally get Java to work on different machines.

2. Java does, however, have a promising future as a better C++. It addresses a number of the problems that plague developers of the latter language by abstracting away a number of its nasty details. For example, in C++, you create a new object via the 'new' operator, and delete it via the 'delete' operator when you are finished with it. It sounds simple and reasonable, but in practice it's hard to get right every time. C++ programmers spend an awful lot of time tracking down the causes of premature object destruction or object leaks, caused by calling 'delete' at the wrong time or forgetting to call it at all. In Java, you create an object via the 'new' operator, but you don't have to figure out when to delete it. The JVM keeps track of all references to the object, and will delete the object automatically when nobody needs it any more. A major cause of headaches and drain of programmer time has been abstracted away by the programming and runtime environment. Java provides similar abstractions in the case of threading and synchronization. Think how hard it is to properly write and test and debug multithreaded, synchronized code in C++. Java abstracts the whole problem away, quite nicely. Java also makes it much easier to access files and other resources over the Internet, which C++ doesn't touch. And if you don't care about platform independence, (and you shouldn't, because it doesn't work) you can compile your Java application for your particular target environment ahead of time, thereby eliminating the overhead of runtime interpretation.

3. Java sounds great; what are the drawbacks? There are two at the time of this writing; one technical and one legal. On the technical side, the high level of abstraction is great as long as it works. But if Java does not properly release all of your objects, say, it leaks one away, there is no good way to debug the problem. The current version of VJ, which is 6.0, is Microsoft's second Java compiler. One of my clients, who is currently using VJ6, says that his team is encountering problems with the JVM not always properly releasing COM objects, as I discuss on page 320. They are writing a large, industrial strength app, and find they need to subscribe to Microsoft's most expensive level of tech support in order to get these low-level internal VJ6 problems addressed in a timely manner. Still, my client reports that he thinks he's still making a profit by choosing Java over C++, albeit a much smaller one than he had hoped. He expects the profit to increase as Java improves and C++ stays mostly static. I would say that Java is where C++ was about ten ago. It looks cool, it's got some great ideas, but no one's managed to do a really good implementation of it yet. It's still mostly for early adopters.

The second problem is legal. As this book goes to press (spring 2000), Sun's lawsuit against Microsoft alleging contract violations in the latter's implementation of Java is still pending, and no one can know the final outcome. Such uncertainty hinders the acceptance of what could become a pretty good tool.

4. Since COM is a language-independent binary standard, it should come as no surprise to learn that you can write both COM clients and servers in Java. In order to accomplish this, you must have a JVM that supports COM. Some, notably Microsoft's, do, while others, notably Sun's and Netscape's, don't. So much for platform independence.

Why would you want to use or implement COM objects in Java? For the same reasons as you use or implement COM objects in other any language. If you are writing a client app in Java, it's because you need to use the functionality that a component vendor has found cost-effective to provide in a language-independent COM fashion, thereby maximizing potential customers, rather than in a language-dependent Java-only fashion that wouldn't sell nearly as many units. If you are a component vendor, it's because that, while Java might be the best language for solving your programming problem, you will sell a lot more units if your customers can use your products from any language.

You will find, as you write COM apps in VJ, that it provides a higher level of abstraction and prefabrication than C++, a level similar to Visual Basic. Unlike VB, however, VJ allows you to access the low-level COM API whenever you need something that hasn't been prefabricated. I think you will find that VJ gives you the ease of use of VB without sacrificing the power of C++. I expect it to really take off in about 2001, provided the lawsuit gets settled favorably.

B. Writing COM Clients in Java

1. I'll use the simplest example I can think to demonstrate the steps needed to write a Java client app that uses COM components. The server in this case is the IDispatch automation server from Chapter 4, that I wrote back in 1994. It is an EXE server that creates a visible window so you can see when it comes and when it goes. It contains a single property, called "HelloMessage", of type BSTR. It also has one method, "SayHello()", which displays this string in the server's main window. Instructions for registering it are given at the end of Chapter 4. The sample client application is found in the directory \Chap14\jhelloclient, and looks like this:

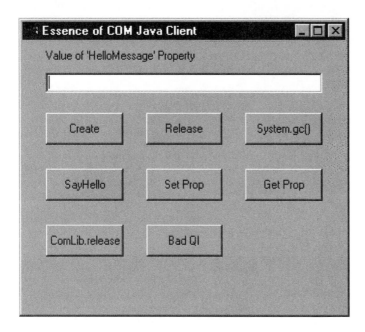

2. VJ accesses COM components by means of Java-language wrapper classes, conceptually similar to the wrapper classes generated by VC++ in response to the #import preprocessor directive. Like VC++, VJ generates its wrapper classes from an object's description in a type library. When you select the "Project — Add COM wrapper..." from the main menu, you will see the COM wrapper selection box shown below. VJ6 is reading the system registry and showing you the list of all the registered type libraries on the system. If you have registered the hello32 server type library correctly, you will see its entry. Thus:

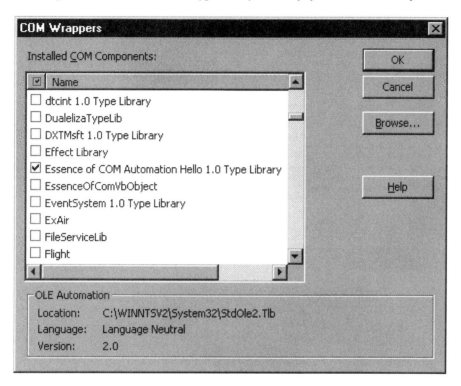

When you select the type library that describes the components you want to use, VJ launches a tool called "Jactivex", which reads the type library, generates a new Java package containing the wrapper classes for all the objects and interfaces described in the library, and adds the new package to your VJ project. The VJ Project Explorer will then look like this:

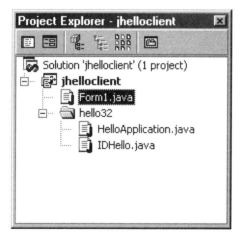

3. Jactivex creates a Java wrapper class for each coclass specified in the type library, in this case HelloApplication, as shown on this page. It also creates a wrapper class for the each interface specified in the type library, in this case the dispinterface IDHello, as shown on the facing page. Note that both classes use comment fields containing the directive **@com**. These provide COM-specific information that the Microsoft JVM uses to figure out the COM attributes of the classes. In the coclass wrapper below, you will find that the @com directives contain the CLSID that the JVM needs to specify when creating the object. You will also find the IID of the dispinterface, and the dispatch ID, name, and type of each method and property for every interface that the object is listed as supporting. If you look at a C++ wrapper class generated by the #import preprocessor directive, it will look very similar. The Java-language representation of COM types, such as GUIDs, are found in the package **com.ms.com**, provided by Microsoft. You will also notice that the COM data types, in this case a BSTR, have been replaced by Jactivex with Java data types, in this case String. Thus:

```
<file HelloApplication.java>

package hello32;
import com.ms.com.*;
import com.ms.com.IUnknown;
import com.ms.com.Variant;
/**
@com.class(classid=6CED2900-A1DD-11CF-8A33-00AA00A58097,DynamicCasts)
@com.interface(iid=6CED2902-A1DD-11CF-8A33-00AA00A58097, thread=AUTO,
    type=DISPATCH) */
public class HelloApplication implements
    IUnknown, com.ms.com.NoAutoScripting, hello32.IDHello
{
    /**
      @com.method(dispid=1, name="HelloMessage", type=PROPGET)
      @com.parameters([type=STRING] return) */

    public native String getHelloMessage();

    /**
      @com.method(dispid=1, name="HelloMessage", type=PROPPUT)
      @com.parameters([in,type=STRING] newValue) */

    public native void setHelloMessage(String newValue);

    /**
      @com.method(dispid=2, type=METHOD, name="SayHello",
            returntype=VOID)
      @com.parameters() */

    public native void SayHello();

  public     static     final     com.ms.com._Guid     iid     =     new
com.ms.com._Guid((int)0x6ced2902,       (short)0xa1dd,       (short)0x11cf,
(byte)0x8a,   (byte)0x33,   (byte)0x0,   (byte)0xaa,   (byte)0x0,   (byte)0xa5,
(byte)0x80,   (byte)0x97);
  public     static     final     com.ms.com._Guid     clsid     =     new
com.ms.com._Guid((int)0x6ced2900,       (short)0xa1dd,       (short)0x11cf,
(byte)0x8a,   (byte)0x33,   (byte)0x0,   (byte)0xaa,   (byte)0x0,   (byte)0xa5,
(byte)0x80,   (byte)0x97);
}
```

```
<file IDHello.java>

package hello32;

import com.ms.com.*;
import com.ms.com.IUnknown;
import com.ms.com.Variant;

    // Dispatch-only interface IDHello

/**
    @com.interface(iid=6CED2902-A1DD-11CF-8A33-00AA00A58097,
      thread=AUTO, type=DISPATCH) */

public interface IDHello extends IUnknown
{

    /**
      @com.method(dispid=1, name="HelloMessage", type=PROPGET)
      @com.parameters([type=STRING] return) */

    public String getHelloMessage();

    /**
      @com.method(dispid=1, name="HelloMessage", type=PROPPUT)
      @com.parameters([in,type=STRING] newValue) */

    public void setHelloMessage(String newValue);

    /**
      @com.method(dispid=2, type=METHOD, name="SayHello",
            returntype=VOID)
      @com.parameters() */

    public void SayHello();


    public    static    final    com.ms.com._Guid    iid    =    new
com.ms.com._Guid((int)0x6ced2902,      (short)0xa1dd,      (short)0x11cf,
(byte)0x8a,  (byte)0x33,  (byte)0x0,  (byte)0xaa,  (byte)0x0,  (byte)0xa5,
(byte)0x80,  (byte)0x97);
    }
```

4. In raw C++, you are used to calling explicit API functions to create COM objects. You must then explicitly call QueryInterface( ) on the object when you want a different interface pointer from it. Finally, you must explicitly call Release( ) on the object when you are finished with it. VJ uses a different strategy, similar to that used by VB, and by smart pointers in VC++. This is demonstrated in the code listing for the sample client app, shown beginning on the facing page. The "try-catch" error handling blocks shown in this listing are described in a later section of this chapter; I'd suggest you ignore them for now.

You probably first want to **import** the hello32 package into your source file, and also com.ms.com. This allows you to refer to the objects within the package by their short names. You create an object in VJ by using the "new" operator to instantiate the corresponding wrapper class object, in this case "HelloApplication". This creates the COM object by calling CoCreateInstance( ) internally, always querying for the IUnknown interface. In VJ, you cannot access this object directly as you did in VB, but only through its interfaces, which is more like the COM way of doing things. To query an object for a specific interface, all you do is cast the existing interface pointer to a variable of another class that represents the desired interface. Assigning the HelloApplication object to the IDHello variable performs an implied cast. You can see this demonstrated in the "btnCreate_click" handler function on the facing page.

You would think, and in fact most documentation has reported, that this would cause the JVM to immediately call QueryInterface( ) on the object asking for the IDHello interface. In fact, this particular query does not happen at the time of the assignment. If you instrument the server's QueryInterface method to display the interfaces requested by the client, you will find that the query for IUnknown happens when the server is launched and the object first created, but the query for IDHello does not take place until just before the first call is made to a method on the interface, that is, when you first clicked the "Set", "Get", or "SayHello" button. The JVM appears to be doing some just-in-time optimization by not querying for an interface until it is actually needed. However, other Java casts call QueryInterface( ) immediately, as explained and demonstrated with the ClassCastException error later in this chapter. Perhaps the JVM is not calling this QueryInterface( ) immediately because the type library indicates that it ought to be successful, so the JVM feels that it may safely wait.

```
/*
Import packages for convenience of using short names.
*/

import com.ms.com.* ;
import hello32.* ;

public class Form1 extends Form
{

/*
This member variable represents the interface we use to control
the client app.
*/

    IDHello m_Hello ;

/*
"Create" button clicked. Create a new HelloApplication object,
which is Java's representation of an abstract connection to the
server. Assign it into an object which represents the interface
so we can actually access its methods.
*/

    private void btn_Create_click(Object source, Event e)
    {
      try
      {
          m_Hello = new HelloApplication() ;
      }
      catch (com.ms.com.ComError ce)
      {
          MessageBox.show  (ce.getMessage(), "create Exception") ;
      }
    }
```

5. Once you have created the interface wrapper that in turn contains the COM object, you simply call the object's methods through the wrapper as if they were straight Java methods, which to your client app they are. There will be one for each method of the underlying object, in this case, "SayHello". Each property will have separate get and set accessor functions, in this case "getHelloMessage" and "setHelloMessage". These calls are made in the "btnSet_click", "btnGet_click", and "btnSayHello_click" event handlers shown below. The JVM handles the packaging of the parameters into a call to IDispatch::Invoke( ), exactly as is done in VB. Thus:

```
/*
"SayHello" button clicked. Call that method on the object.
*/
    private void btn_SayHello_click(Object source, Event e)
    {
      m_Hello.SayHello() ;
    }


/*
"Set" button clicked. Get the string from the edit control and set
its value into the object's "HelloMessage" property.
*/
    private void btn_SetProp_click(Object source, Event e)
    {
      m_Hello.setHelloMessage (edit1.getText()) ;
    }


/*
"Get" button clicked. Get the value of the "HelloMessage" property
and display it in the edit control.
*/
    private void btn_GetProp_click(Object source, Event e)
    {
      edit1.setText (m_Hello.getHelloMessage( )) ;
    }
```

6. VJ uses smart pointers for all of its object references. To delete a COM object in VJ, you set its interface pointer to null, or simply allow it to go out of scope. The sample app does the former when you click the "Release" button, but you will notice that the server's window does not immediately disappear. The reason for this is that while your client app has forever released its own right to use that particular object, the JVM does not actually call Release( ) on the underlying interface until it's good and ready. It's probably thinking that someone else might ask for another object from that server and it doesn't want to waste the overhead of starting it again. When all the references to an object have been set to null, the JVM will call the object's Release( ) method at the next garbage collection. You can force this by clicking the "System.gc" button, which calls that Java function to force an immediate garbage collection. When you do that, the server's window finally disappears.

```
/*
"Release" button clicked. Set the interface pointer to null. The
external object will be released and the server shut down at the
next system garbage collection.
*/

    private void btn_Release_click(Object source, Event e)
    {
      m_Hello = null ;
    }

/*
"System.gc" button clicked. Force an immediate system garbage
collection which will release any unused objects.
*/

    private void btn_SystemGc_click(Object source, Event e)
    {
      System.gc( ) ;
    }
```

WARNING: While it sounds really cool, this object release mechanism is not reliable in the current release of VJ. See the next page for details.

7. Unfortunately, the garbage collection mechanism for releasing objects described on the previous page is not reliable in the current version. The documentation recommends that you explicitly release every COM object via the function **ComLib.release( )**, as shown below. The sample app demonstrates this with a button labeled "ComLib.release". When you click it, the server window disappears immediately. The documentation states that:

"[Releasing COM objects via the garbage collection mechanism] is not guaranteed due to the threading limitations of many COM objects. That is, many COM objects [those which are single or apartment threaded] can only be called on the thread on which they were created. Because garbage collection occurs at unpredictable times, the required thread may have expired or may be no longer responding to messages by the time garbage-collection reclaims the object. In addition, this unpredictability can obscure true memory leaks and/or tie up important system resources. For these reasons, it is recommended that you use explicit releases in order to free COM objects in a timely and predictable fashion. "

My clients in the field confirm that the documentation is correct, that this problem really does occur at least occasionally. To my mind, this is a serious flaw. One of the features that I like best about Java over C++ is automatic garbage collection. The correct functioning of that garbage collection is one of my chief worries as I make the switch to Java. It seems to me that allowing a thread to die while objects still exist that need to be serviced by that particular thread is a bug. In the ThreadDB sample app of my apartment threading article (MSJ February 1997, page 31, bottom left) I dealt with exactly this issue, explaining the necessity for the thread to stay alive and showing you how to do it.

Having ComLib.release( ) available for the times when you want it is useful. For example, sometimes you might not want to take the time for a full garbage collection. You just want to blow away a single object, but you want it done right now. I just wish that they hadn't made it mandatory because they couldn't fix the bugs with threads. Maybe in the next release. Sigh.

```
/*
User has clicked the ComLib.release( ) button. Call that library
function to force an immediate release of the object without doing
a full system garbage collection.
*/

    private void btn_ComLibRelease_click(Object source, Event e)
    {
      ComLib.release(m_Hello) ;
    }
```

This page intentionally contains no text other than this sentence.

C. CREATING A COM SERVER IN JAVA

1. If you like the Java language itself, you will like using it for COM servers. In this example, I show you how to write a Java COM server that provides the same functionality as the "Hello, World" automation server from Chapter 4. You will find the sample code in the directory \Chap14\jhellodll. When you tell VJ that you want to create a COM DLL, it adds a COM-enabled class to your project. Thus:

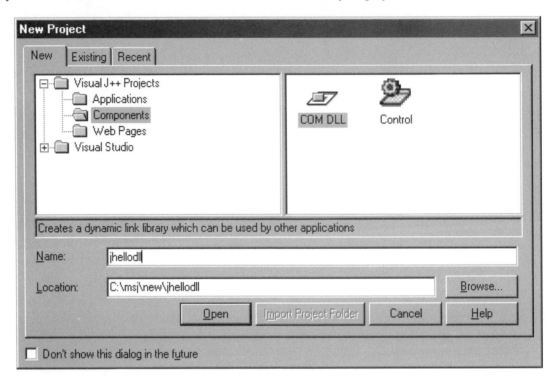

Microsoft's JVM, "msjava.dll", prefabricates just about all of the infrastructure needed for a COM server. It contains the necessary code for making registry entries. It contains an implementation of IUnknown and IDispatch. It also contains a class factory that creates Java classes in response to requests from COM. You simply write the Java class that implements your custom methods and properties.

2. To add other COM-enabled classes, simply choose the "Project – Properties" menu item and designate those classes as COM-enabled. Thus:

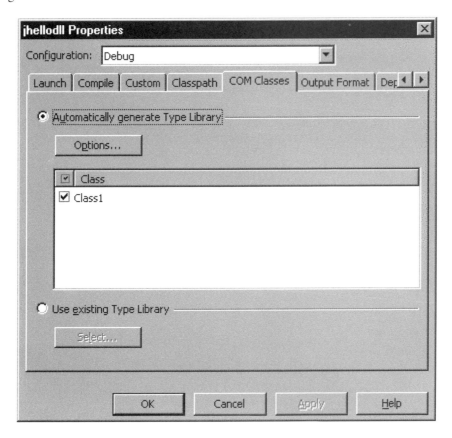

3. You now simply add the methods that you want to your Java class. By marking it as a COM class, you have told the JVM to be ready to wrap it up in a complete prefabricated COM shell, that maps all the incoming COM calls into Java-specific calls without your having to think further about it. Thus:

```
/**
 * This class is designed to be packaged with a COM DLL output format.
 * The class has no standard entry points, other than the constructor.
 * Public methods will be exposed as methods on the COM interface.

    @com.register ( clsid=5C7C2401-FB22-11D2-92FD-006097402523,
      typelib=5C7C2402-FB22-11D2-92FD-006097402523 )
 */

public class Class1
{
    public String HelloMessage = "Hello, World" ;

/*
Caller wants us to say hello. Pop up a message box containing
the current value of the "HelloMessage" property.
*/

    public synchronized void  SayHello ( )
    {
      com.ms.wfc.ui.MessageBox.show (HelloMessage, "jhellodll") ;
    }

/*
Caller wants to set the value of the "HelloMessage" property. Remember
the new value.
*/

    public synchronized void setHelloMessage (String msg)
    {
      HelloMessage = msg ;
    }

/*
Caller wants to get the value of the "HelloMessage" property.
*/

    public synchronized String getHelloMessage ( )
    {
      return HelloMessage ;
    }
}
```

4. By default, VJ will generate a type library describing the methods and properties that your class exposes to the world. The .IDL listing below shows the contents of the type library generated by VJ for the code in this example. Note that the methods and properties are, by default, exposed via an IDispatch interface only. Also note that a number of VJ's internal class methods, such as toString( ) and getClass( ), are exposed on this interface even though you didn't ask for that, and there's no good way to get them out. If you do not want them listed in your type library to confuse your client, you must write your own type library outside of VJ and tell VJ to include it in your DLL by selecting the "Use existing Type Library" radio button on the "Properties" dialog box shown previously.

```
[uuid(5C7C2402-FB22-11D2-92FD-006097402523), version(1.0)]

library jhellodll
{

    importlib("StdOle2.Tlb");

    [uuid(2B1F10AD-50BC-11D3-8779-00C04FB92AFD)]
    dispinterface Class1_Dispatch {
        properties:
        methods:
            [id(0x00000068), helpstring("toString")]
            BSTR toString();
            [id(0x00000067), helpstring("notifyAll")]
            void notifyAll();
            [id(0x00000066), helpstring("hashCode")]
            long hashCode();
            [id(0x00000064)]
            VARIANT wait(
                            [in, out] VARIANT* Parameter0,
                            [in, out] VARIANT* Parameter1);
            [id(0x00000070), propget, helpstring("helloMessage")]
            BSTR helloMessage();
            [id(0x00000070), propput, helpstring("helloMessage")]
            void helloMessage([in] BSTR rhs);
            [id(0x0000006f), helpstring("SayHello")]
            void SayHello();
            [id(0x0000006e), helpstring("setHelloMessage")]
            void setHelloMessage([in] BSTR Parameter0);
            [id(0x0000006d), helpstring("notify")]
            void notify();
            [id(0x0000006b), helpstring("equals")]
            VARIANT_BOOL equals([in] IDispatch* Parameter0);
            [id(0x0000006a), helpstring("getHelloMessage")]
            BSTR getHelloMessage();
            [id(0x00000069), helpstring("getClass")]
            IDispatch* getClass();
    };

    [uuid(5C7C2401-FB22-11D2-92FD-006097402523)]
    coclass Class1
    {
        [default] dispinterface Class1_Dispatch;
    };
```

5. If you want to implement a VTBL or dual interface in VJ, instead of the default dispatch-only interface shown on the previous page, you can do that via VJ's **implements** keyword. To demonstrate, I added another class to this sample application and made it implement the ITypeLibMarshaledEliza interface from Chapter 3. I took the type library describing that interface and generated a Java wrapper class for it, as shown previously in this chapter. The Java class is shown below. Note the parameters to the **@com.method** compiler directive that specifies the construction of the interface's VTBL.

```
package typelibmarshaled;

import com.ms.com.*;
import com.ms.com.IUnknown;
import com.ms.com.Variant;

// VTable-only interface ITypeLibMarshaledEliza

/**
    @com.interface (iid=088AFA02-DB7C-11D0-9121-00608C86B89C,
       thread=AUTO)
*/

public interface ITypeLibMarshaledEliza extends IUnknown
{

  /** @com.method(vtoffset=0, addFlagsVtable=4)
      @com.parameters([in,type=STRING] bstrIn, [out,size=1,type=ARRAY]
           pbstrOut)
  */

    public void Complain(String bstrIn, String[] pbstrOut);

    public static final com.ms.com._Guid iid =
       new com.ms.com._Guid((int)0x88afa02, (short)0xdb7c,
       (short)0x11d0, (byte)0x91, (byte)0x21, (byte)0x0, (byte)0x60,
       (byte)0x8c, (byte)0x86, (byte)0xb8, (byte)0x9c);
}
```

6. You then declare your java class using the keyword **implements** to specify the fact that the class is implementing an interface defined elsewhere. Thus:

```
/**
 * @com.register ( clsid=2B00121B-50BC-11D3-8779-00C04FB92AFD,
     typelib=5C7C2402-FB22-11D2-92FD-006097402523)
 */

public class Eliza implements typelibmarshaled.ITypeLibMarshaledEliza
{
  public void Complain(String bstrIn, String[] pbstrOut)
  {
    com.ms.wfc.ui.MessageBox.show (bstrIn, "jhellodll") ;

    String out = "What the heck are you complaining about?" ;
    pbstrOut [0] = out  ;
  }
}
```

NOTE: VJ6 does not properly handle the output type library when you use this mechanism. Even though the class does properly implement the VTBL as specified in the type library you originally imported, the type library generated by VJ will describe a dispatch-only interface similar to that shown previously in this chapter. Use the type library viewer to examine the sample DLL to see this. You will need to write your own type library outside of VJ to provide to your external clients.

7. The component that you write in VJ knows how to make the standard registry entries that the SCM needs to locate it. Thus:

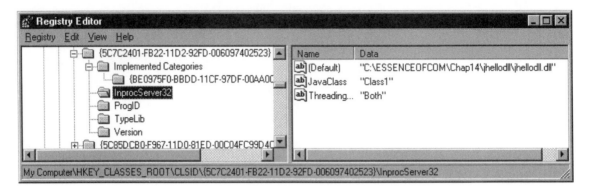

You may also add your own registration code for making any non-standard registry entries. The DLL self-registration code that Microsoft provides in its JVM will look for and call a method called onCOMRegister( ), passing a flag that tells you whether your object is being registered or unregistered. To use it, simply add this method to your class, and write your own code for adding or removing your desired registry entries. Thus:

```
public static void onCOMRegister(boolean register)
{
    if (register = true)
    {
      < registration code goes here >
    }
    else
    {
      < unregistration code goes here >
    }
}
```

This page intentionally contains no text other than this sentence.

D. COM ERROR HANDLING IN JAVA

1. COM's binary standard calls for methods to signal their success or failure with simple result codes. Because exceptions are language dependent, and also very hard to implement across different processes and different machines, COM doesn't support them. While COM does provide limited context-based error handling (see the API functions SetErrorInfo( ) and GetErrorInfo( )), it's not packaged in the form of an exception. And many COM objects don't even use these, relying instead on simple HRESULTs. However, Java language programming depends heavily on exceptions to signal errors, and Java programming would be difficult and unwieldy if you couldn't use them. Fortunately, Microsoft's JVM automatically and transparently converts between these two divergent world views.

Microsoft provides the Java class **com.ms.com.ComFailException** to signal the failure of a COM function or method call. Whenever a Java applet makes a COM call, if the return HRESULT has its high bit set, thereby signaling an error, the JVM will create and throw an exception of this type. An applet that cares about error return codes will use Java's standard **try-catch** syntax to catch this exception as shown below.

The ComFailException object contains the methods **getHResult( )** and **getMessage( )**. The former provides you with the COM error code value used throughout this book, and should be valid at all times. The latter is inherited from the Java base class RuntimeException, from which ComFailException derives. Thus:

```
/*
"SayHello" button clicked. Call that method on the object.
*/
    private void btn_SayHello_click(Object source, Event e)
    {
      try
      {
            m_Hello.SayHello() ;
      }
      catch (ComFailException cfe)
      {
            MessageBox.show (cfe.getMessage(), "SayHello") ;
      }
    }
```

2. From the server side, all Java class methods that implement COM interface methods are implicitly defined as throwing a ComFailException. When your Java COM server method encounters an error that it wants to signal, you allocate an object of this class, fill in its elements, and throw it. The JVM will catch the exception, convert it back to a COM HRESULT, and pass it back as the return value of your method in the manner the COM client is expecting. The JVM will also use the COM error function SetErrorInfo( ) to make additional context information available to any client that is paying attention to it. Thus:

```java
public class Class1
{
    public String HelloMessage = "Hello, World" ;
    private String BadWords = "heck darn Netscape" ;
    final int E_FAIL = 0x80004005 ;

/*
Caller wants to set the value of the "HelloMessage" property.
*/

    public synchronized void setHelloMessage (String msg)
    {
/*
Make sure someone doesn't say a dirty word.
Take exception if they do.
*/

        if (BadWords.indexOf (msg) != -1)
        {
            com.ms.com.ComFailException cfe =
                new com.ms.com.ComFailException
                    (E_FAIL, "You said a naughty word!") ;

            throw cfe ;
        }
/*
Otherwise remember the new value.
*/

        HelloMessage = msg ;
    }
```

NOTE: You will occasionally see a COM method, such as IPersistStream::IsDirty( ), return an HRESULT of S_FALSE, whose hex value is 0x00000001. This represents a funny intermediate state between success and failure. It essentially means that "Yes, I was able to successfully find out what you wanted to know, and the answer to your question is 'No'." Java provides a separate class to handle this case called ComSuccessException. Use it exactly as you would a ComFailException.

E. USING THE COM API FROM JAVA

1. Both VB and VJ feature very high levels of abstraction that make it easier to program COM by abstracting away a lot of the repetitive operations. A COM object used in either language looks more or less like a native object in that language. The problem with VB, however, is that you can't step outside that abstraction layer when you want to do something that it doesn't cover. VJ does allow you to do this. I demonstrate this by writing a running object table viewer in Java, as shown below. You will find the code for this in the sample code subdirectory \Chap14\jrotview.

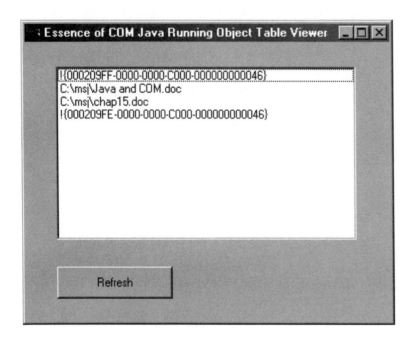

NOTE: VJ6 actually provides a wrapper for the running object table and the IMoniker interface in the package com.ms.com, which abstracts away the necessity for writing code as shown in this particular example. I am showing it to a) demonstrate what Microsoft has done on your behalf, and b) demonstrate what you must do in similar situations.

2. The sample app needs to call the API functions GetRunningObjectTable( ) and CreateBindCtx( ), both of which reside in the system DLL "OLE32.DLL", and both of which return COM interface pointers. Calling a Windows API function from within Java requires using the J/Direct calling mechanism, found under the "View — Other Windows" menu, to construct the import declarations that allow VJ6 to call functions from DLLs. If you've ever used the "Declare Function" statement in VB for importing a DLL function, it will seem very similar. The only problem was that the J/Direct call builder's data file has declarations for most standard Win32 API functions, but not for those that live in the system file OLE32.DLL, as these do.   I had to work by example from the on-line documentation.

Since they have a consistent calling style of their own, VJ6 imports functions from OLE32.DLL and OLEAUT32.DLL somewhat differently than other API functions. For example, normal API functions called from Java return their normal error codes. Most COM functions, on the other hand, return an HRESULT, which the JVM translates into a Java exception if it is anything other than S_OK. The function signatures are different as well. The last parameter passed to a COM function is generally an output parameter. Java treats this as if it were marked with the [retval] attribute, which tells a compliant programming language to pass a hidden pointer and treat the result as the return value of the function. The function prototype in the API is:

```
HRESULT GetRunningObjectTable (int, IRunningObjectTable *)
```

In Java, it is

```
static native IRunningObjectTable  GetRunningObjectTable (int)
```

The compiler directive @dll.import specifies a call to an external DLL. The parameter "ole" tells it to interpret the call according to the rules of COM functions, which VJ refers to as "OLE Mode". Thus:

```
    /**
     * @dll.import("OLE32", ole)
     */
public static native IBindCtx CreateBindCtx (int i) ;

    /**
     * @dll.import("OLE32", ole)
     */
public static native IRunningObjectTable GetRunningObjectTable(int i);
```

3. Once I had imported the functions, I needed Java wrapper classes to handle the interfaces for my running object table operations, which are IRunningObjectTable, IEnumMoniker, IMoniker, and IBindCtx. You will remember that Jactivex creates them from type libraries. The problem then became finding an existing type library containing definitions of these interfaces. A little searching on the disk showed me that the DirectAnimation library "danim.dll" already contained such a thing. If it hadn't, I would have built it myself from the .IDL files that come with Visual Studio. I imported this type library as shown in the client app example, and had the Java wrapper classes that I needed (along with about 200 others that I didn't care about that just slowed down compilation. I simply deleted these).

Once I had my wrapper classes, I started coding. It was pretty simple, very much like VB or VC with smart pointers. The only tricky part was getting parameters back from object methods by reference. The method IRunningObjectTable::EnumRunning( ), for example, requires the address of an IEnumMoniker interface for its output. Java doesn't support pointers, so I had to instantiate a one-member array, which Java passes by reference. I had to do this in a few other places as well. I expect that in the future, more developers will be declaring their output variables with the [retval] attribute, which will eliminate the need for this workaround.

```
    private void RefreshList ( )
    {
/*
Clear list box.
*/

    listBox1.removeAll ( ) ;


/*
Get the current running object table from the
operating system.
*/

    IRunningObjectTable rot = GetRunningObjectTable (0) ;


    <continued on next page>
```

<continued from previous page>

```
/*
Call the method IRunningObjectTable::EnumRunning to get an
IEnumMoniker interface that we will use to enumerate the names
of all the entries in it.

Since this interface is returned by an output pointer, we need
to pass a single-element array to receive it.
*/

        IEnumMoniker enum [] = new IEnumMoniker [1] ;
        rot.EnumRunning(enum) ;

        int fetched [] = new int [1] ;
        IMoniker moniker [] = new IMoniker [1] ;



        while (true)
        {
/*
Get next moniker in the table.
If we've gotten them all, break out of the loop.
*/

            enum [0].RemoteNext (1, moniker, fetched) ;
            if (fetched[0] != 1)
            {
                break ;
            }
/*
Create a bind context object for the moniker to use while
composing its human-readable display name.
*/
            String str [] = new String [1] ;
            IBindCtx ctx = CreateBindCtx (0) ;
            moniker[0].GetDisplayName (ctx, null, str) ;


/*
Add the name to the list box.
*/

            listBox1.addItem (str[0]) ;
        }
    }
```

F. COM THREADING IN JAVA

1. The topic of COM threading fascinates me. I still remember the light bulb going off in my head when I finally figured out what the apartment threading model was really doing and why. So when I started writing this chapter on Java, the first thing that I wanted to investigate was how it handled threads. Java is unique in that threads come and go behind the scenes without your thinking about it. So it makes sense that the connection between threading and COM would be handled behind the scenes as well, without your having to think about it.

The first thing I wanted to do was to see what threading model a Java client app would use. To do this, I wrote an ATL server DLL that contains 4 different classes of objects, one each for the single, apartment, free, and both threading models. You will find this in the directory \Chap14\threadsv. You need to register the server DLL "threadsv.dll" before working with the sample client app. The controls each expose the same interface, IGetCurrentThreadId, which contains a single read-only property called CurrentThreadId, which uses the API function GetCurrentThreadId( ) to report the ID of the thread on which the object receives the call. The sample Java client app lives in the directory \jthreadcl and is shown below. At startup, it reports the ID of its own UI thread. You specify which threading model you want, and it creates an object of the class that supports that model. It then calls IGetCurrentThreadId::getCurrentThreadId( ), which reports the thread on which the object receives the call.

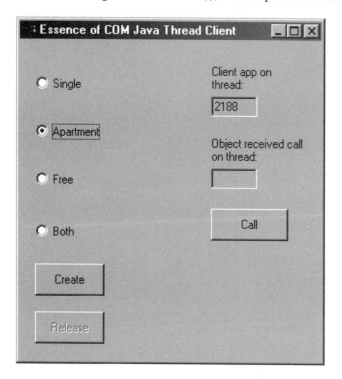

You will find that a Java client app creates a thread that calls CoInitialize( ) and maintains a message pump, thereby becoming the legacy STA thread. You can see this as you create and then call the Single threading model demo object. The form itself runs on a different STA thread, which you can see if you create and then call the Apartment demo object.

Other threads that you create in a Java client app will, by default, be MTA threads. If you want to create other STA threads, you must call the function com.ms.com.ComLib.declareMessagePumpThread( ) in the thread's Run( ) method, and then write and manage your own Windows message pump. The SDK documentation contains an example.

2. On the server side, COM objects created in VJ6 mark themselves as supporting both threading models, as shown in this screen shot:

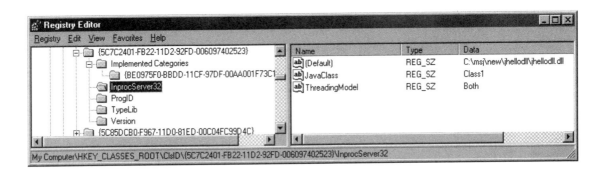

This means that VJ COM objects are always created in the apartment of the thread that creates them, whether that is an STA or the process's lone MTA. This means that every object needs to provide its own synchronization code to protect itself against concurrent accesses from different threads to the extent that it requires. In C++, this requires writing some fairly nasty code involving critical sections or other Win32 synchronization primitives. In Java, the JVM is required to support the keyword **synchronized**. A method that is declared with this keyword may be accessed by only one thread at a time. That's all you have to do or can do in Java. Thus:

```
/*
Caller wants to set the value of the "HelloMessage" property. Remember
the new value.
*/

    public synchronized void setHelloMessage (String msg)
    {
      HelloMessage = msg ;
    }
```

Lab Exercises
Chapter 14
COM Support in Visual Java

Directory: \EssenceOfCOM\chap14

1. To test the Java COM client application, first register the completed "Hello32" server from the \Chap04\HELLOAU directory. Then run the client application \Chap14\jhelloclient\jhelloclient.exe. The sample program should work as explained in the text.

2. To test the Java server application, register the DLL \Chap14\jhellodll\jhellodll using regsvr32.exe. Then run the client app \Chap14\jhellodll\vbtest\project1.exe. A sample program will provide easy access to create the COM objects implemented in the Java dll. Don't expect Eliza to be too sympathetic.

3. To test the running object table viewer, bring up an application that makes an entry in the running object table. Office applications do this when they open a saved file, although not usually when they open an unsaved default file on startup. VC++ also does this, putting its CLSID into the running object table. Run the sample program \Chap14\jrotview.exe. It will show you the contents of the running object table as described in the text.

4. To test the threading sample programs, first register the DLL \Chap14\threadsv\threadsv.dll using regsvr32.exe. Then run the sample program \Chap14\jthreadcl\jsthreadcl.exe. Use the sample program to create and call an object using each of the threading models. Note the thread on which each call is received, indicating the apartment in which each object lives.

EXTRA CREDIT: Create your own thread inside the client application and have it create the threading objects and report the results. Unless you have gone out of your way to make it an STA thread, it will be an MTA thread. The "free" and "both" objects that it creates will live in its apartment (the MTA), while the "single" and "apartment" objects will live in STAs. Are they the same STA, or different ones?

EXTRA EXTRA CREDIT: Create your own thread inside the client application, and this time go out of your way to make it an STA thread. Call the function com.ms.com.ComLib.declareMessagePumpThread( ) and implement the message loop. Try creating each type of object to see which apartment it lives in.

Appendix

Containment and Aggregation

A. CONCEPTS AND DEFINITIONS

1. "Code reuse" is the holy grail of the software industry, and much is made of COM as a mechanism for promoting this Good Thing. In one sense, an application programmer does this every time he uses a COM object, such as a calendar control, that he bought from some vendor instead of writing it himself. In another sense, developers would very much like to assemble COM components out of other components, instead of building the entire component from scratch. This section deals with two mechanisms for assembling COM objects into larger, hopefully more functional and profitable COM objects.

Though frequently presented and discussed together, a philosophy that goes back to the first edition of Kraig Brockschmidt's *Inside OLE* (Microsoft Press, 1993), aggregation and containment really exist to do superficially similar things at different times for different reasons. Containment exists to wire separate interfaces together at compile time, where the developer knows all the interfaces but doesn't want to write code to implement one of them. Aggregation exists to wire separate interfaces together at runtime, in ways that the original developer never thought of.

2. Throughout this book, when I wanted an object to support more than one interface, I've done it with multiple inheritance. This is the easiest way to do things if you have to write all the methods yourself. And usually I've had to do exactly that, because the interfaces shared common data. The interfaces were not independent black-box components, they were different views of the same thing. Consider the example at the end of Chapter 8, where one object supported both IDataObject and IPersistFile. The two interfaces did different things to the same data. That's usually the case in COM; when you are writing one component, it is relatively rare to find a prefabricated black box component that does useful things for you without needing to know your intimate details. There are a few, but it's much less common than seekers of holy grails would like to admit. That's why I've put these two techniques in an appendix, instead of their own separate chapter. Having said that, I have to admit that in the relatively few cases where you need them, nothing else will work.

B. CONTAINMENT

1. One way to reuse components is via containment, shown in the diagram below. The component consists of an outer object and an inner object. The outer object is the original CTimeData object, rewritten to add support for the IDispatch interface and therefore renamed CTimeDataDispatch. Its declaration is shown on the next page.

In the previous multiple inheritance examples, I've placed the code for implementing all the interfaces in the same object. The difference now is that the IDispatch VTBL on the outer object is an empty shell. The outer object provides a VTBL, but it accomplishes the work by creating a component, the inner or contained object, and delegating the IDispatch method calls to this object. Thus:

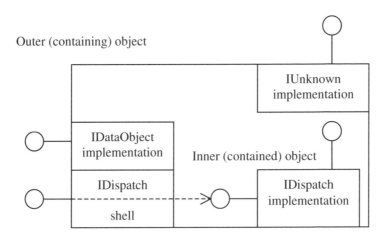

Containment is relatively easy to write. The contained object does not need any special functionality to support it as is the case with aggregation; you can contain any object that can stand alone. Neither the outer object's client nor the inner object itself know or care that containment is taking place. Containment can also work with objects that live in separate processes or even on separate machines, whereas aggregation only works for in-process objects.

Better yet, the outer object can do all kinds of things to enhance the behavior of the inner object. For example, the outer object could inspect and modify method parameters before passing them to the inner object. Maybe the inner object speaks English and the outer object translates its input to and from French. Maybe the inner object provides useful functionality and the outer object meters it and bills the client. If you think of subclassing a window in the Windows API, this is the COM version of it.

2. The outer object provides VTBLs for both interfaces via multiple inheritance as before. Thus:

```
class CTimeDataDispatch : public IDataObject, public IDispatch
{

    public:
       ULONG                    m_RefCount ;
/*
Pointer to inner object held by the outer object.
*/
       IDispatch *              m_pInnerDispatch ;

       < rest of declaration omitted >
};
```

When the outer object is constructed, it creates the inner object via CoCreateInstance( ). Alternatively, the outer object could wait until the client actually queried for the inner object's interface and create it on demand. It releases the inner object in its destructor. Thus:

```
/*
Constructor/destructor
*/

CTimeDataDispatch::CTimeDataDispatch()
{
    m_RefCount = 1 ;
    g_ObjectCount ++ ;
/*
Create inner contained IDispatch
*/
    CLSID clsid ;
    CLSIDFromProgID (L"EssenceOfCOM.HelloAutomation", &clsid) ;

    CoCreateInstance (
      clsid, NULL, CLSCTX_SERVER, IID_IDispatch,
      (LPVOID *) &m_pInnerDispatch) ;

    return;
}

CTimeDataDispatch::~CTimeDataDispatch(void)
{
    g_ObjectCount -- ;

/*
Release inner contained IDispatch
*/
    if (m_pInnerDispatch)
    {
      m_pInnerDispatch->Release( ) ;
    }
    return;
}
```

3. The outer object in this example implements the IDispatch interface by simply delegating the call to the inner object. If you wanted to mess with the parameters or do other work around this call, it would go here. Thus:

```
STDMETHODIMP CTimeDataDispatch::Invoke(DISPID dispidMember,
    REFIID riid,  LCID lcid, WORD wFlags, DISPPARAMS *pDispParams,
    VARIANT *pVarResult, EXCEPINFO *pExcepInfo, UINT *puArgErr)
{

/*
If inner dispatch interface pointer exists and is valid, delegate the
call to it.
*/

    if (m_pInnerDispatch)
    {
      return m_pInnerDispatch->Invoke (dispidMember, riid, lcid,wFlags,
          pDispParams, pVarResult, pExcepInfo, puArgErr) ;
    }
/*
If not, fail the call.
*/

    else
    {
      return E_FAIL ;
    }
}
```

C. AGGREGATION

1. Aggregation is not really about development-time code reuse. Containment does a better and more flexible job of that and is easier to write. Using aggregation for code reuse gets airplay far out of proportion to its importance. Kraig Brockschmidt himself said that he gave it far too much emphasis in the first edition of his book, and he downplayed it considerably in the second edition.

Instead, you use aggregation to wire together at runtime interfaces that you didn't know about at development time. For example, in Chapter 10, when setting a callback to be notified of the completion of an asynchronous method, you pass an ISynchronize interface pointer to the method ICallFactory::CreateCall( ). The call factory wires the ISynchronize interface into the call object that it creates. The COM geeks at Microsoft who wrote the call factory didn't know about your ISynchronize interface at compile time; instead it got wired in at runtime. For another example, objects that are used in the COM+ object pool (not discussed in this book, see my *Understanding COM+* from Microsoft Press) are required to support aggregation. The pool manager wires another interface onto the pool object to keep track of administrative information pertaining to that particular instance. Aggregation exists to mash into the same identity interfaces that didn't know about each other at development time.

Aggregation differs from containment in that in the former, the inner object's interface is not wrapped by the outer object, but instead exposes its interface directly. The two object's IUnknown interfaces are wired together so that the inner object's IUnknown delegates its calls to the outer IUnknown. Thus:

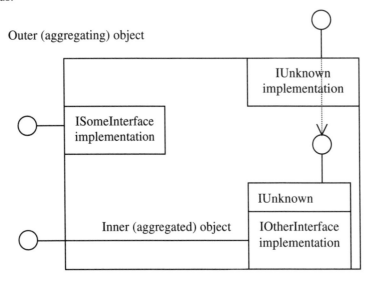

Another difference from containment is that to reuse an object via aggregation, the object must have been written to support it, and not all of them are. An object that is aggregatable is trickier to write than one that isn't. Although the ATL and VJ provide prefabricated support that makes aggregation easy, Visual Basic doesn't do it at all. Furthermore, in aggregation, the outer object doesn't get the chance to examine or modify the calls to the inner. Plus, aggregation works only for in-process objects.

2. The code for aggregation looks like this. The outer object provides a VTBL only for its own interface, in this case IDataObject. Thus:

```
class CSomeInterfaceOuter : public ISomeInterface
{

    public:
      ULONG       m_RefCount ;
      IUnknown*   m_pInnerUnknown ;

    <rest of class declaration omitted>
} ;
```

The outer object creates the inner object via CoCreateInstance( ) with two major new additions. First, when setting up aggregation, the outer object must pass a pointer to its IUnknown interface as the second parameter to CoCreateInstance( ). This will be passed to the class factory so that the inner object will know who it's inside of. Second, in aggregation, the outer object **MUST ask for the IUnknown interface** and only IUnknown when creating the inner object. Thus:

```
CSomeInterfaceOuter:: CSomeInterfaceOuter ()
{
    m_RefCount = 1 ;
    g_ObjectCount ++ ;

/*
Create inner object, passing pointer to outer object and requesting
IUnknown interface.
*/


    CoCreateInstance (
      CLSID_InnerObject,
      this,                 // outer IUnknown for aggregation
      CLSCTX_INPROC_SERVER, // only works for in-proc
      IID_IUnknown,      // in aggregation, must always ask for IUnknown
      (LPVOID *) &m_pInnerUnknown) ;

    return;
}
```

3. The outer object also modifies its QueryInterface( ). When the client queries for an interface, the outer object first tries to satisfy it. If not, then it delegates to the inner IUnknown to see if maybe the inner aggregated object supports the requested interface. This can be done for any number of aggregated inner IUnknowns. You could also check the inner object first, which would allow the inner interface to replace an outer interface if that's what you wanted. Thus:

```
HRESULT CSomeInterfaceOuter::QueryInterface(REFIID riid, LPVOID *ppv)
{
    if (riid == IID_IUnknown || riid == IID_ISomeInterface)
    {
        *ppv = (LPVOID)this;
        AddRef();
        return S_OK ;
    }
    else
    {
      return m_pInnerUnknown->QueryInterface (riid, ppv) ;
    }
}
```

4. Writing an inner object for aggregation is a somewhat tricky task. The coding isn't interesting, just tedious, and no one writes one on his own any more anyway. I've decided to leave it out of this edition of the book. You can find a sample of it in the platform SDK.

INDEX

347

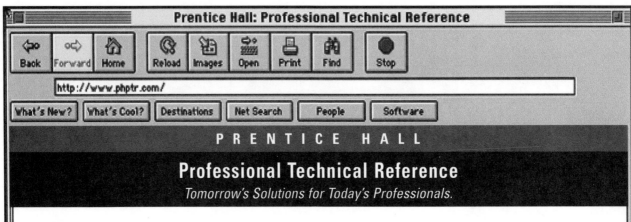